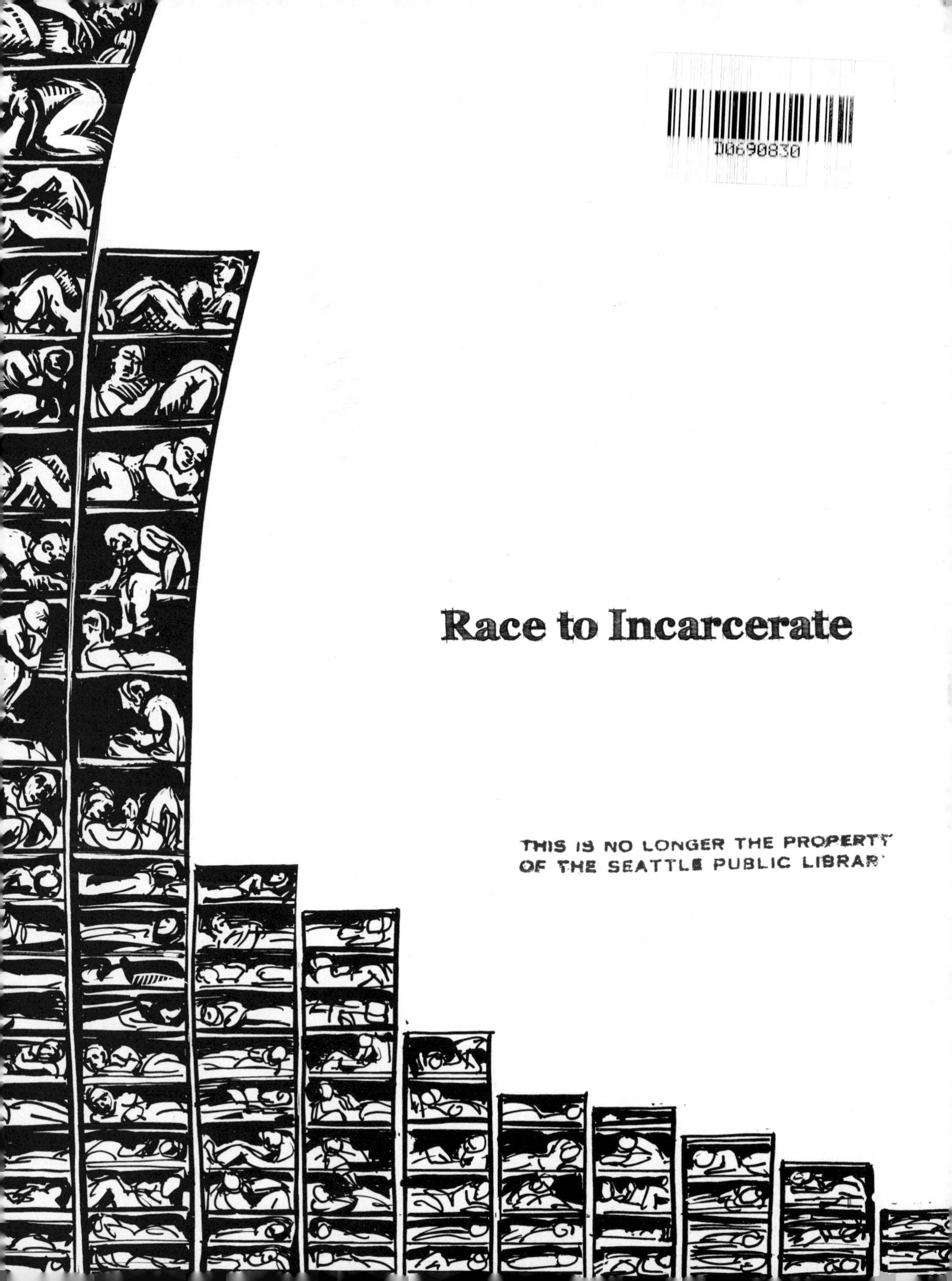

Race to Incarcerate

Also by Sabrina Jones
Isadora Duncan: A Graphic Biography

Also by Marc Mauer
Race to Incarcerate

Invisible Punishment:
The Collateral Consequences
of Mass Imprisonment
(edited with Meda Chesney-Lind)

Race to Incarcerate

A
Graphic
Retelling

SABRINA JONES and MARC MAUER

20
YEARS

THE NEW PRESS

Requests for permission to reproduce
selections from this book should be mailed to:
Permissions Department, The New Press, 38 Greene Street,
New York, NY 10013.

Published in the United States by
The New Press, New York, 2013
Distributed by Perseus Distribution

ISBN 978-1-59558-541-7 (pb)
ISBN 978-1-59558-893-7 (e-book)
CIP data is available

The New Press publishes books that promote and enrich
public discussion and understanding of the issues vital to
our democracy and to a more equitable world. These books
are made possible by the enthusiasm of our readers; the
support of a committed group of donors, large and small; the
collaboration of our many partners in the independent media
and the not-for-profit sector; booksellers, who often hand-sell
New Press books; librarians; and above all by our authors.

www.thenewpress.com

Printed in the United States of America

10 9 8 7 6 5 4 3 2 1

Contents

Foreword by Michelle Alexander

DO NOT underestimate the power of the book you are holding in your hands. Years ago, back when I was working as a civil rights lawyer and advocate challenging racial profiling by law enforcement, investigating patterns of drug law enforcement, and launching media campaigns designed to raise awareness about skyrocketing incarceration rates and the devastating toll that "get tough" policies were having on our communities, there was one book—only one—that I viewed as utterly indispensable to my work: *Race to Incarcerate.* I had multiple copies on my shelf, one that had more yellow highlighting than black and white text. It was so frayed that the cover was nearly falling off. The other copies of the book were part of my lending library. When politicians, reporters, or community folks would ask me questions like "Where did you get those statistics?" or "How do you know that?" I would tell them to read *Race to Incarcerate.* I'd jot down their addresses and then send them a copy of the book, sometimes through overnight mail. There was no doubt in my mind that anyone who wanted to understand how and why we became the world leader in imprisonment had to read that book, and had to read it fast. The fate of our communities, indeed our nation, literally depended on it.

Looking back, I realize that I rarely shared the book with young people. It's not that young people weren't asking a lot of good questions and eager to understand why so many in our poorest communities, particularly young black and brown men, were locked in cages. In fact, some of the best, most penetrating questions about our system of mass incarceration came from young people who were quick to grasp that the system made a mockery of our nation's claim that we are "the land of the free." The problem was that *Race to Incarcerate* was not designed for young people. Its intended audience was policy makers, scholars, and people who were in the habit of reading policy analysis. Instinctively I grasped for other sources—magazine articles, videos, or films—when trying to help young people understand the radical changes that had occurred in our penal system. I never felt satisfied with what I had to offer and wished that someone would write a book that would be engaging and accessible to young readers and people of all walks of life, not just to policy wonks like myself.

I could not be more thrilled that the book that fueled so much of my own civil rights work and advocacy is now available in a graphic form designed for the very generation that, I am confident, will build and lead the movement to end mass incarceration in America. I hope you will use this book the way I used the original, as a tool for consciousness-raising, organizing, and advocacy. The time is long overdue for America to wake up and face the truth about the human rights nightmare that is occurring right here, right now, on our soil. Read this book and then pass it on. Buy copies for your friends. Organize study circles. And then get to work building the movement. The fate of generations to come depends on people like you, people who are curious enough to pick up a book like this and put it to good use. The future belongs to those who understand that knowledge *is* power.

December 2012

Preface by Marc Mauer

THIS EDITION of *Race to Incarcerate* represents the continuation of a personal journey for me, beginning with the publication of the first edition of the book in 1999. To be honest, it had never occurred to me to try to write a book, but the editors at The New Press convinced me that there was a book inside my head waiting to be written, and I'm very grateful to them for having planted that suggestion.

I assumed that was the end of my publishing career. But the book was well received and helped to stimulate dialogue on criminal justice policy, so several years later my editors came back with a proposal for a second edition. The passage of time allowed me to think about changes in the world of criminal justice and to extend the analysis of the first edition. Surely that was the end of the story—or so I thought.

But now, thanks to the talents of Sabrina Jones, here we have the story of *Race to Incarcerate* told as a graphic novel. This provides us with an opportunity to frame the policy arguments in a format that attempts to appeal to both our intellectual and our emotional capacities. And it does so in a political climate on criminal justice policy that is evolving in intriguing ways.

Fourteen years after the original edition, it's important to examine what has changed—for better or worse—during this period and how we might assess the challenges that currently confront the movement for criminal justice reform.

In many respects, there is now reason for cautious optimism about the accomplishments and prospects for reform. The streets and neighborhoods of America are generally safer than they were in the 1990s. A relatively steady decline in crime since the early 1990s means that rates of both property and violent crime have declined by more than 40 percent, down to the lowest levels in forty years. While there is debate about *why* crime rates are down (more on this later), it is a welcome development in any case.

After nearly four decades of sustained growth, prison populations appear to be stabilizing, and even declining in some states. The first overall national decline, albeit a modest 0.6 percent, occurred in 2010, but states such as New York and New Jersey have registered reductions in the 20 percent range since 2000, and a handful of others are beginning to produce significant reductions as well.

Foremost among these is California, ordered by the U.S. Supreme Court in 2011 to reduce its prison population by 46,000, the result of litigation in which the court concluded that severe overcrowding in the state's prisons produced a level of medical care so poor that it was unconstitutional. The state is now in the midst of what can be conceived as a grand social experiment, whereby substantial numbers of lower-level offenders and parole violators are being supervised in local counties. How this experiment plays out should be of great interest to all of us by providing insight into the scale of population reductions that are possible and their effect on crime. It seems likely to be a messy experiment, though, with broad variations in impact by county and limited resources to provide services at the local level.

The most significant national reductions in population are taking place in the juvenile justice system, where the number of young people in detention has declined by a third since the late 1990s. Some of this reflects the overall reduction in youth crime over the past decade, and some appears to be a product of conscious policy decisions to reduce the use of secure confinement in favor of greater community-based approaches to supervision and services.

One of the key driving forces of the prison-building era—"get tough" sentencing policies—is also an area where encouraging breakthroughs are beginning to emerge. We've seen this most prominently with the two most high-profile manifestations of mandatory sentencing policy for drug offenses. In New York, the notorious Rockefeller drug laws, adopted in 1973, served in many respects as the template for the punitive excesses of the war on drugs. Under its provisions, persons convicted of selling two ounces of narcotics or possessing four ounces would receive a minimum prison term of fifteen years. After decades of critique and activism, the state legislature finally scaled back the law considerably in 2009.

At the federal level, the broad disparity between sentences for drug offenses involving crack cocaine and those involving powder cocaine had come to symbolize the harsh unfairness of drug sentencing policy. Originally adopted by Congress in 1986, the mandatory sentencing policy punished crack cocaine offenses far more harshly than powder cocaine offenses, using a drug quantity ratio of 100:1 to distinguish the two forms of cocaine. Eighty percent of those prosecuted for crack cocaine offenses were African American and subject to a mandatory prison term of five years for possessing as little as five grams of the drug—about the weight of two pennies. In 2010, a bipartisan coalition came together in Congress to pass the Fair Sentencing Act, reducing the disparity ratio from 100:1 to 18:1. Although it wasn't the equalization of penalties that many had called for, it was still a substantial change that will benefit many future defendants.

Developments in the courts are also encouraging, none more so than a series of decisions by the U.S. Supreme Court regarding the sentencing of juveniles. Three decisions in particular—*Roper v. Simmons* in 2005, *Graham v. Florida* in 2010, and *Miller v. Alabama* and *Jackson v. Hobbs* in 2012—successively ruled unconstitutional the death penalty as applied to juveniles; the imposition of life without parole in non-homicide cases; and, finally, sentences of juvenile life without parole imposed in a mandatory way by statute.

Perhaps most promising is the shift in public dialogue about criminal justice policy. At the risk of sounding overly optimistic, it seems clear that the "tough on crime" political environment of the 1980s and 1990s is, if not extinguished, at least undergoing a substantial shift. The relatively new concepts—and, in many cases, implementation—of reentry and justice reinvestment programming have brought together practitioners and political leadership from all parts of the political spectrum in a constructive approach to producing better outcomes for persons convicted of crimes.

One can see this in the political dialogue around public safety issues as well. On reentry issues, for example, the Second Chance Act, adopted by Congress in 2008, provided funding for demonstration projects, including employment services and substance-abuse treatment programs for people leaving prison. Particularly intriguing about this development was the political coalition that came together to promote the legislation. In the House, leadership came from members of the Congressional Black Caucus who had been longtime champions of such reform; in the Senate, however, the key sponsor was then-senator Sam Brownback, a Republican from Kansas and one of the most conservative members of the body. Brownback, a deeply religious man, has a strong belief in forgiveness and redemption, and thus viewed reentry programming as a natural outgrowth of such a worldview.

These developments largely predated the fiscal crises of recent years, but the economic situation has made a focus on reform even more salient. Governors and legislative leaders of both major parties now actively seek strategies that can produce cost-saving reductions in incarceration without adversely affecting public safety.

Taken together, these developments certainly suggest that there has in fact been a shift in the political dialogue on crime policy. We've also seen the development of programming and policies designed to scale back harsh punishments in favor of more constructive approaches to sentencing.

As welcome as these changes may be, we also need to recognize the enormous scale of the problem at hand. After nearly four decades of steadily rising imprisonment, reducing our level of incarceration to anything reasonable will require far more than just tinkering with sentencing and parole policy. A few examples illustrate these challenges.

Over the past decade, the states of New York and New Jersey have led the nation in reducing their prison populations, both in the range of 20 percent. Considering that almost all other states experienced an increase in their populations during this period, this is a significant development. Yet even if all states were to achieve such declines, the national rate of incarceration would be reduced to about 580 per 100,000 citizens—still roughly four times the average in western Europe.

Or imagine that advocates of drug legalization achieved their goal and we were to empty the prisons and jails of anyone awaiting trial or serving time for a drug conviction. Substantial as this would be, it would only reduce the number of people behind bars from about 2.3 million to 1.8 million. A significant reduction, of course, but hardly on the scale that would end mass incarceration.

While some of the problem is due to the relatively limited extent of alternative sentencing and diversion programming within the court system, the more fundamental problem is that we have come to rely on the criminal justice system as our primary approach to social problems, particularly in low-income communities of color. This is most obvious in the war on drugs, whereby drug law enforcement targets such neighborhoods while drug users and sellers in middle-income communities largely escape the clutches of the justice system.

But it is not only the drug war that produces such distorted outcomes. Even when considering how to respond to people who have committed violent or other serious crimes, it is far too narrow a vision to ask only how much punishment is appropriate. In typical policy discussions, we focus only on the crimes people in prison have committed. Doing so tells us that about half of that population is serving time for a violent offense. For many people, that stops the conversation.

But we could also ask a different set of questions that might illuminate some of the factors that have contributed to these outcomes. Such an approach would reveal that about three-quarters of the people in prison have a history of substance abuse, and about one in six has a history of mental illness. There are below-average levels of educational attainment and work histories among people behind bars and significant levels of physical and sexual abuse among women in particular. Looking at the problem this way suggests that there might be interventions that could have reduced the propensity for serious harm, and that focusing on punishment alone comes into play only after the harm has been done.

Just to be clear, this argument does not suggest that individuals have no responsibility for their actions, no matter how impoverished their circumstances may be. But such a framework does tell us that the structures and supports we provide in a community may very well influence public safety outcomes. And if our goal is to reduce victimization, then punishment for its own sake does not get us very far.

There are those who would argue, of course, that mass incarceration policies have in fact reduced victimization, and so, while distasteful to some, they are necessary for continued gains in public safety. This relationship, though, is much more murky than often believed. The best studies of this issue to date suggest that rising imprisonment in the 1990s may have been responsible for between 10 to 25 percent of the decline in violent crime. Such an impact is not insignificant, of course, but it also suggests that 75 to 90 percent of the decline was *not* the result of sending more people to prison.

Why, then, did crime begin to decline in the 1990s? While there is no definitive answer, it appears to have been a result of a number of factors. These include a relatively healthy economy during the 1990s that created more job opportunities, particularly for people in the low-wage labor market; the waning of the crack cocaine epidemic and its associated violence by the early 1990s; strategic policing initiatives in some cities; teenagers in urban neighborhoods learning to avoid sites of potential conflict; and, yes, more incarceration.

Even conceding the limited extent that incarceration contributed to the decline in crime does not necessarily suggest that this was the *most* effective means of accomplishing this objective. Research on a variety of interventions, such as enhanced preschool education, high school completion programs, and substance abuse treatment, demonstrates that such initiatives can be more cost-effective in reducing crime than expanded incarceration.

But suppose for the moment we had reason to believe that most of the reduction in crime had been due to putting more people behind bars. Would we then need to conclude that such a policy is the right one to pursue? If one believes this to be the case, then one must also acknowledge that such a policy implicitly lends support to an outcome where one in three black males and one in six Latino males does time in prison, as research from the Department of Justice demonstrates. It's hard to imagine a society that viewed itself as rational and compassionate would choose such a policy.

*

As noted, this is the third iteration of *Race to Incarcerate* and certainly not a version that I would ever have anticipated. My appreciation first to Carnell Hunnicutt, currently serving a long prison sentence, whose voluminous comic book renditions of prison issues originally gave me the idea that my story could be told this way, too. Appreciation to my colleague Lois Ahrens as well for insight and support in conceptualizing such a project. Thanks once again to The New Press—to our editor Sarah Fan and longtime colleague Diane Wachtell—for their vision and support and for their commitment to developing the intellectual critique of mass incarceration. Their books have made a difference. And to my collaborator Sabrina Jones for being so gracious in working with my limited artistic abilities, for being able to conceptualize a visual portrait of a text that is heavy on policy and data analysis, and to make that text come alive in new ways.

Thanks, too, to my colleagues on the board and staff of The Sentencing Project. People are frequently surprised to learn that we have a relatively modest budget and staff size and note that our productivity is befitting of a much larger organization. Those observations only confirm my view that we have a particularly dedicated and creative group of people here, all of whom combine their passion for social justice with strong skills in research and advocacy.

And finally, thanks once again to my family for all their support, for being the people they are, and for the contributions they make to the world in their own ways.

Race to Incarcerate

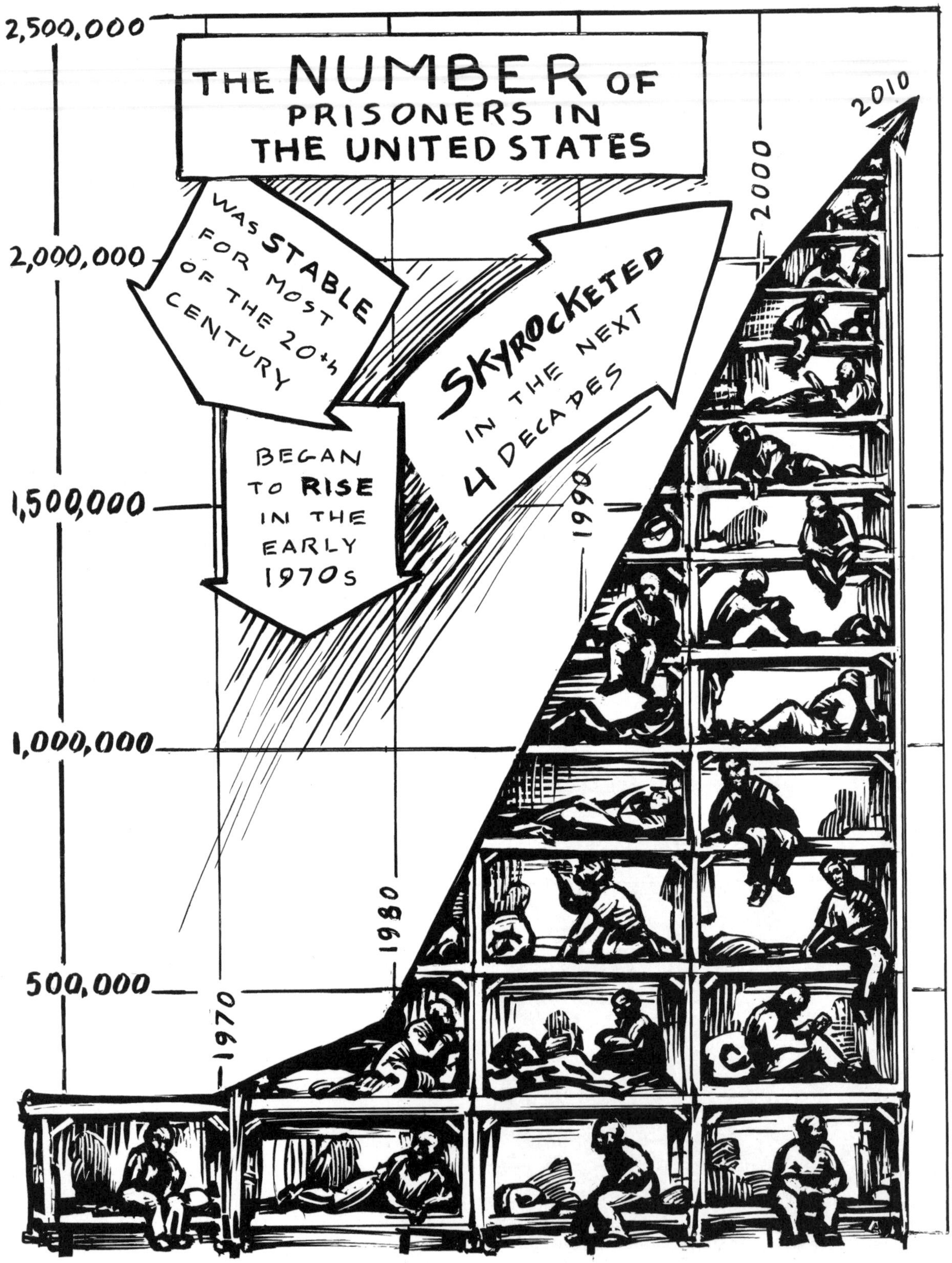
THE NUMBER OF PRISONERS IN THE UNITED STATES
WAS STABLE FOR MOST OF THE 20th CENTURY
BEGAN TO RISE IN THE EARLY 1970s
SKYROCKETED IN THE NEXT 4 DECADES
2,500,000
2,000,000
1,500,000
1,000,000
500,000
1970
1980
1990
2000
2010

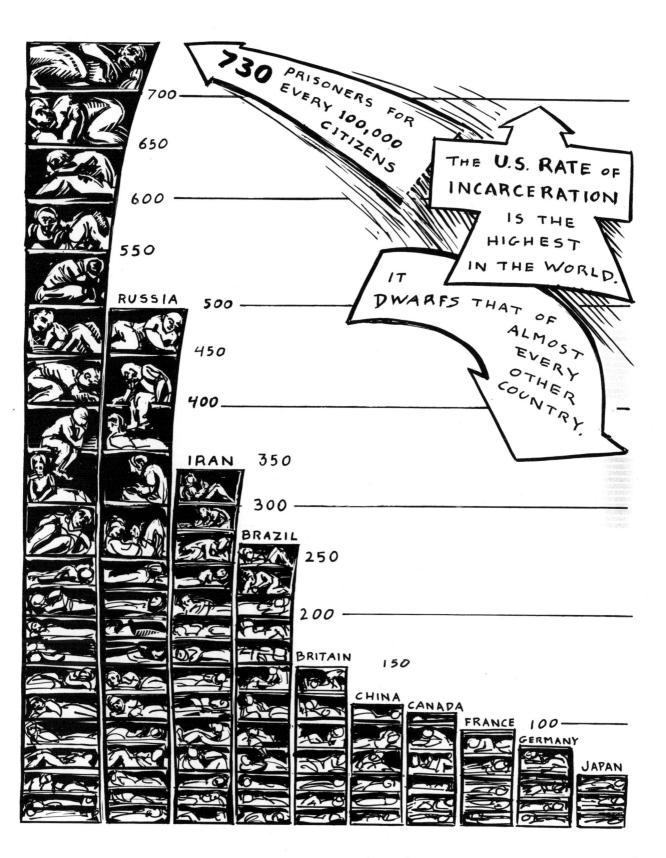

730 PRISONERS FOR EVERY **100,000** CITIZENS

THE **U.S. RATE** OF **INCARCERATION** IS THE HIGHEST IN THE WORLD.

IT **DWARFS** THAT OF ALMOST EVERY OTHER COUNTRY.

700
650
600
550
RUSSIA 500
450
400
IRAN 350
300
BRAZIL 250
200
BRITAIN 150
CHINA CANADA
FRANCE 100
GERMANY
JAPAN

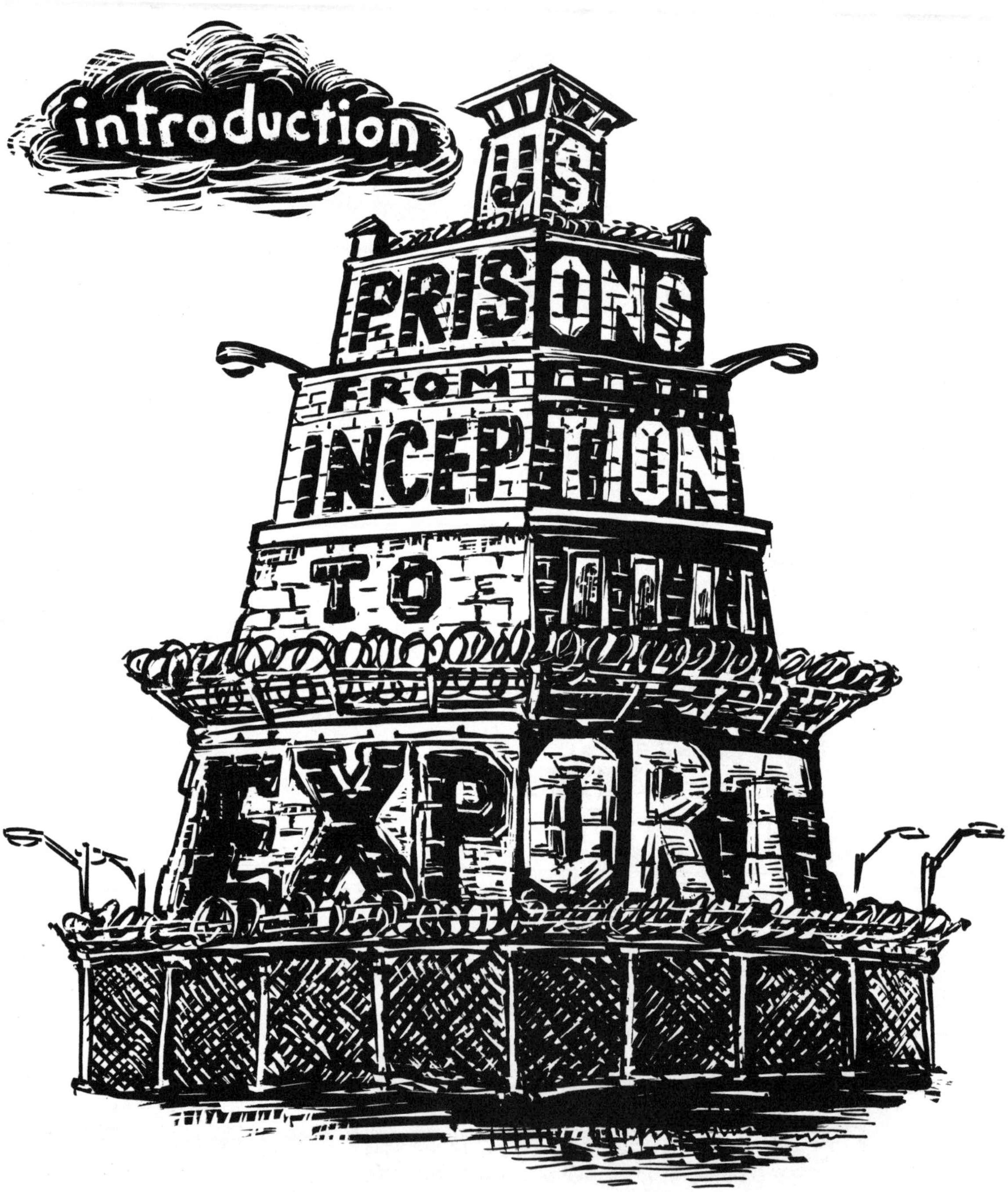
introduction
US
PRISONS
FROM
INCEPTION
TO
EXPORT

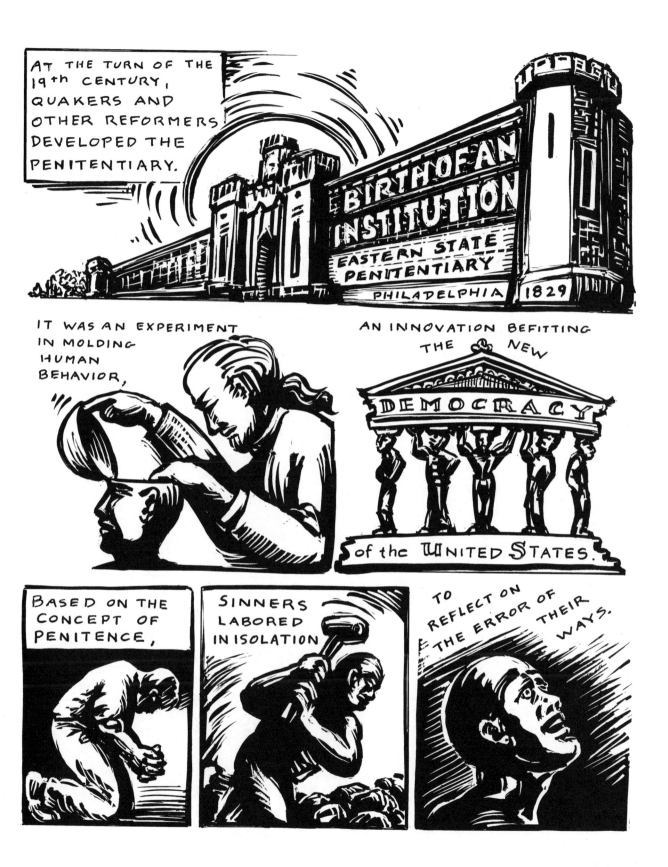

AT THE TURN OF THE 19th CENTURY, QUAKERS AND OTHER REFORMERS DEVELOPED THE PENITENTIARY.

BIRTH OF AN INSTITUTION

EASTERN STATE PENITENTIARY

PHILADELPHIA 1829

IT WAS AN EXPERIMENT IN MOLDING HUMAN BEHAVIOR,

AN INNOVATION BEFITTING THE NEW DEMOCRACY of the UNITED STATES.

BASED ON THE CONCEPT OF PENITENCE,

SINNERS LABORED IN ISOLATION

TO REFLECT ON THE ERROR OF THEIR WAYS.

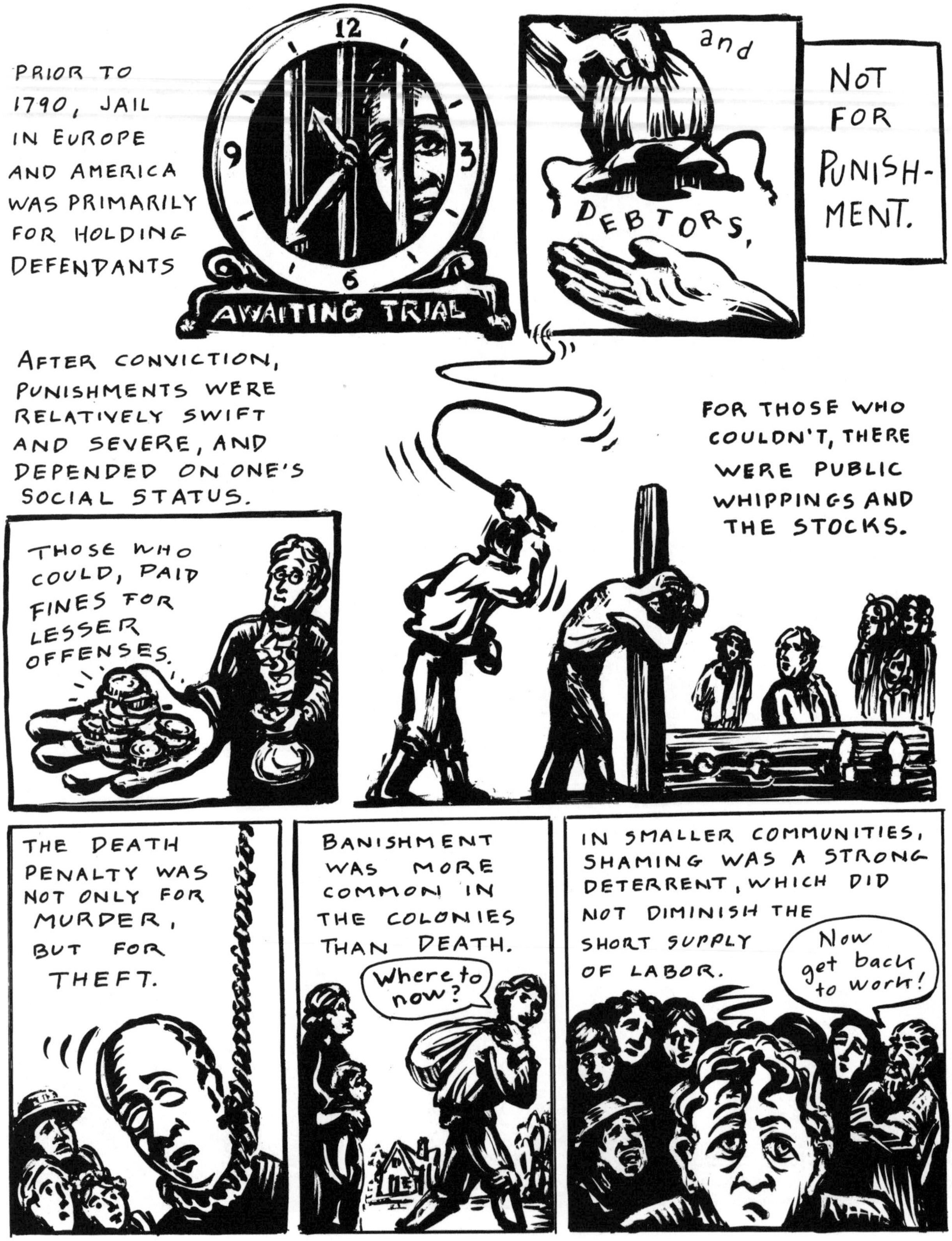
PRIOR TO 1790, JAIL IN EUROPE AND AMERICA WAS PRIMARILY FOR HOLDING DEFENDANTS
AWAITING TRIAL
and
DEBTORS,
NOT FOR PUNISHMENT.
AFTER CONVICTION, PUNISHMENTS WERE RELATIVELY SWIFT AND SEVERE, AND DEPENDED ON ONE'S SOCIAL STATUS.
THOSE WHO COULD, PAID FINES FOR LESSER OFFENSES.
FOR THOSE WHO COULDN'T, THERE WERE PUBLIC WHIPPINGS AND THE STOCKS.
THE DEATH PENALTY WAS NOT ONLY FOR MURDER, BUT FOR THEFT.
BANISHMENT WAS MORE COMMON IN THE COLONIES THAN DEATH.
Where to now?
IN SMALLER COMMUNITIES, SHAMING WAS A STRONG DETERRENT, WHICH DID NOT DIMINISH THE SHORT SUPPLY OF LABOR.
Now get back to work!

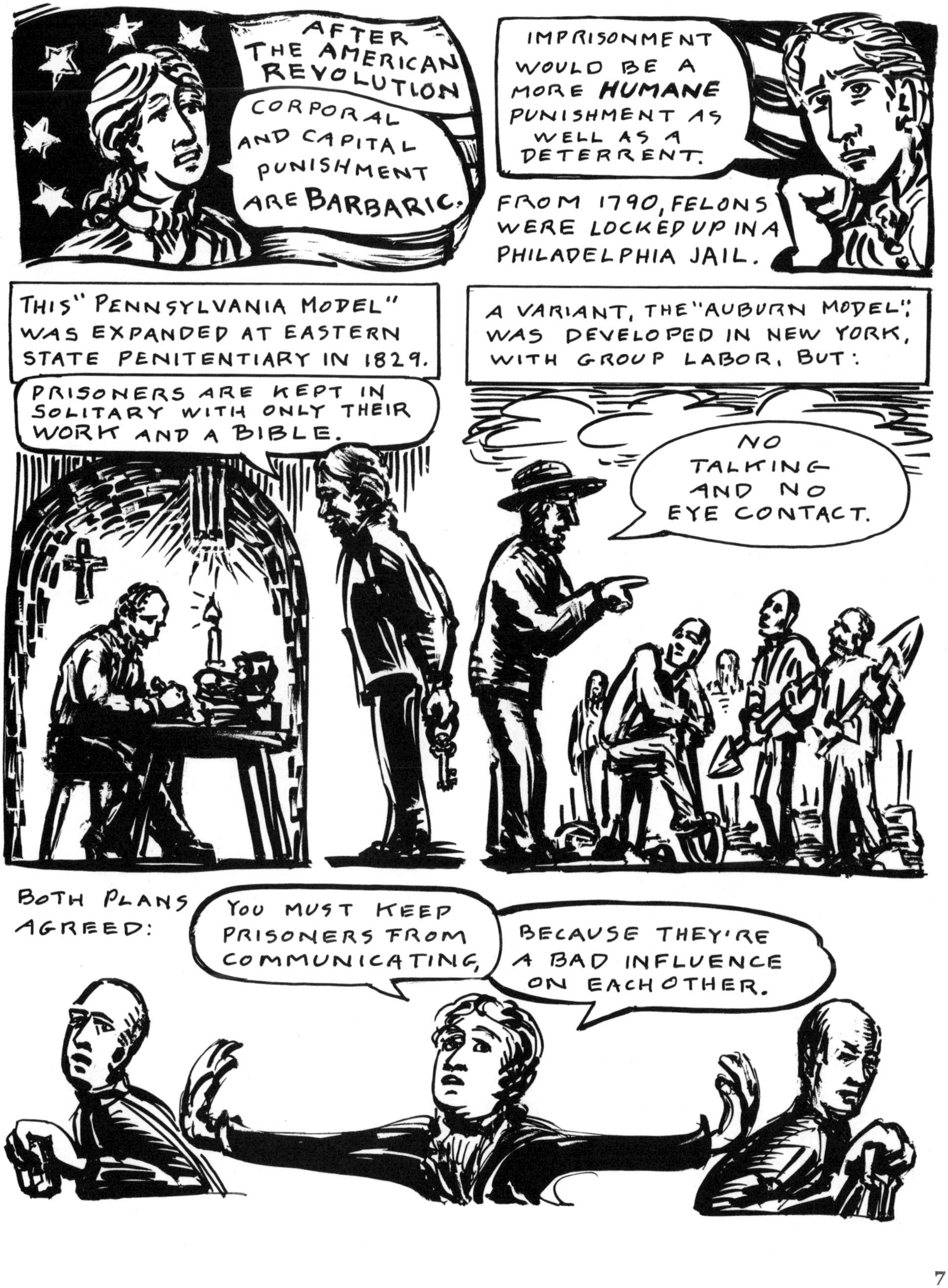
AFTER THE AMERICAN REVOLUTION
CORPORAL AND CAPITAL PUNISHMENT ARE BARBARIC.
IMPRISONMENT WOULD BE A MORE HUMANE PUNISHMENT AS WELL AS A DETERRENT.
FROM 1790, FELONS WERE LOCKED UP IN A PHILADELPHIA JAIL.
THIS "PENNSYLVANIA MODEL" WAS EXPANDED AT EASTERN STATE PENITENTIARY IN 1829.
PRISONERS ARE KEPT IN SOLITARY WITH ONLY THEIR WORK AND A BIBLE.
A VARIANT, THE "AUBURN MODEL", WAS DEVELOPED IN NEW YORK, WITH GROUP LABOR, BUT:
NO TALKING AND NO EYE CONTACT.
BOTH PLANS AGREED:
YOU MUST KEEP PRISONERS FROM COMMUNICATING,
BECAUSE THEY'RE A BAD INFLUENCE ON EACHOTHER.

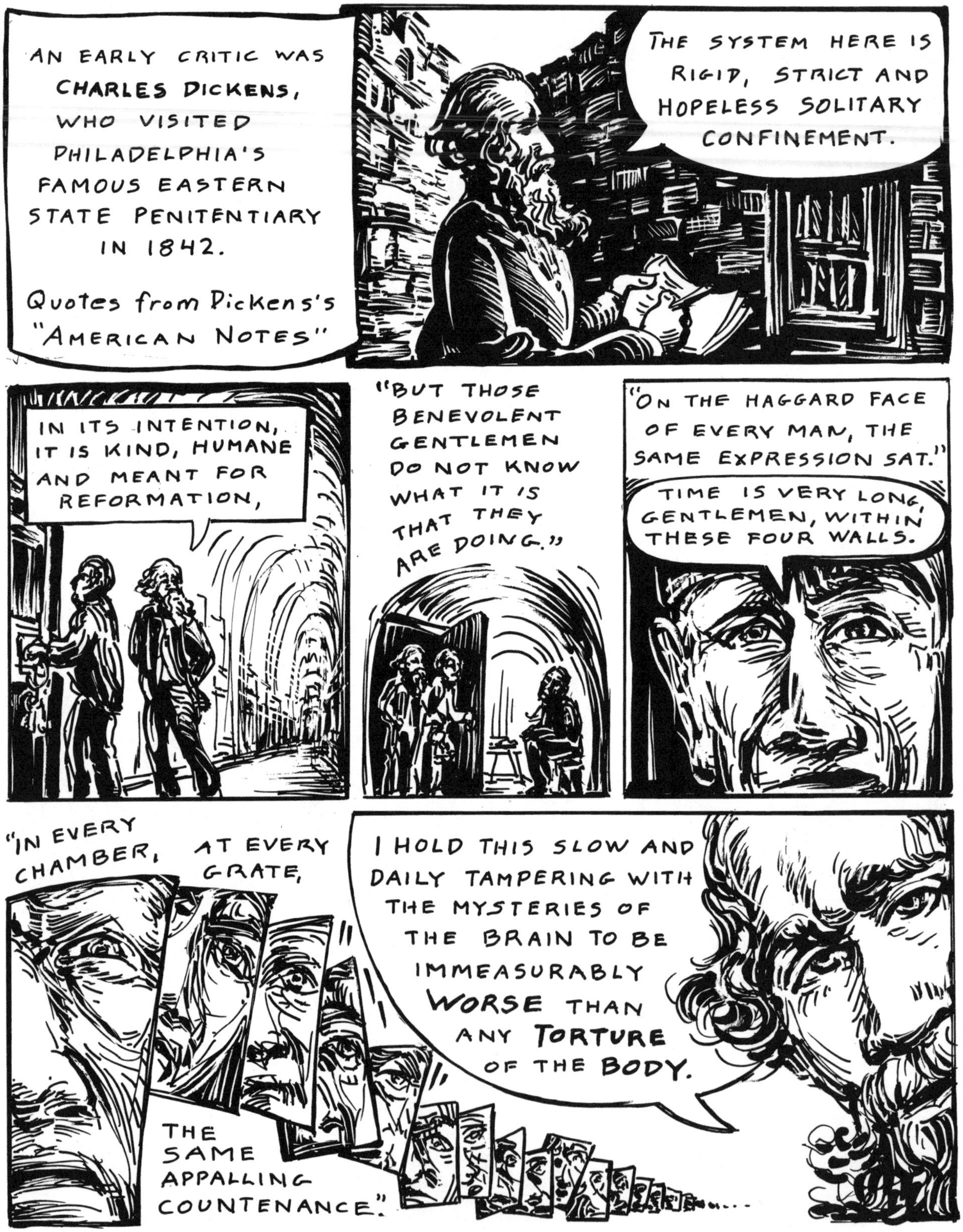
AN EARLY CRITIC WAS CHARLES DICKENS, WHO VISITED PHILADELPHIA'S FAMOUS EASTERN STATE PENITENTIARY IN 1842.
Quotes from Dickens's "AMERICAN NOTES"
THE SYSTEM HERE IS RIGID, STRICT AND HOPELESS SOLITARY CONFINEMENT.
IN ITS INTENTION, IT IS KIND, HUMANE AND MEANT FOR REFORMATION,
"BUT THOSE BENEVOLENT GENTLEMEN DO NOT KNOW WHAT IT IS THAT THEY ARE DOING."
"ON THE HAGGARD FACE OF EVERY MAN, THE SAME EXPRESSION SAT."
TIME IS VERY LONG, GENTLEMEN, WITHIN THESE FOUR WALLS.
"IN EVERY CHAMBER, AT EVERY GRATE,
THE SAME APPALLING COUNTENANCE."
I HOLD THIS SLOW AND DAILY TAMPERING WITH THE MYSTERIES OF THE BRAIN TO BE IMMEASURABLY WORSE THAN ANY TORTURE OF THE BODY.

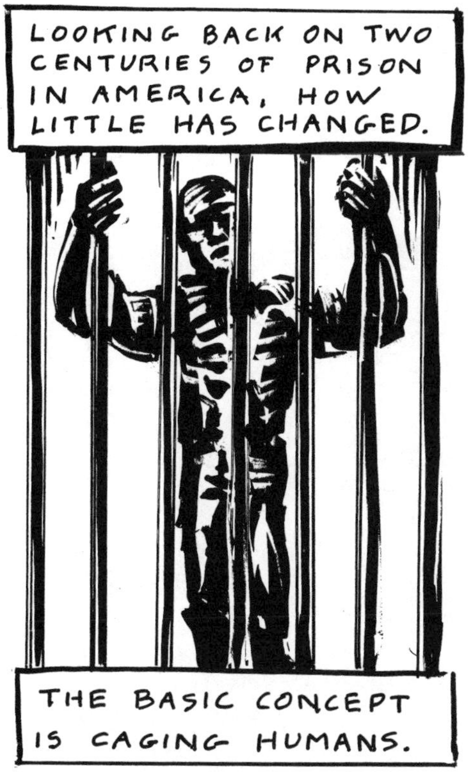
LOOKING BACK ON TWO CENTURIES OF PRISON IN AMERICA, HOW LITTLE HAS CHANGED.
THE BASIC CONCEPT IS CAGING HUMANS.

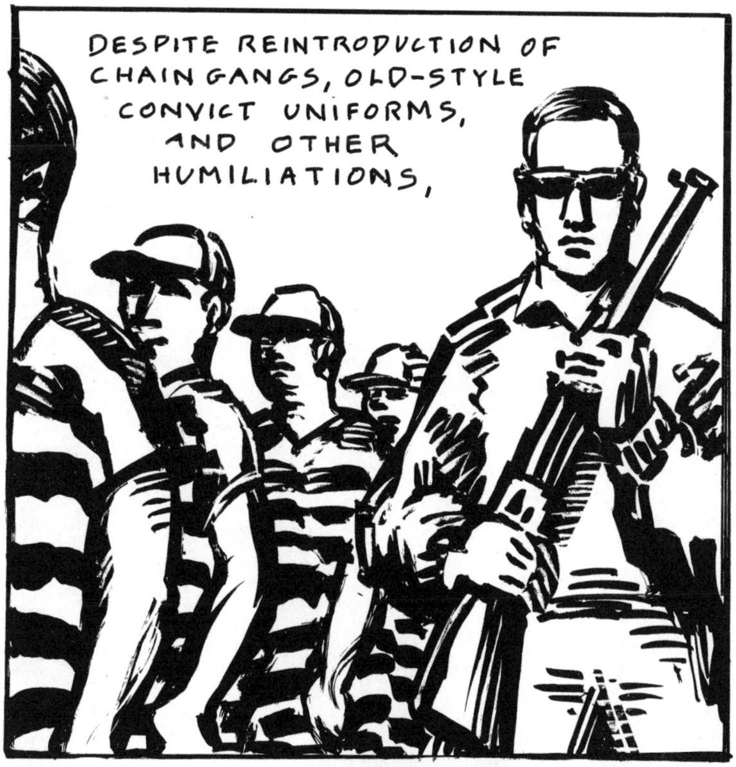
DESPITE REINTRODUCTION OF CHAINGANGS, OLD-STYLE CONVICT UNIFORMS, AND OTHER HUMILIATIONS,

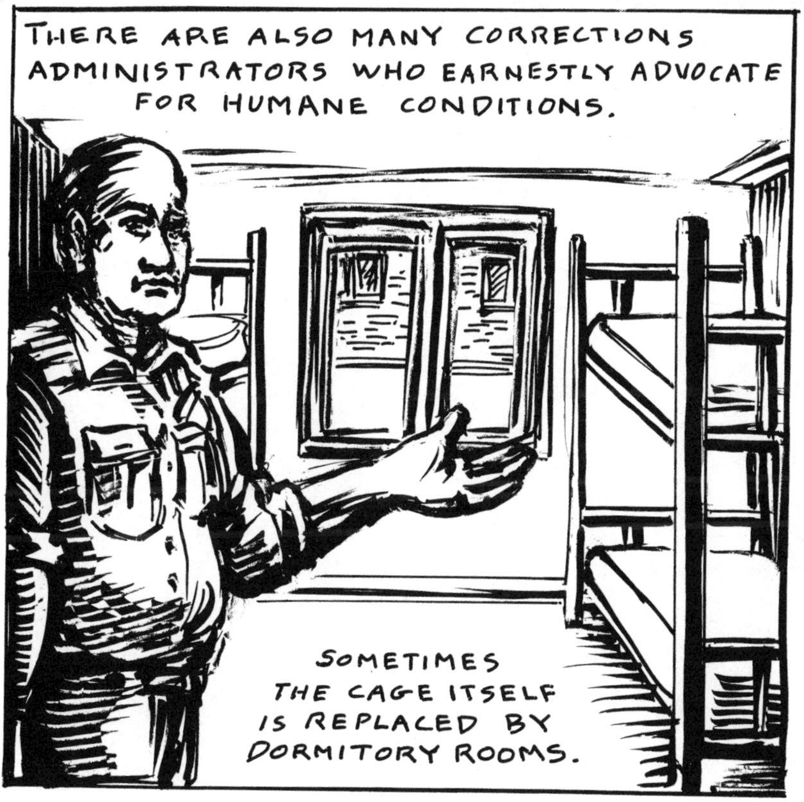
THERE ARE ALSO MANY CORRECTIONS ADMINISTRATORS WHO EARNESTLY ADVOCATE FOR HUMANE CONDITIONS.
SOMETIMES THE CAGE ITSELF IS REPLACED BY DORMITORY ROOMS.

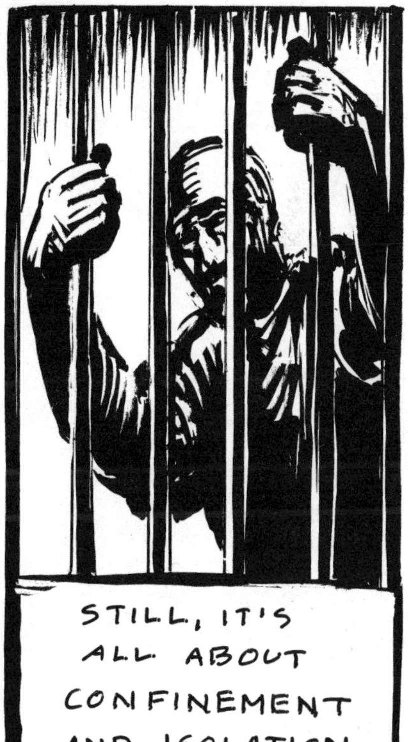
STILL, IT'S ALL ABOUT CONFINEMENT AND ISOLATION.

THE CRIMINAL JUSTICE SYSTEM IS **REACTIVE** AND PUNITIVE. IT ONLY COMES INTO PLAY **AFTER**

A CRIME IS COMMITTED · VICTIM CALLS 911 · POLICE INVESTIGATE · SUSPECT IS ARRESTED · PROSECUTOR CHARGES · TRIAL OR PLEA BARGAIN · SENTENCING · PRISON · PROBATION · PAROLE · RESTRICTIONS AFTER RELEASE

THIS MAY SEEM LIKE THE ONLY WAY, WHEN **CRIMINALS** ARE SEEN AS **ALIEN** TO THE **REST** OF **US.**

BUT THERE ARE ALSO **PROACTIVE** WAYS TO INFLUENCE BEHAVIOR **WITHIN** FAMILIES AND COMMUNITIES.

EDUCATION, RELIGION, AND PARENTING ARE WAYS TO ENCOURAGE GOOD BEHAVIOR.

SCHOOL

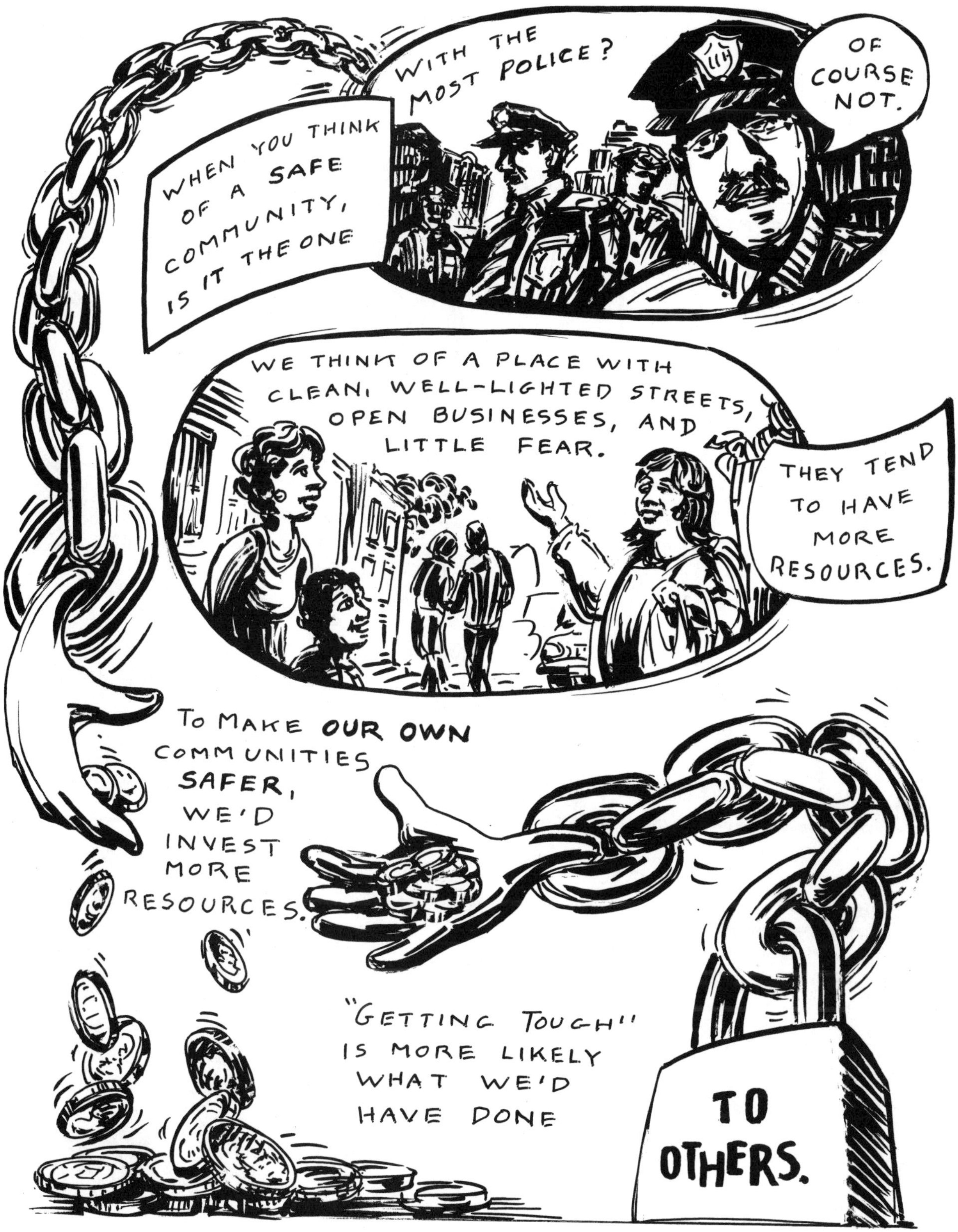
WHEN YOU THINK OF A SAFE COMMUNITY, IS IT THE ONE
WITH THE MOST POLICE?
OF COURSE NOT.
WE THINK OF A PLACE WITH CLEAN, WELL-LIGHTED STREETS, OPEN BUSINESSES, AND LITTLE FEAR.
THEY TEND TO HAVE MORE RESOURCES.
TO MAKE OUR OWN COMMUNITIES SAFER, WE'D INVEST MORE RESOURCES.
"GETTING TOUGH" IS MORE LIKELY WHAT WE'D HAVE DONE
TO OTHERS.

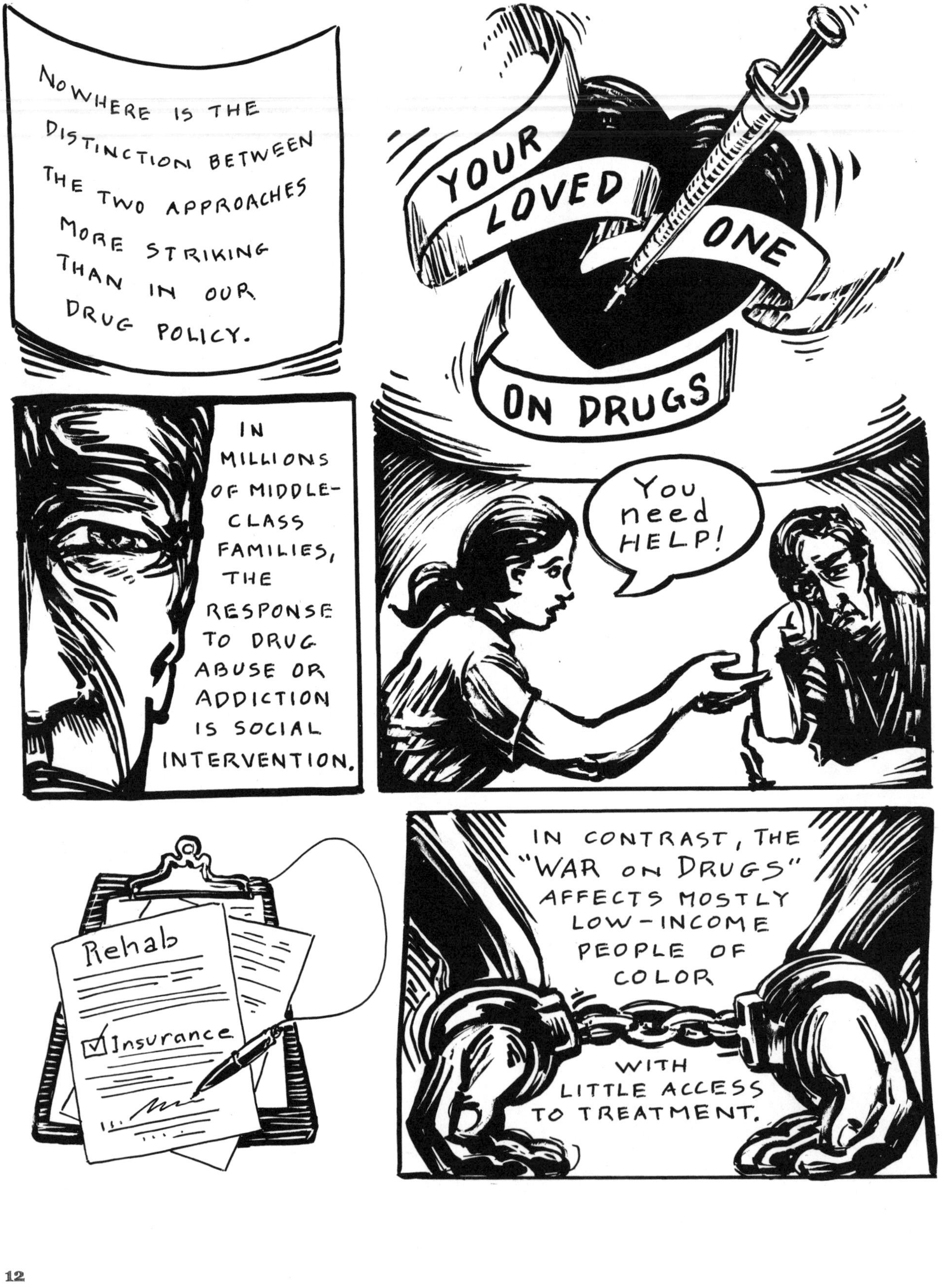
Nowhere is the distinction between the two approaches more striking than in our drug policy.
Your loved one on drugs
In millions of middle-class families, the response to drug abuse or addiction is social intervention.
You need HELP!
Rehab
Insurance
In contrast, the "War on Drugs" affects mostly low-income people of color
with little access to treatment.

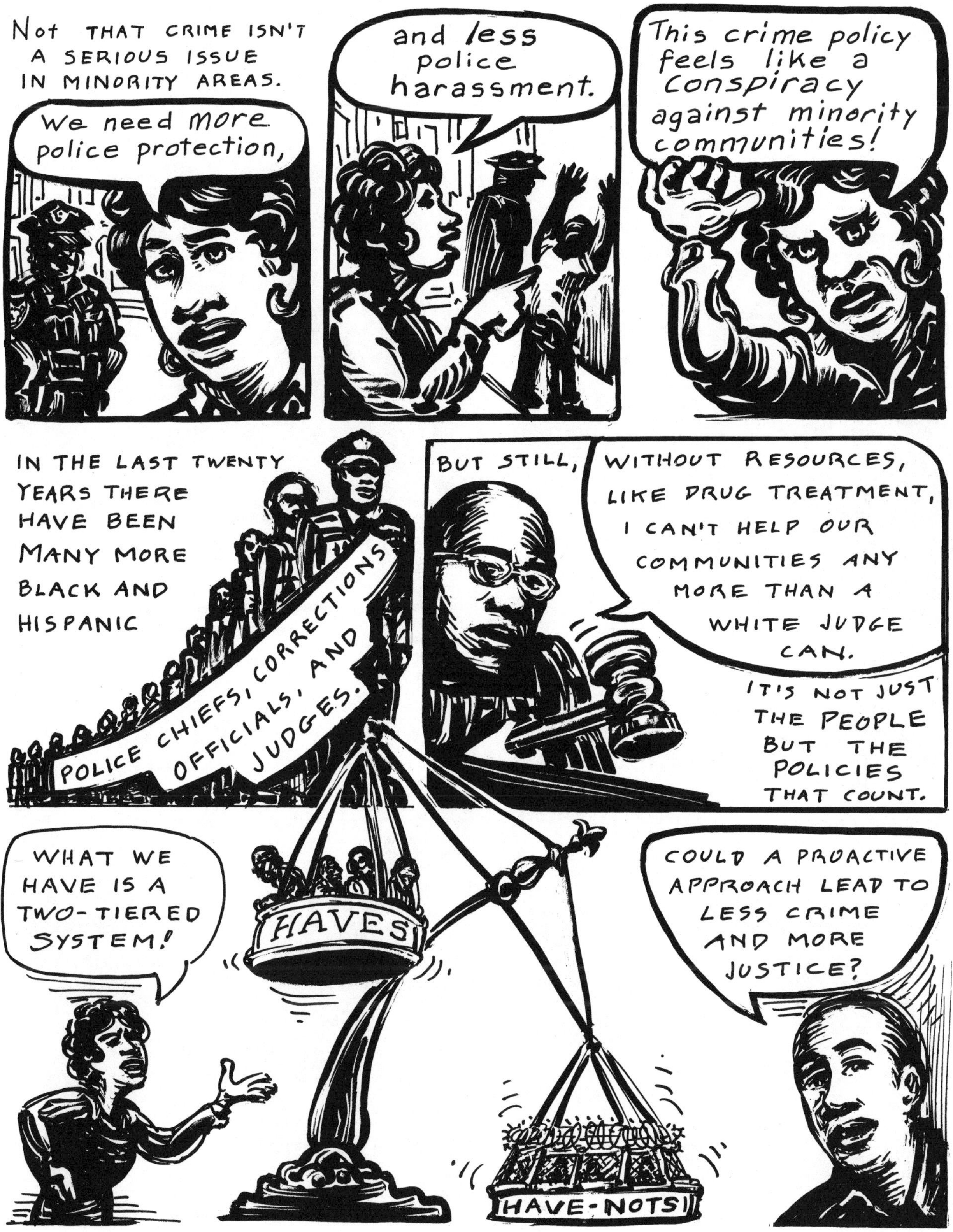

Not THAT CRIME ISN'T A SERIOUS ISSUE IN MINORITY AREAS.
We need more police protection,
and less police harassment.
This crime policy feels like a conspiracy against minority communities!
IN THE LAST TWENTY YEARS THERE HAVE BEEN MANY MORE BLACK AND HISPANIC
POLICE CHIEFS, CORRECTIONS OFFICIALS, AND JUDGES.
BUT STILL,
WITHOUT RESOURCES, LIKE DRUG TREATMENT, I CAN'T HELP OUR COMMUNITIES ANY MORE THAN A WHITE JUDGE CAN.
IT'S NOT JUST THE PEOPLE BUT THE POLICIES THAT COUNT.
WHAT WE HAVE IS A TWO-TIERED SYSTEM!
HAVES
HAVE-NOTS
COULD A PROACTIVE APPROACH LEAD TO LESS CRIME AND MORE JUSTICE?

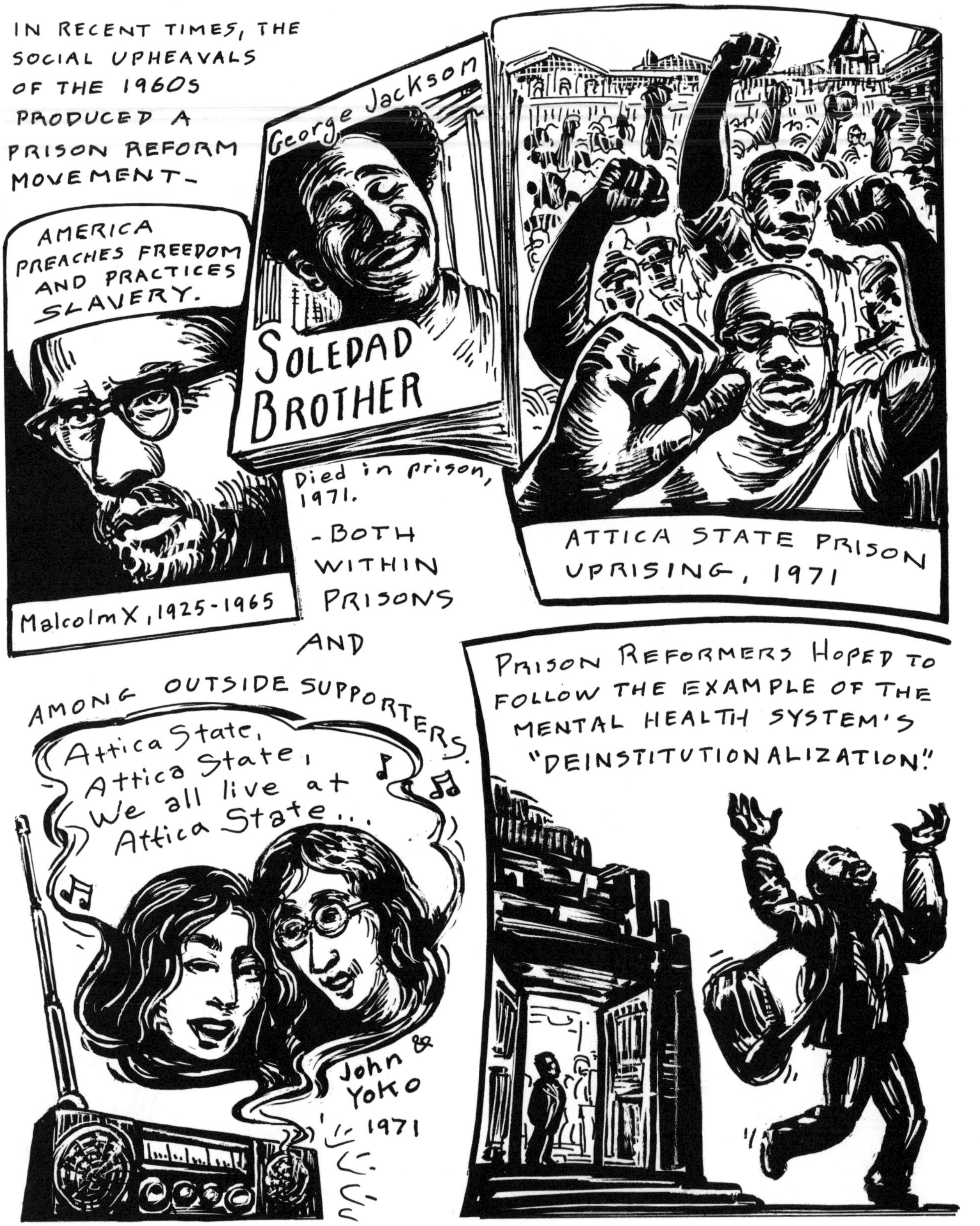
IN RECENT TIMES, THE SOCIAL UPHEAVALS OF THE 1960S PRODUCED A PRISON REFORM MOVEMENT–
AMERICA PREACHES FREEDOM AND PRACTICES SLAVERY.
Malcolm X, 1925-1965
George Jackson
SOLEDAD BROTHER
Died in prison, 1971.
ATTICA STATE PRISON UPRISING, 1971
-BOTH WITHIN PRISONS
AND
AMONG OUTSIDE SUPPORTERS.
Attica State, Attica State, We all live at Attica State...
John & Yoko 1971
PRISON REFORMERS HOPED TO FOLLOW THE EXAMPLE OF THE MENTAL HEALTH SYSTEM'S "DEINSTITUTIONALIZATION."

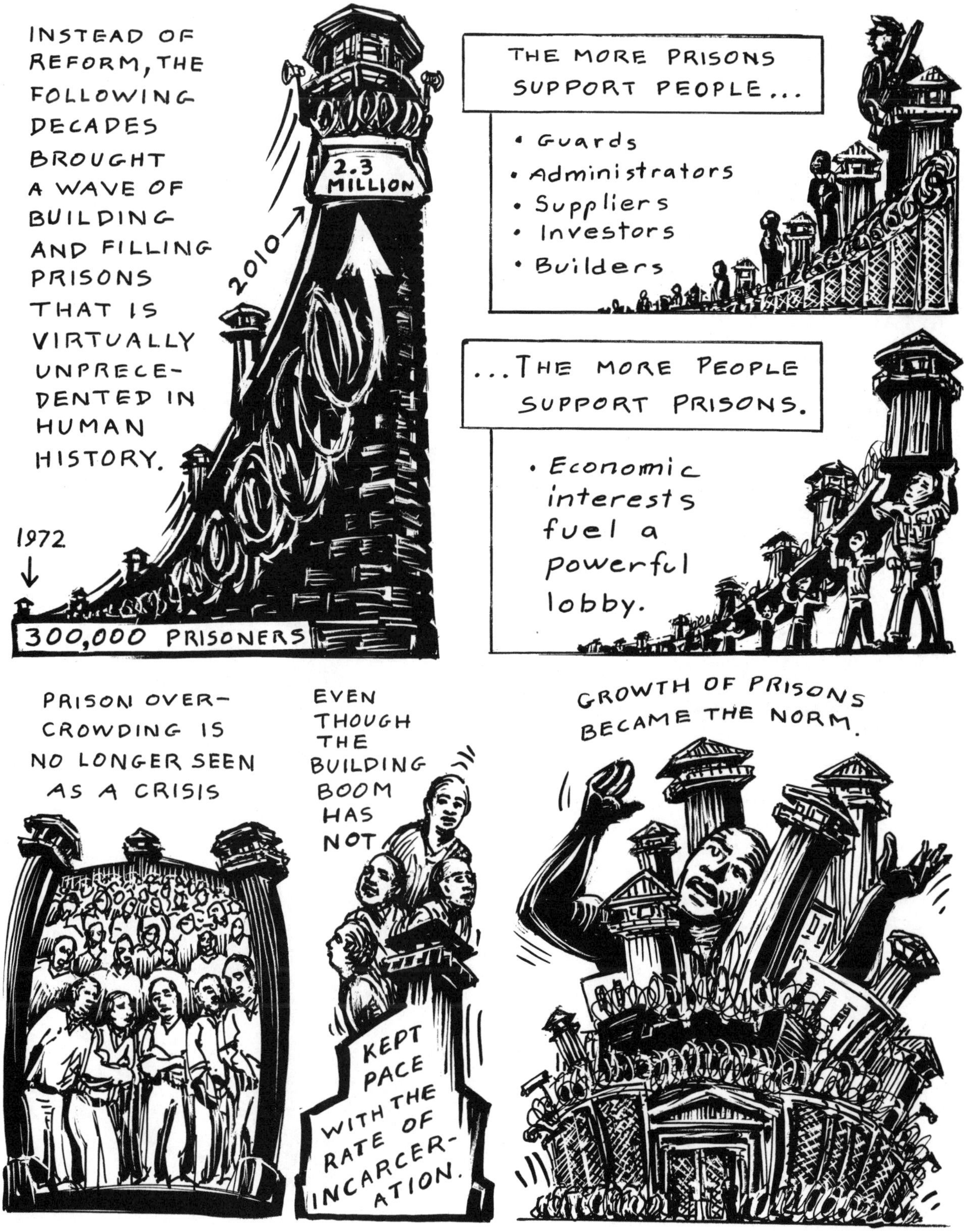
INSTEAD OF REFORM, THE FOLLOWING DECADES BROUGHT A WAVE OF BUILDING AND FILLING PRISONS THAT IS VIRTUALLY UNPRECE-DENTED IN HUMAN HISTORY.
2.3 MILLION
2010
1972
300,000 PRISONERS
THE MORE PRISONS SUPPORT PEOPLE...
• Guards
• Administrators
• Suppliers
• Investors
• Builders
...THE MORE PEOPLE SUPPORT PRISONS.
• Economic interests fuel a powerful lobby.
PRISON OVER-CROWDING IS NO LONGER SEEN AS A CRISIS
EVEN THOUGH THE BUILDING BOOM HAS NOT
KEPT PACE WITH THE RATE OF INCARCER-ATION.
GROWTH OF PRISONS BECAME THE NORM.

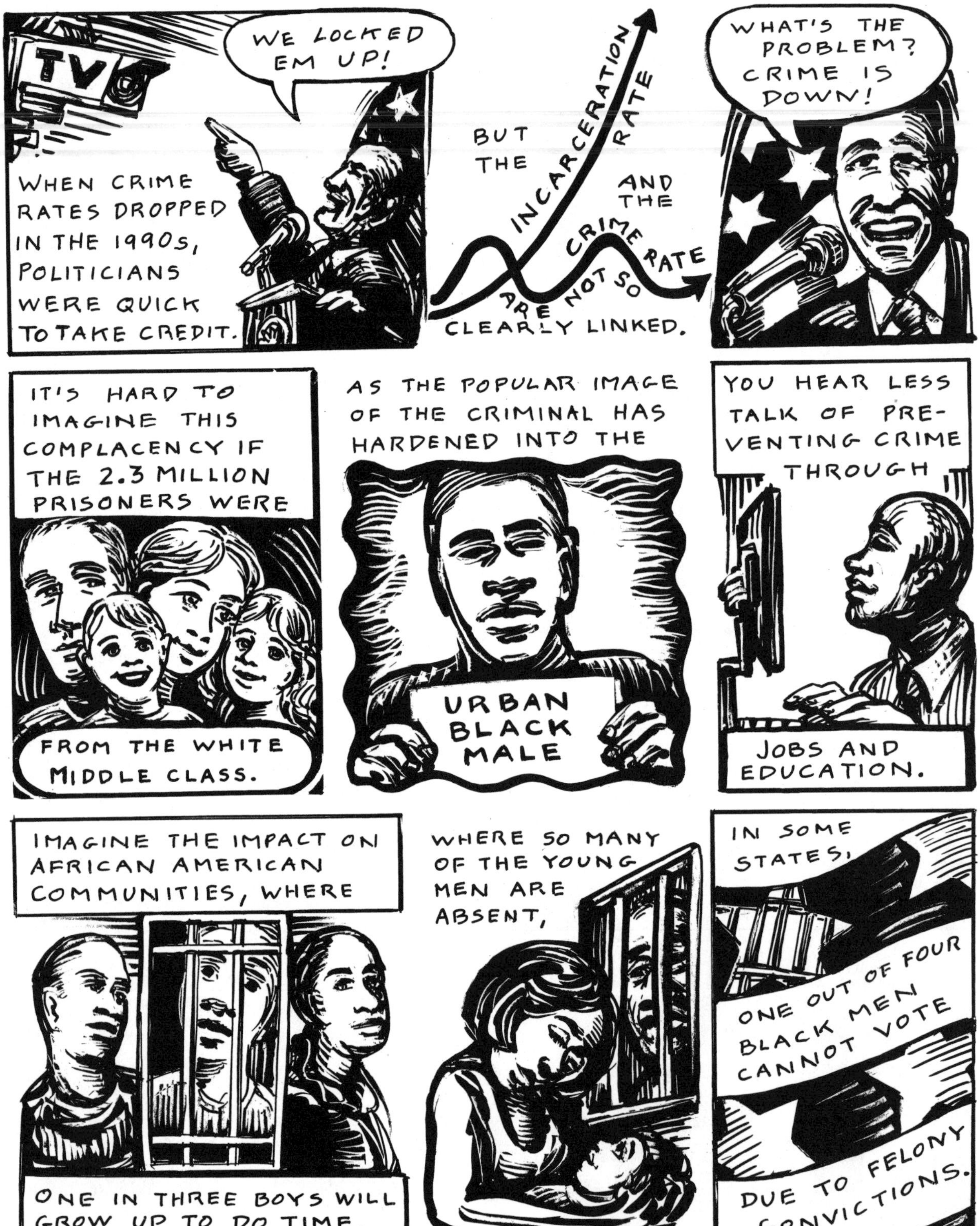
TV
WE LOCKED EM UP!
WHEN CRIME RATES DROPPED IN THE 1990s, POLITICIANS WERE QUICK TO TAKE CREDIT.
BUT THE
INCARCERATION RATE
AND THE
CRIME RATE
ARE NOT SO CLEARLY LINKED.
WHAT'S THE PROBLEM? CRIME IS DOWN!
IT'S HARD TO IMAGINE THIS COMPLACENCY IF THE 2.3 MILLION PRISONERS WERE
FROM THE WHITE MIDDLE CLASS.
AS THE POPULAR IMAGE OF THE CRIMINAL HAS HARDENED INTO THE
URBAN BLACK MALE
YOU HEAR LESS TALK OF PRE- VENTING CRIME THROUGH
JOBS AND EDUCATION.
IMAGINE THE IMPACT ON AFRICAN AMERICAN COMMUNITIES, WHERE
ONE IN THREE BOYS WILL GROW UP TO DO TIME,
WHERE SO MANY OF THE YOUNG MEN ARE ABSENT,
IN SOME STATES,
ONE OUT OF FOUR BLACK MEN CANNOT VOTE
DUE TO FELONY CONVICTIONS.

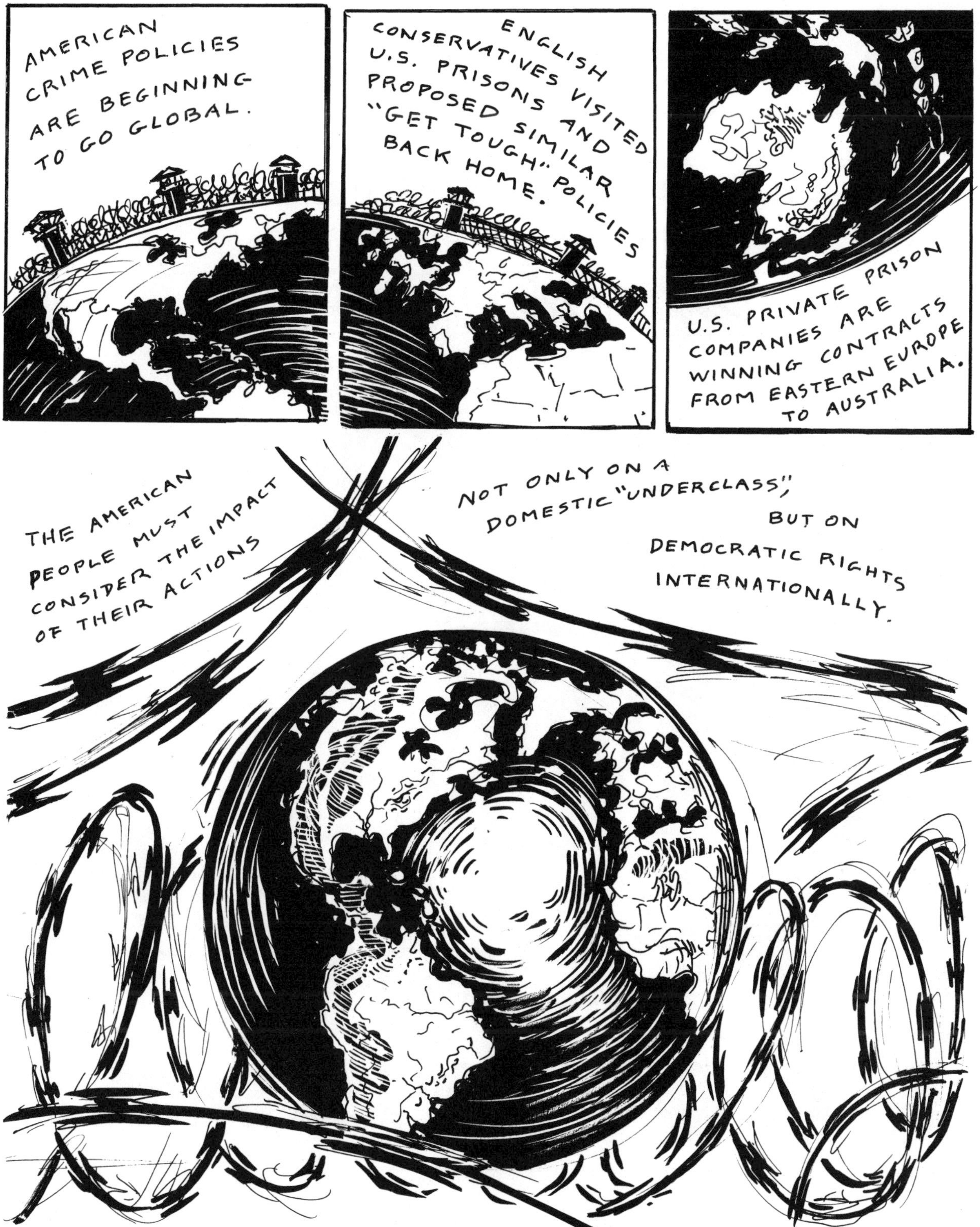
AMERICAN CRIME POLICIES ARE BEGINNING TO GO GLOBAL.
ENGLISH CONSERVATIVES VISITED U.S. PRISONS AND PROPOSED SIMILAR "GET TOUGH" POLICIES BACK HOME.
U.S. PRIVATE PRISON COMPANIES ARE WINNING CONTRACTS FROM EASTERN EUROPE TO AUSTRALIA.
THE AMERICAN PEOPLE MUST CONSIDER THE IMPACT OF THEIR ACTIONS
NOT ONLY ON A DOMESTIC "UNDERCLASS,"
BUT ON DEMOCRATIC RIGHTS INTERNATIONALLY.

THE RISE OF THE

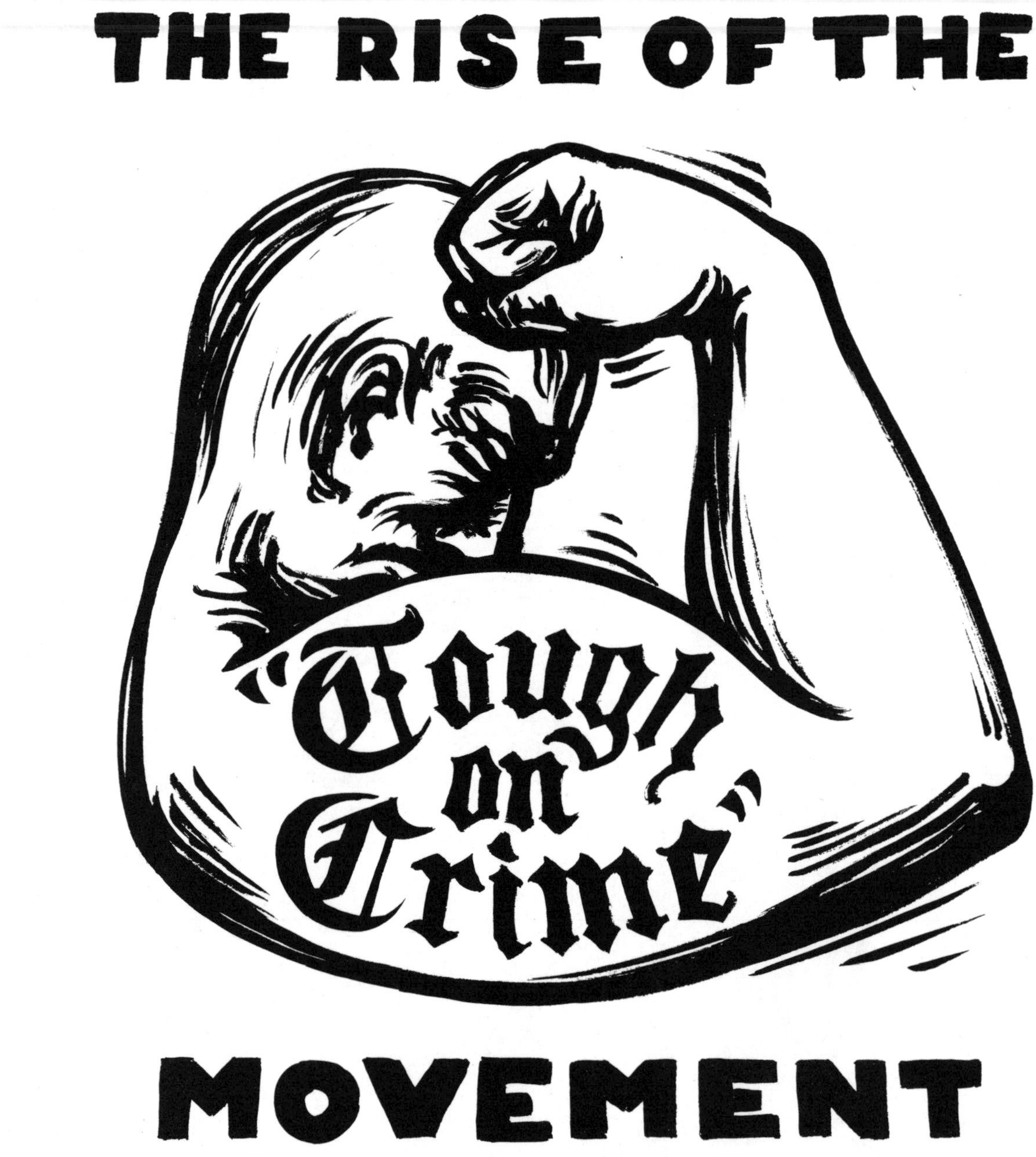
"Tough on Crime"

MOVEMENT

THE RACE TO INCARCERATE FORMALLY BEGAN IN **1973** WITH THE RISE OF THE PRISON POPULATION, BUT ITS ROOTS CAN BE TRACED BACK TO THE PREVIOUS DECADE WITH THE CRITIQUE OF REHABILITATION.

PRISONS HAVE CHANGED VERY LITTLE OVER THE LAST TWO CENTURIES, BUT OUR IDEA OF THEIR PURPOSE HAS UNDERGONE SHIFTS.

DETERRENCE

REHABILITATION

AMERICA'S POST-WWII PROSPERITY FUELED A MOOD OF OPTIMISM

IN WHICH PUBLIC POLICY BECAME MORE GENEROUS AND COMPASSIONATE.

THE DEATH PENALTY, WHICH HAD PEAKED IN THE 1930s, IN THE DEPRESSION,

FELL INTO DECLINE AND WAS ABOLISHED IN PRACTICE BY LEGAL CHALLENGES IN 1972.

IN 1968, 72% OF AMERICANS TOLD POLLSTERS THE GOAL OF PRISON SHOULD BE REHABILITATION.

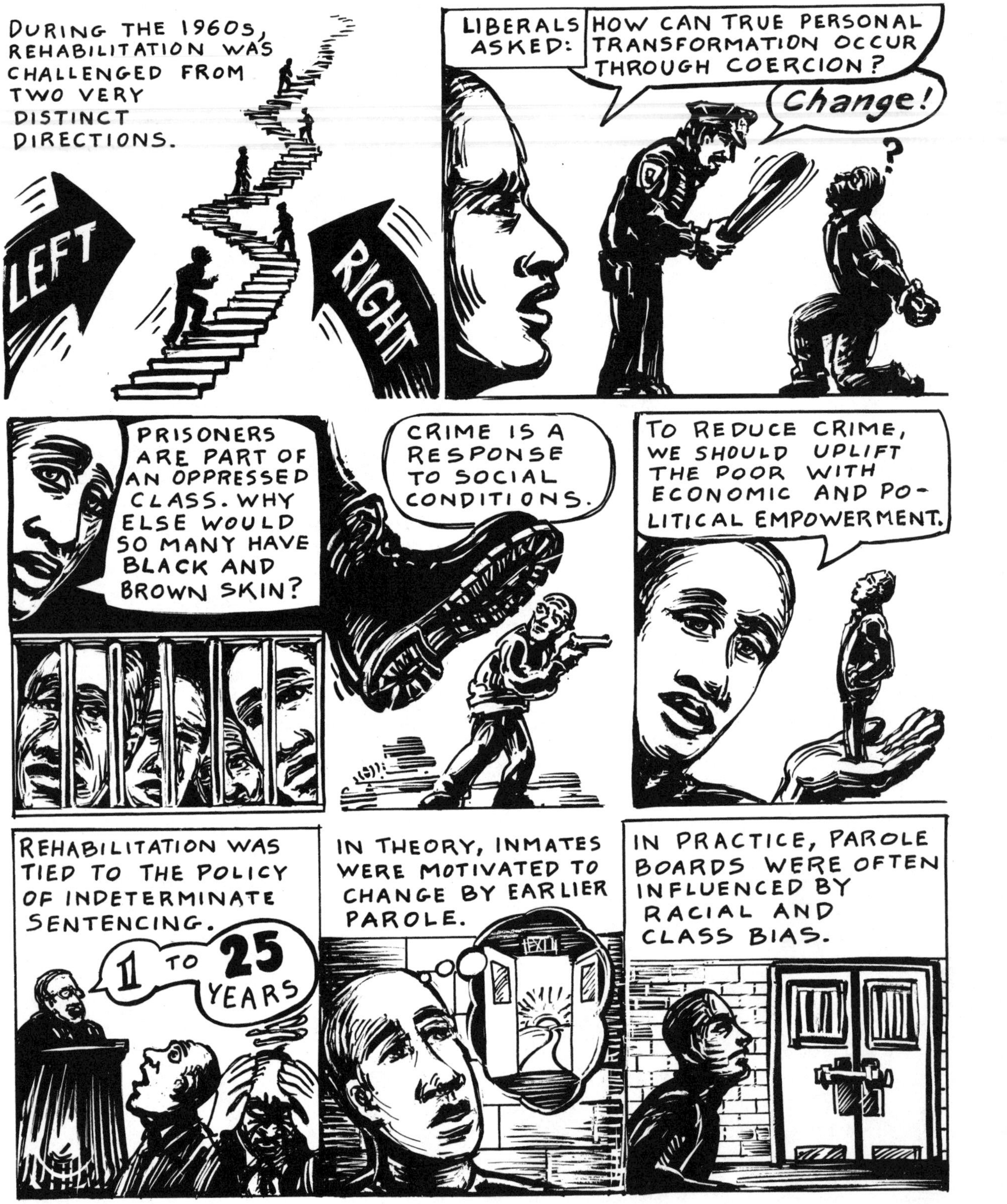
DURING THE 1960S, REHABILITATION WAS CHALLENGED FROM TWO VERY DISTINCT DIRECTIONS.
LEFT
RIGHT
LIBERALS ASKED:
HOW CAN TRUE PERSONAL TRANSFORMATION OCCUR THROUGH COERCION?
Change!
?
PRISONERS ARE PART OF AN OPPRESSED CLASS. WHY ELSE WOULD SO MANY HAVE BLACK AND BROWN SKIN?
CRIME IS A RESPONSE TO SOCIAL CONDITIONS.
TO REDUCE CRIME, WE SHOULD UPLIFT THE POOR WITH ECONOMIC AND POLITICAL EMPOWERMENT.
REHABILITATION WAS TIED TO THE POLICY OF INDETERMINATE SENTENCING.
1 TO 25 YEARS
IN THEORY, INMATES WERE MOTIVATED TO CHANGE BY EARLIER PAROLE.
EXIT
IN PRACTICE, PAROLE BOARDS WERE OFTEN INFLUENCED BY RACIAL AND CLASS BIAS.

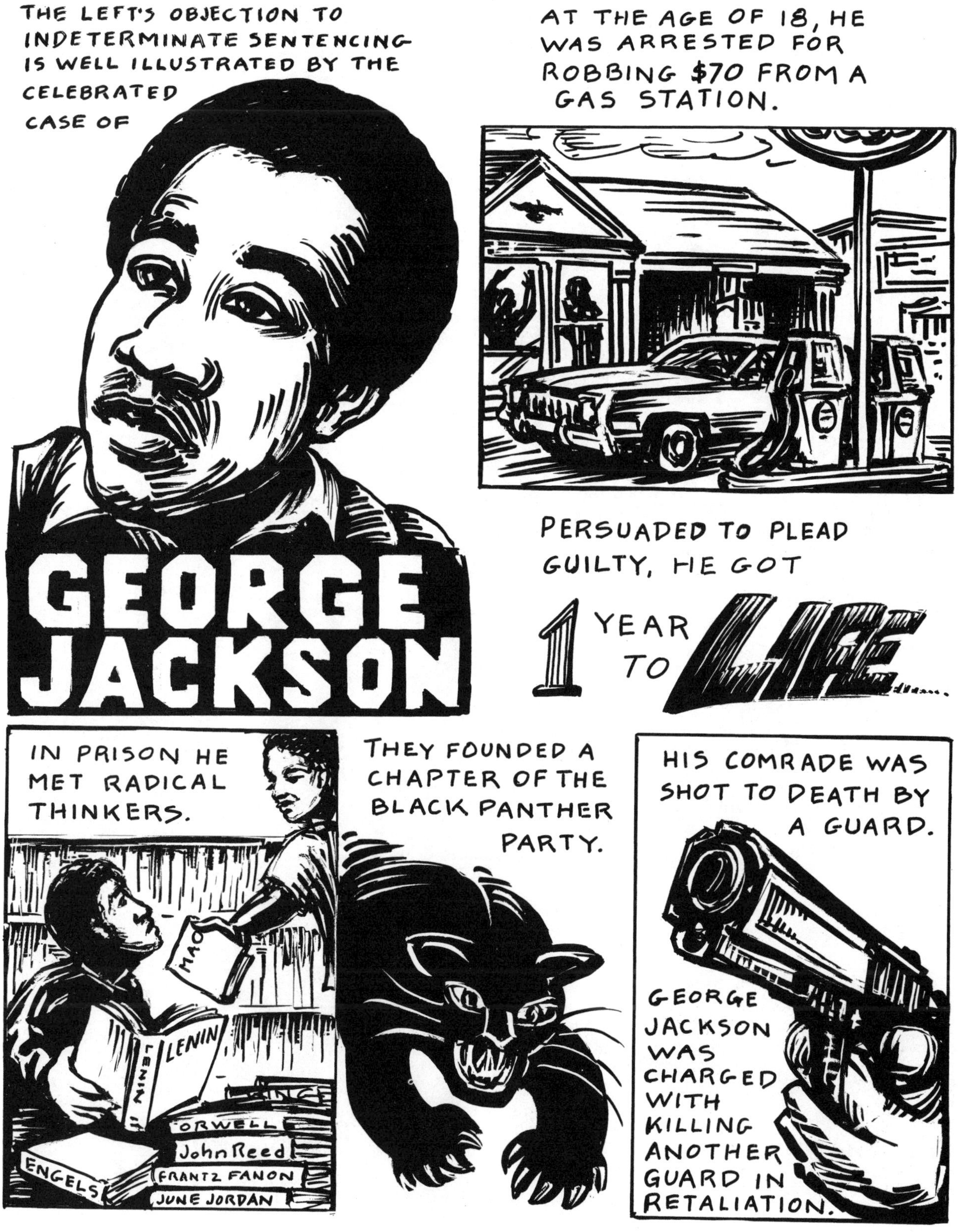

THE LEFT'S OBJECTION TO INDETERMINATE SENTENCING IS WELL ILLUSTRATED BY THE CELEBRATED CASE OF
GEORGE JACKSON
AT THE AGE OF 18, HE WAS ARRESTED FOR ROBBING $70 FROM A GAS STATION.
PERSUADED TO PLEAD GUILTY, HE GOT
1 YEAR TO LIFE...
IN PRISON HE MET RADICAL THINKERS.
MAO
LENIN
LENIN
ORWELL
John Reed
ENGELS
FRANTZ FANON
JUNE JORDAN
THEY FOUNDED A CHAPTER OF THE BLACK PANTHER PARTY.
HIS COMRADE WAS SHOT TO DEATH BY A GUARD.
GEORGE JACKSON WAS CHARGED WITH KILLING ANOTHER GUARD IN RETALIATION.

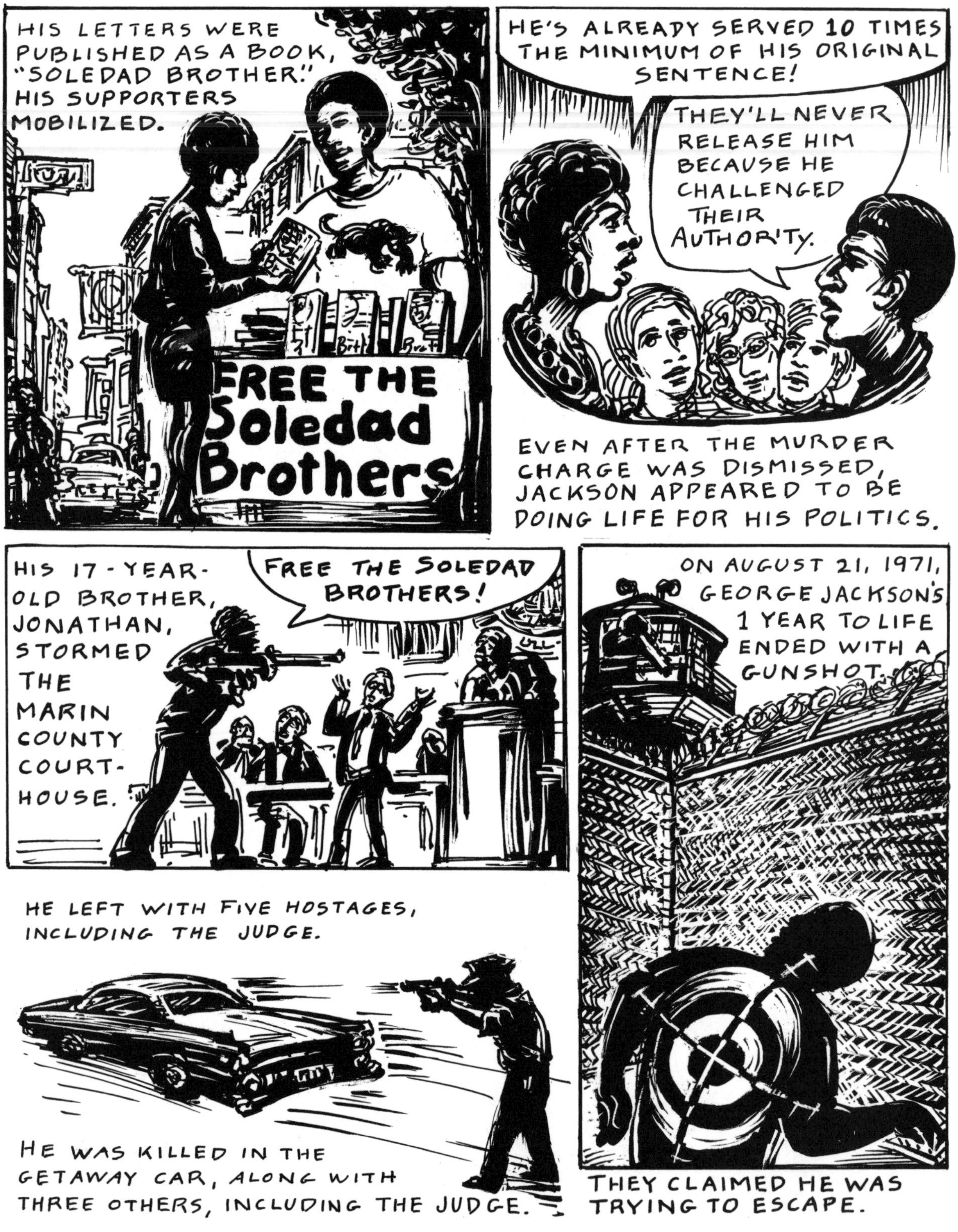

HIS LETTERS WERE PUBLISHED AS A BOOK, "SOLEDAD BROTHER." HIS SUPPORTERS MOBILIZED.
FREE THE Soledad Brothers
HE'S ALREADY SERVED 10 TIMES THE MINIMUM OF HIS ORIGINAL SENTENCE!
THEY'LL NEVER RELEASE HIM BECAUSE HE CHALLENGED THEIR AUTHORITY.
EVEN AFTER THE MURDER CHARGE WAS DISMISSED, JACKSON APPEARED TO BE DOING LIFE FOR HIS POLITICS.
HIS 17-YEAR-OLD BROTHER, JONATHAN, STORMED THE MARIN COUNTY COURTHOUSE.
FREE THE SOLEDAD BROTHERS!
HE LEFT WITH FIVE HOSTAGES, INCLUDING THE JUDGE.
HE WAS KILLED IN THE GETAWAY CAR, ALONG WITH THREE OTHERS, INCLUDING THE JUDGE.
ON AUGUST 21, 1971, GEORGE JACKSON'S 1 YEAR TO LIFE ENDED WITH A GUNSHOT.
THEY CLAIMED HE WAS TRYING TO ESCAPE.

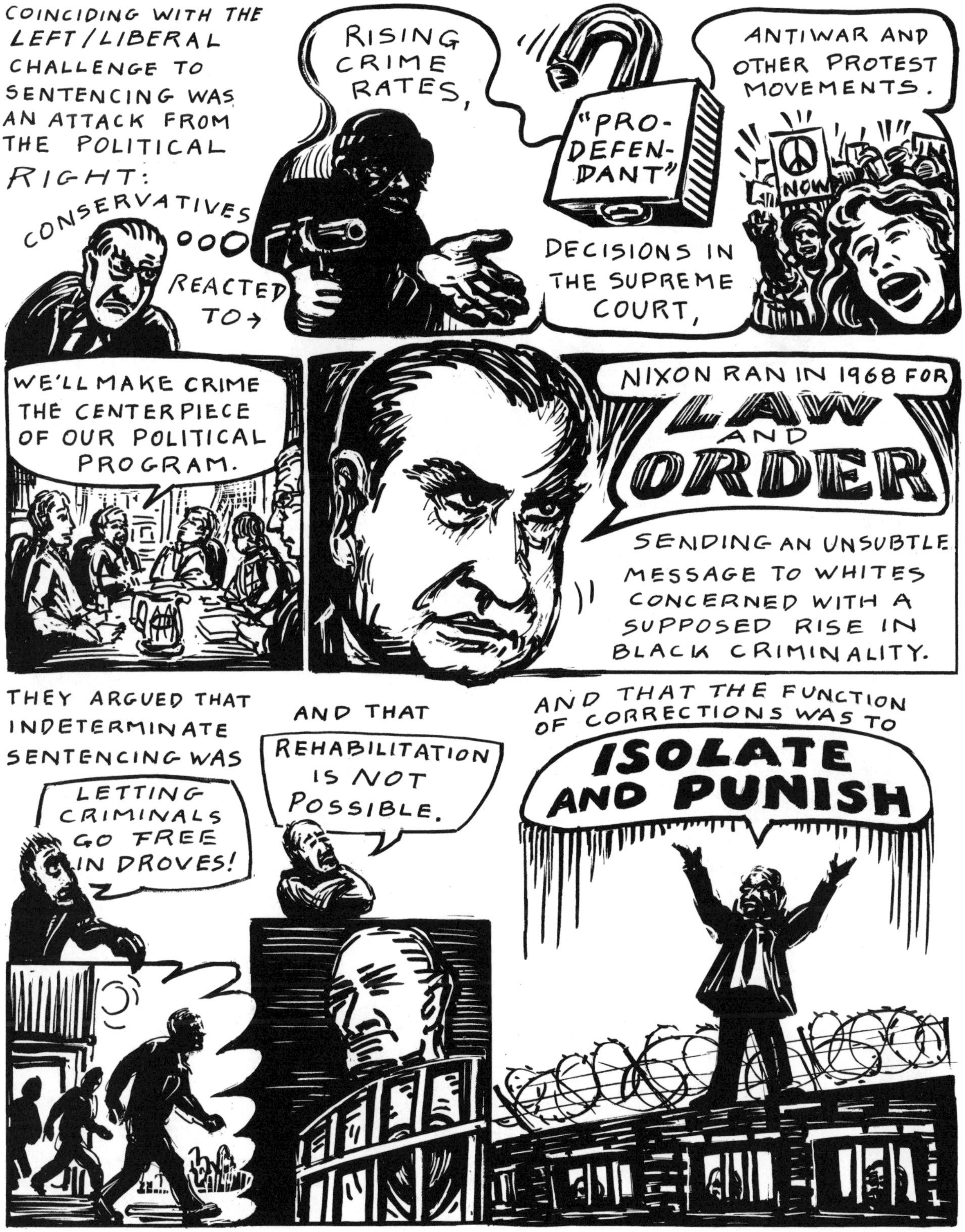

COINCIDING WITH THE LEFT/LIBERAL CHALLENGE TO SENTENCING WAS AN ATTACK FROM THE POLITICAL RIGHT:
CONSERVATIVES
REACTED TO→
RISING CRIME RATES,
"PRO-DEFENDANT"
DECISIONS IN THE SUPREME COURT,
ANTIWAR AND OTHER PROTEST MOVEMENTS.
NOW
WE'LL MAKE CRIME THE CENTERPIECE OF OUR POLITICAL PROGRAM.
NIXON RAN IN 1968 FOR
LAW AND ORDER
SENDING AN UNSUBTLE MESSAGE TO WHITES CONCERNED WITH A SUPPOSED RISE IN BLACK CRIMINALITY.
THEY ARGUED THAT INDETERMINATE SENTENCING WAS
LETTING CRIMINALS GO FREE IN DROVES!
AND THAT
REHABILITATION IS NOT POSSIBLE.
AND THAT THE FUNCTION OF CORRECTIONS WAS TO
ISOLATE AND PUNISH

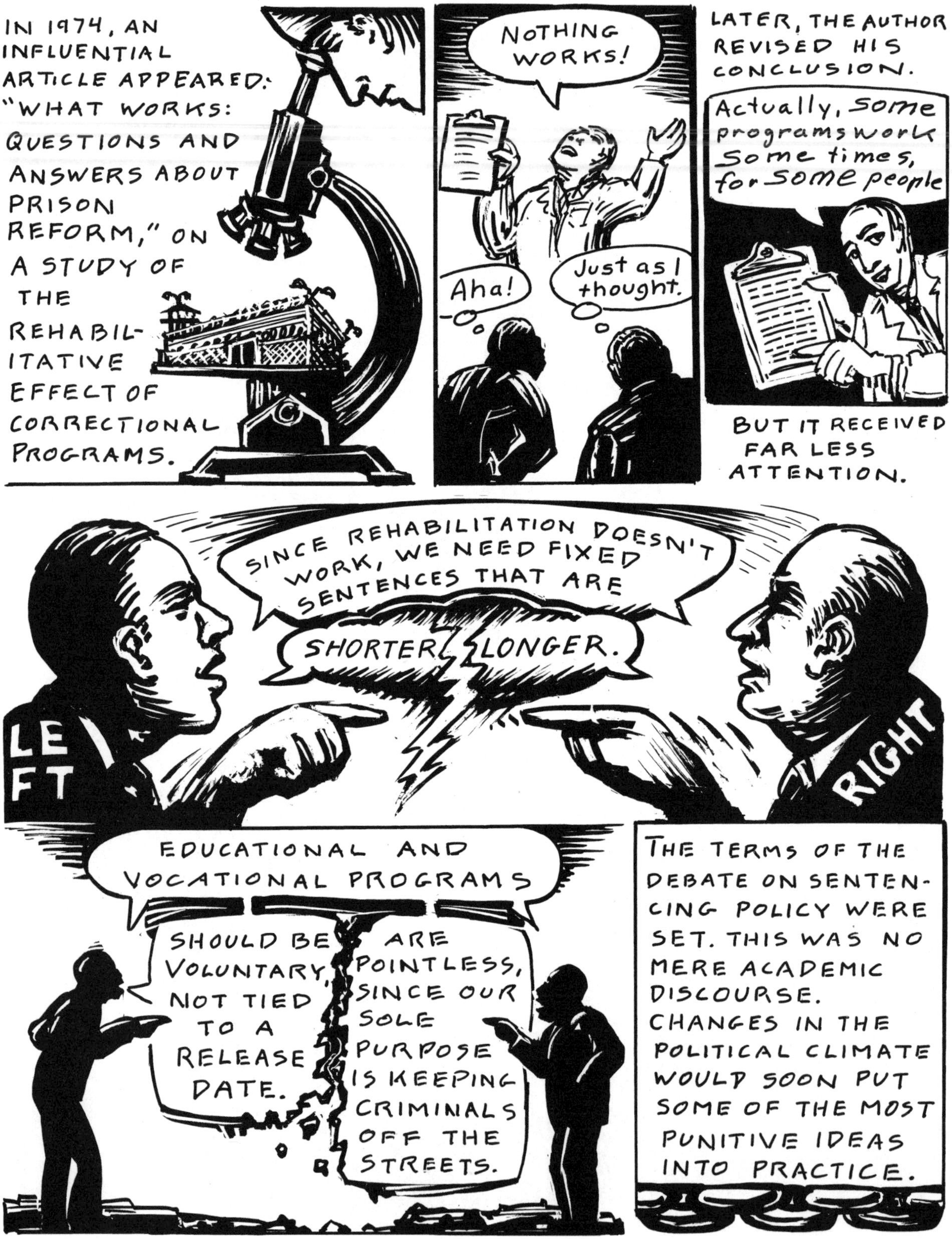
IN 1974, AN INFLUENTIAL ARTICLE APPEARED: "WHAT WORKS: QUESTIONS AND ANSWERS ABOUT PRISON REFORM," ON A STUDY OF THE REHABILITATIVE EFFECT OF CORRECTIONAL PROGRAMS.
NOTHING WORKS!
Aha!
Just as I thought.
LATER, THE AUTHOR REVISED HIS CONCLUSION.
Actually, some programs work some times, for some people
BUT IT RECEIVED FAR LESS ATTENTION.
SINCE REHABILITATION DOESN'T WORK, WE NEED FIXED SENTENCES THAT ARE
SHORTER.
LONGER.
LEFT
RIGHT
EDUCATIONAL AND VOCATIONAL PROGRAMS
SHOULD BE VOLUNTARY, NOT TIED TO A RELEASE DATE.
ARE POINTLESS, SINCE OUR SOLE PURPOSE IS KEEPING CRIMINALS OFF THE STREETS.
THE TERMS OF THE DEBATE ON SENTENCING POLICY WERE SET. THIS WAS NO MERE ACADEMIC DISCOURSE. CHANGES IN THE POLITICAL CLIMATE WOULD SOON PUT SOME OF THE MOST PUNITIVE IDEAS INTO PRACTICE.

THE TRIUMPH OF

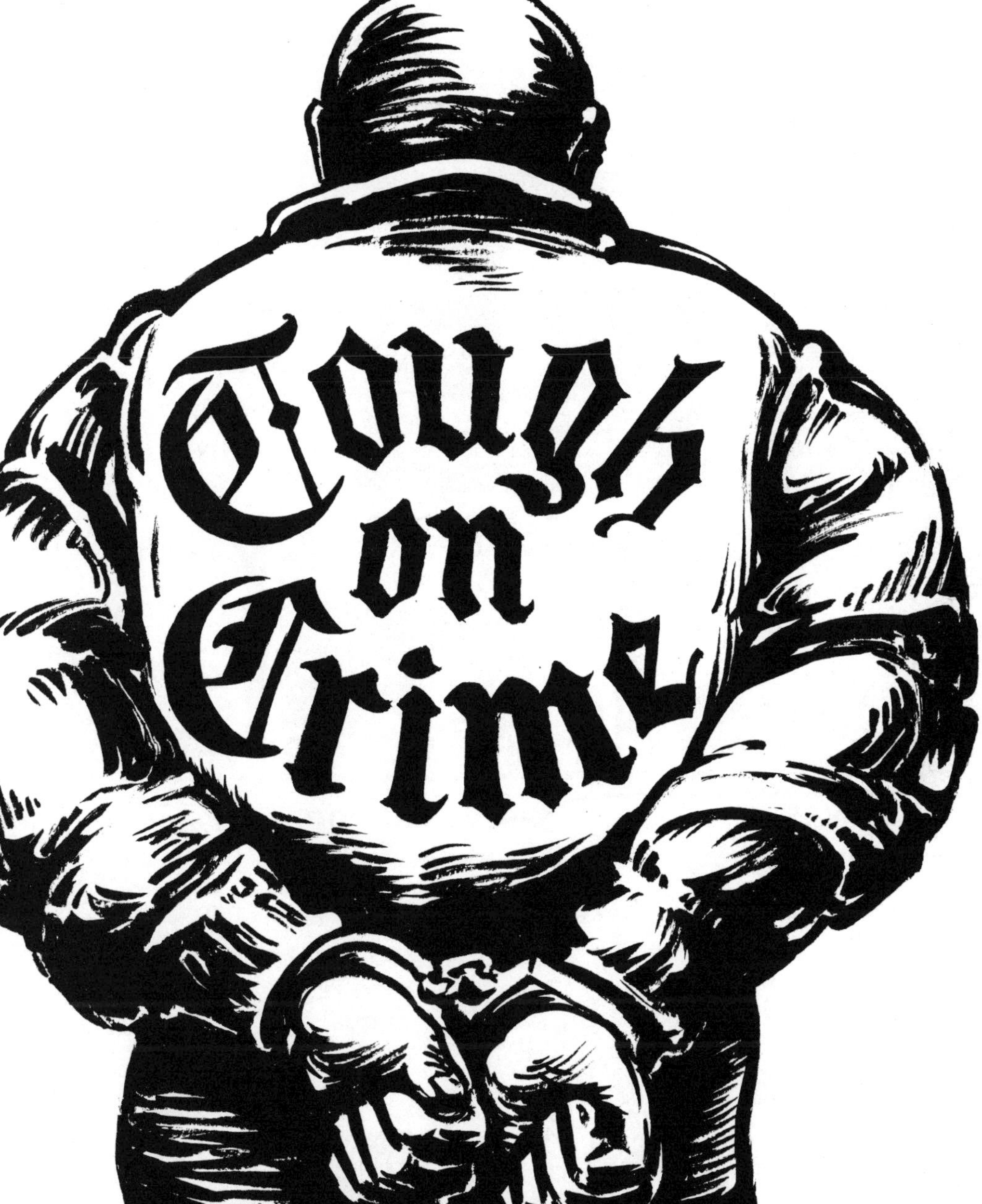
Tough
on
Crime

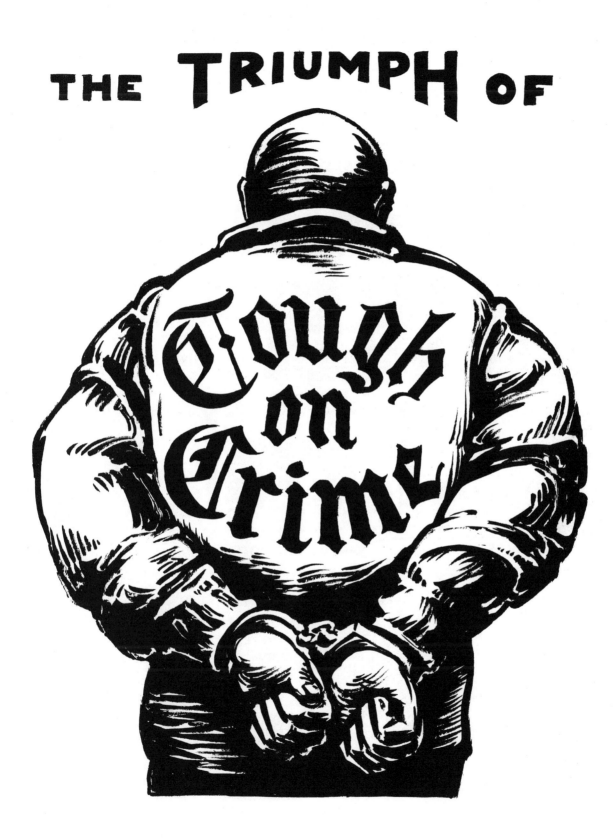

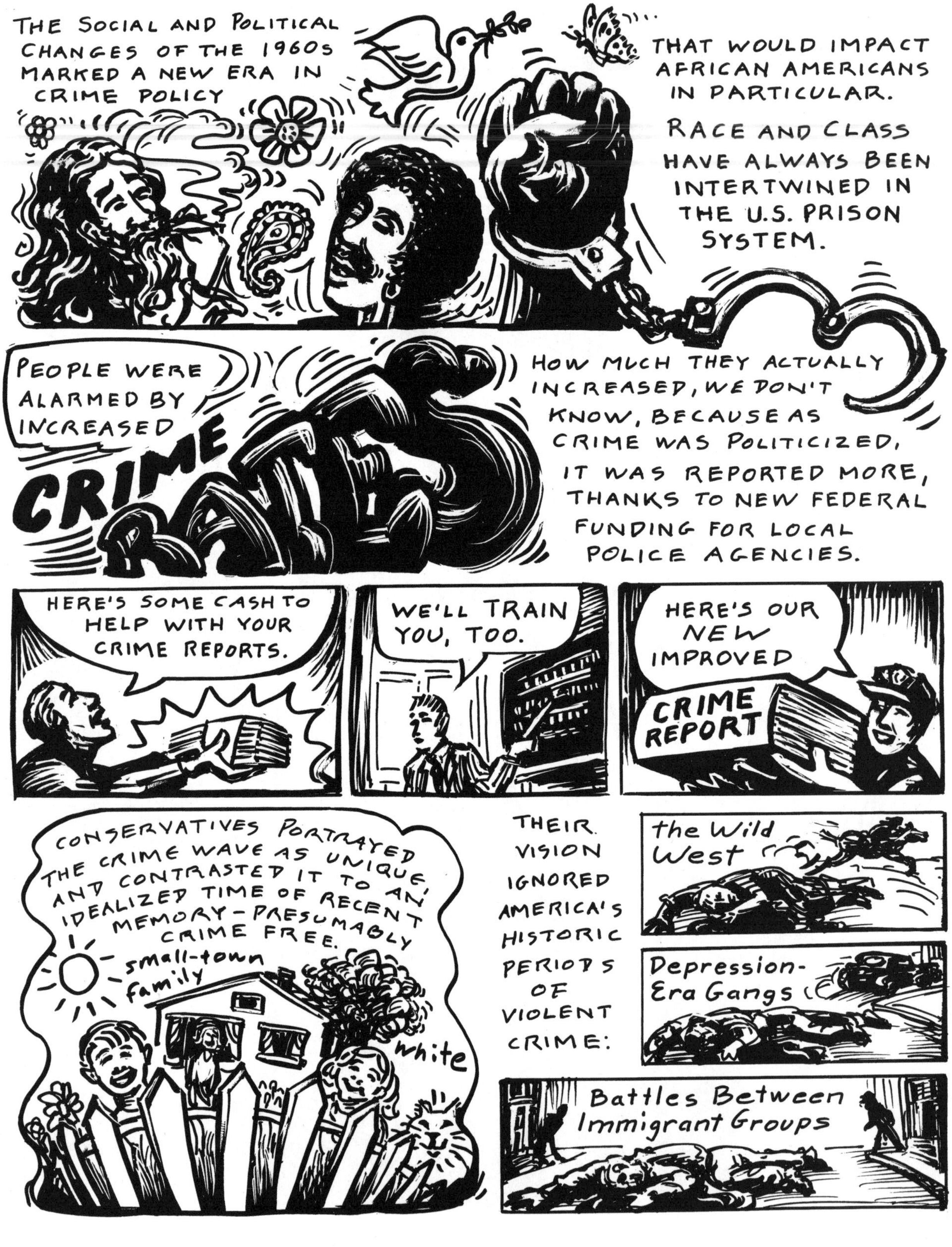
THE SOCIAL AND POLITICAL CHANGES OF THE 1960s MARKED A NEW ERA IN CRIME POLICY
THAT WOULD IMPACT AFRICAN AMERICANS IN PARTICULAR.
RACE AND CLASS HAVE ALWAYS BEEN INTERTWINED IN THE U.S. PRISON SYSTEM.
PEOPLE WERE ALARMED BY INCREASED
CRIME RATES
HOW MUCH THEY ACTUALLY INCREASED, WE DON'T KNOW, BECAUSE AS CRIME WAS POLITICIZED, IT WAS REPORTED MORE, THANKS TO NEW FEDERAL FUNDING FOR LOCAL POLICE AGENCIES.
HERE'S SOME CASH TO HELP WITH YOUR CRIME REPORTS.
WE'LL TRAIN YOU, TOO.
HERE'S OUR NEW IMPROVED
CRIME REPORT
CONSERVATIVES PORTRAYED THE CRIME WAVE AS UNIQUE, AND CONTRASTED IT TO AN IDEALIZED TIME OF RECENT MEMORY—PRESUMABLY CRIME FREE.
small-town
family
white
THEIR VISION IGNORED AMERICA'S HISTORIC PERIODS OF VIOLENT CRIME:
the Wild West
Depression-Era Gangs
Battles Between Immigrant Groups

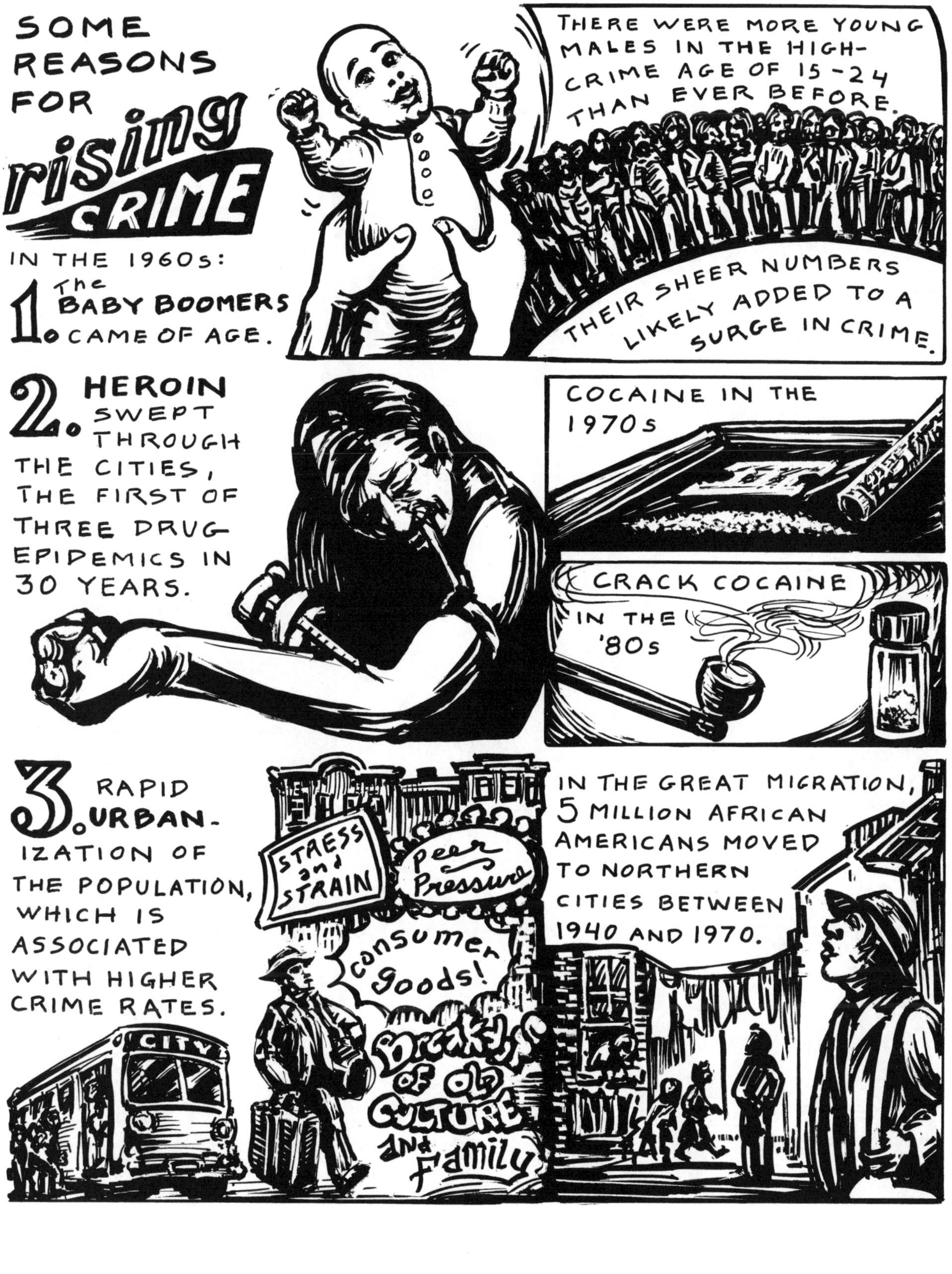
SOME REASONS FOR rising CRIME IN THE 1960s:
1. The BABY BOOMERS CAME OF AGE.
THERE WERE MORE YOUNG MALES IN THE HIGH-CRIME AGE OF 15-24 THAN EVER BEFORE.
THEIR SHEER NUMBERS LIKELY ADDED TO A SURGE IN CRIME.
2. HEROIN SWEPT THROUGH THE CITIES, THE FIRST OF THREE DRUG EPIDEMICS IN 30 YEARS.
COCAINE IN THE 1970s
CRACK COCAINE IN THE '80s
3. RAPID URBANIZATION OF THE POPULATION, WHICH IS ASSOCIATED WITH HIGHER CRIME RATES.
CITY
STRESS and STRAIN
Peer Pressure
consumer goods!
Breakdowns of Old Culture and Family
IN THE GREAT MIGRATION, 5 MILLION AFRICAN AMERICANS MOVED TO NORTHERN CITIES BETWEEN 1940 AND 1970.

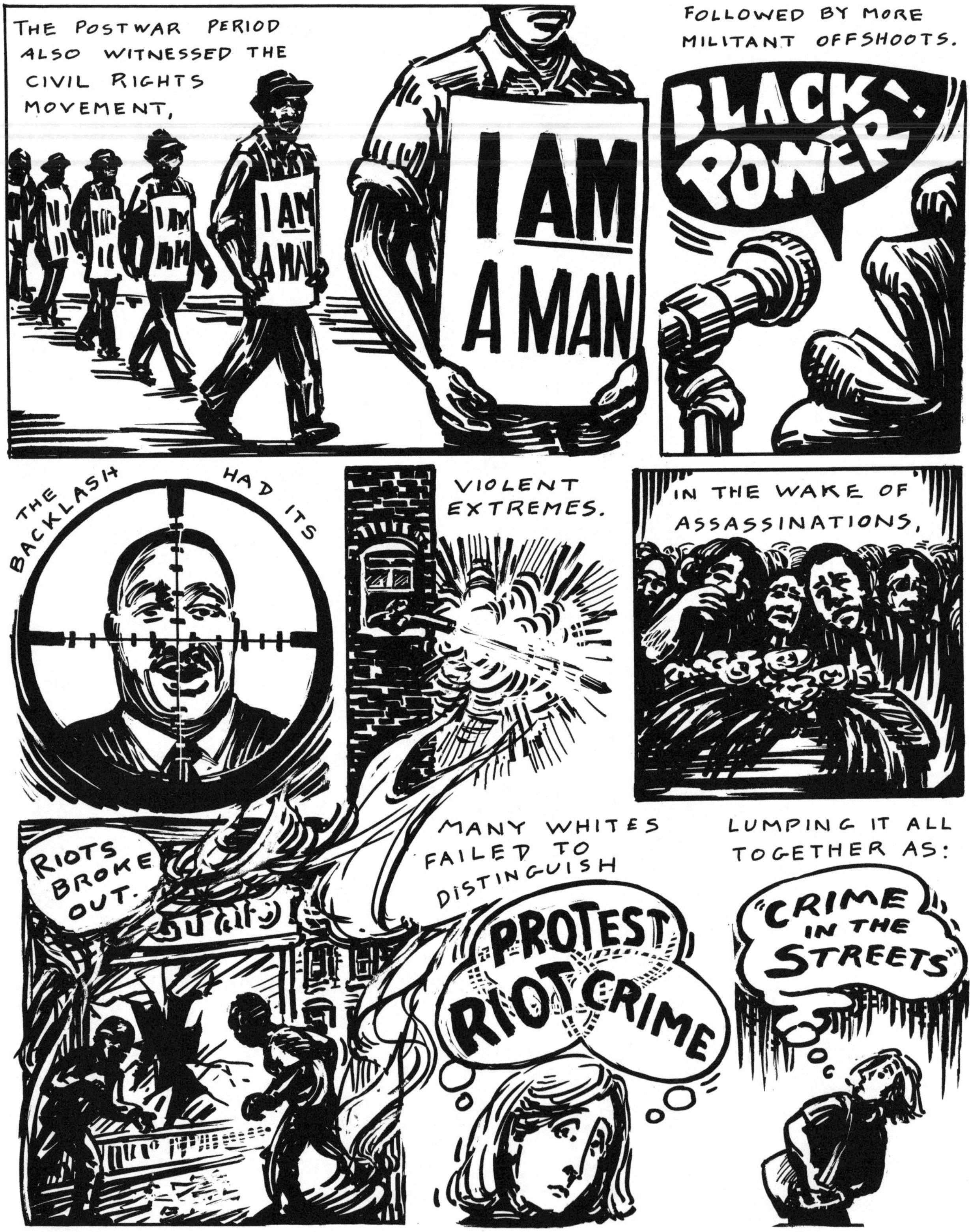
THE POSTWAR PERIOD ALSO WITNESSED THE CIVIL RIGHTS MOVEMENT,
I AM A MAN
FOLLOWED BY MORE MILITANT OFFSHOOTS.
BLACK POWER!
THE BACKLASH HAD ITS
VIOLENT EXTREMES.
IN THE WAKE OF ASSASSINATIONS,
RIOTS BROKE OUT.
MANY WHITES FAILED TO DISTINGUISH
PROTEST RIOT CRIME
LUMPING IT ALL TOGETHER AS:
"CRIME IN THE STREETS"

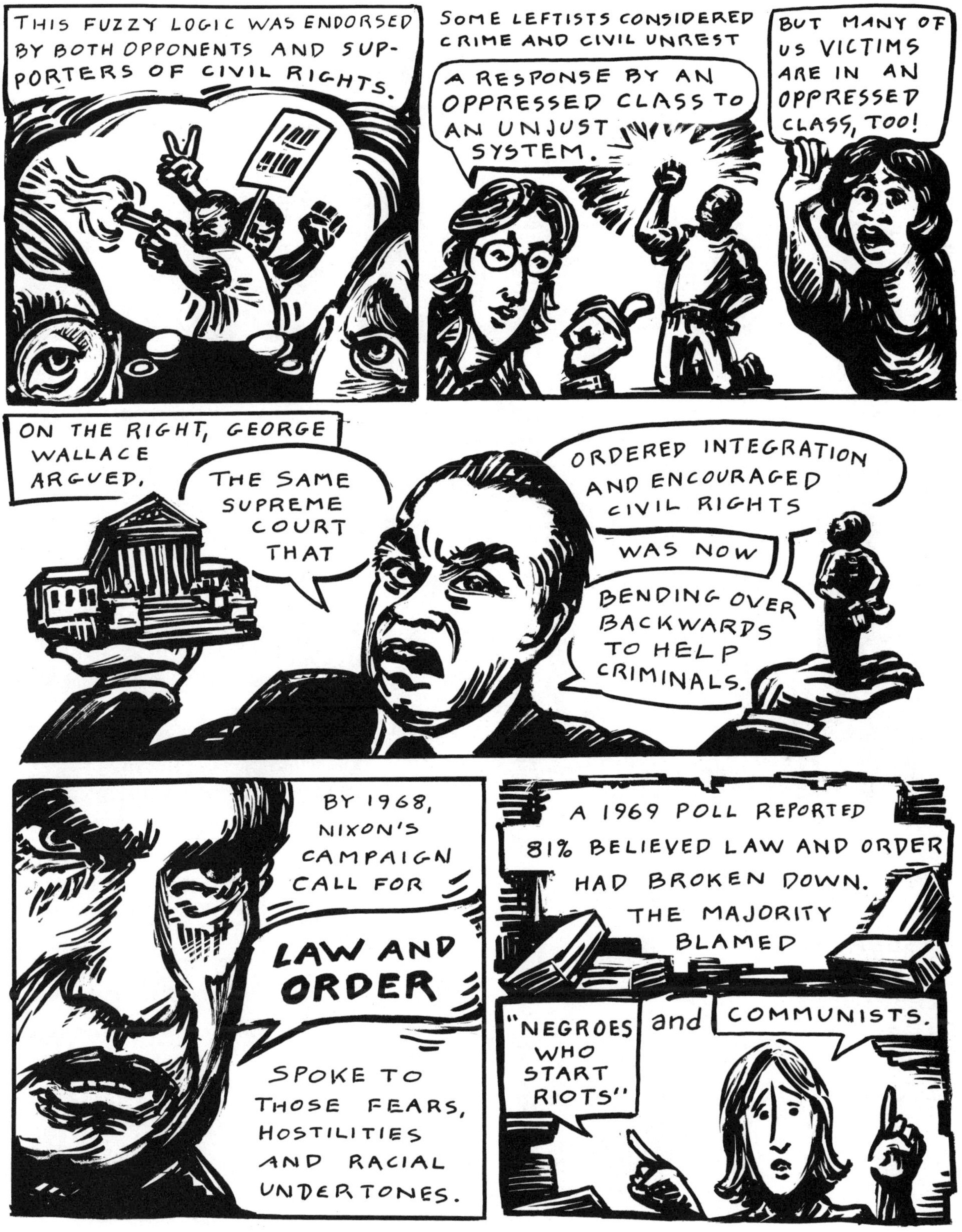
THIS FUZZY LOGIC WAS ENDORSED BY BOTH OPPONENTS AND SUPPORTERS OF CIVIL RIGHTS.
SOME LEFTISTS CONSIDERED CRIME AND CIVIL UNREST
A RESPONSE BY AN OPPRESSED CLASS TO AN UNJUST SYSTEM.
BUT MANY OF US VICTIMS ARE IN AN OPPRESSED CLASS, TOO!
ON THE RIGHT, GEORGE WALLACE ARGUED,
THE SAME SUPREME COURT THAT
ORDERED INTEGRATION AND ENCOURAGED CIVIL RIGHTS
WAS NOW
BENDING OVER BACKWARDS TO HELP CRIMINALS.
BY 1968, NIXON'S CAMPAIGN CALL FOR
LAW AND ORDER
SPOKE TO THOSE FEARS, HOSTILITIES AND RACIAL UNDERTONES.
A 1969 POLL REPORTED 81% BELIEVED LAW AND ORDER HAD BROKEN DOWN.
THE MAJORITY BLAMED
"NEGROES WHO START RIOTS"
and
COMMUNISTS.

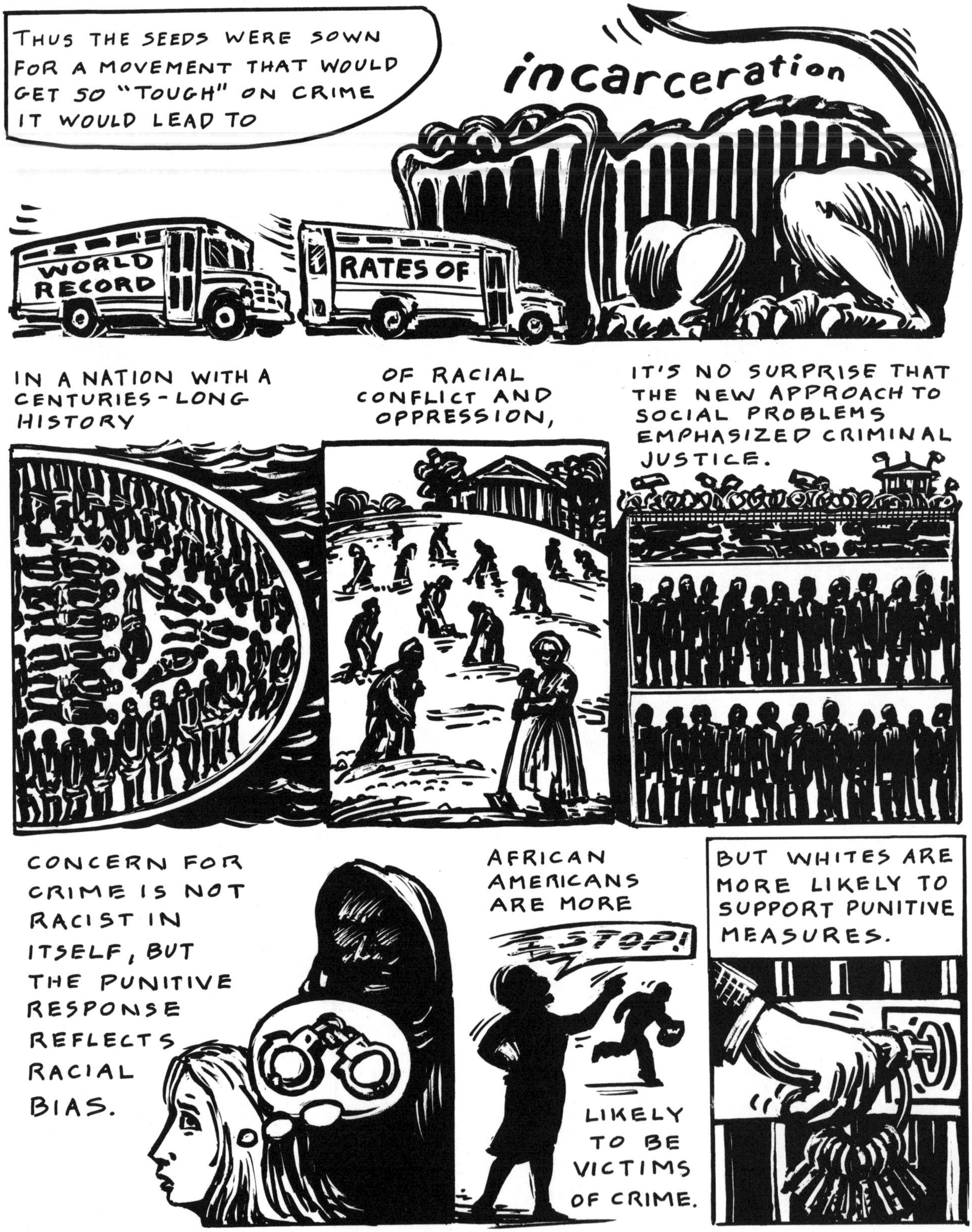
THUS THE SEEDS WERE SOWN FOR A MOVEMENT THAT WOULD GET SO "TOUGH" ON CRIME IT WOULD LEAD TO
WORLD RECORD
RATES OF
incarceration
IN A NATION WITH A CENTURIES-LONG HISTORY
OF RACIAL CONFLICT AND OPPRESSION,
IT'S NO SURPRISE THAT THE NEW APPROACH TO SOCIAL PROBLEMS EMPHASIZED CRIMINAL JUSTICE.
CONCERN FOR CRIME IS NOT RACIST IN ITSELF, BUT THE PUNITIVE RESPONSE REFLECTS RACIAL BIAS.
AFRICAN AMERICANS ARE MORE
STOP!
LIKELY TO BE VICTIMS OF CRIME.
BUT WHITES ARE MORE LIKELY TO SUPPORT PUNITIVE MEASURES.

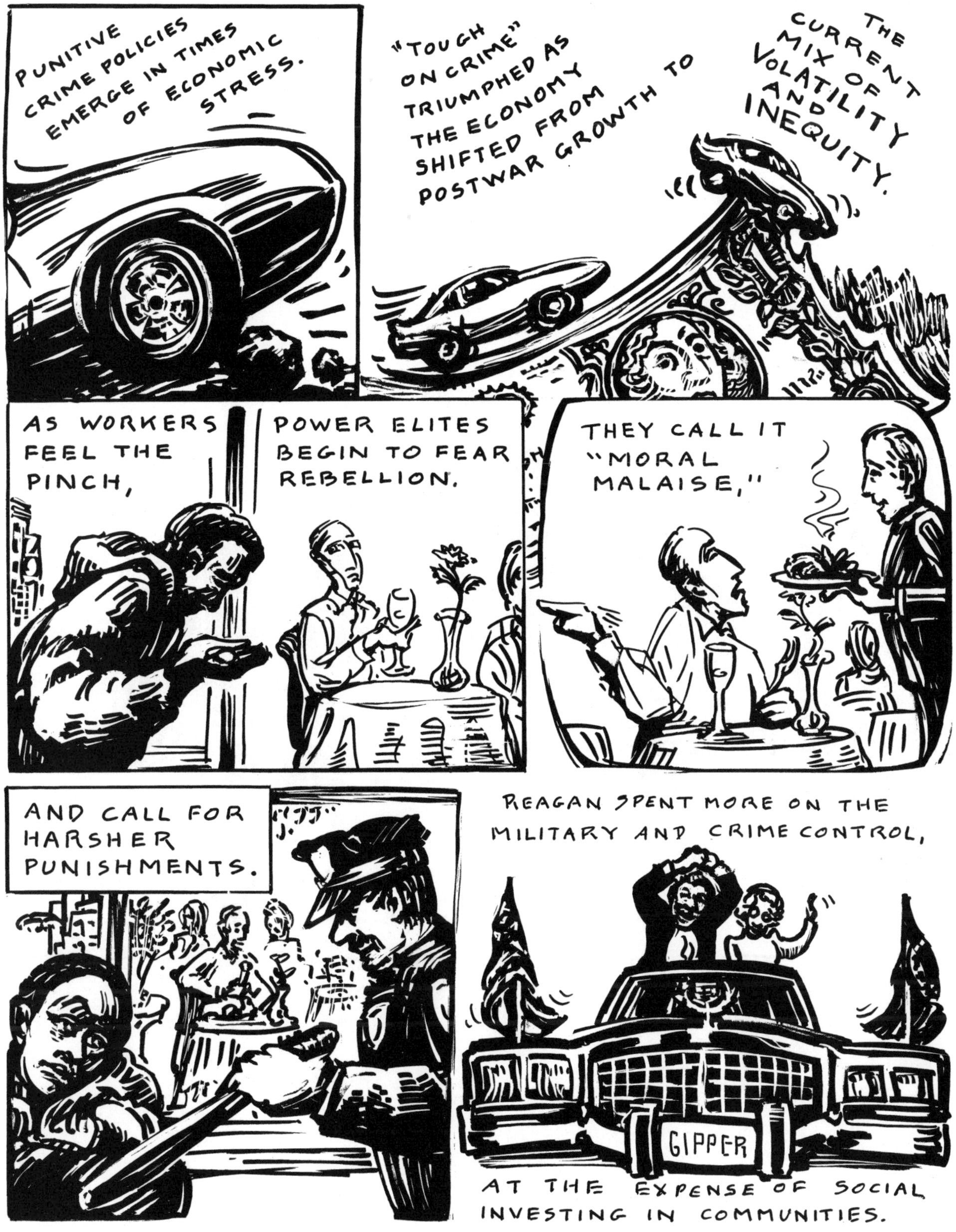
PUNITIVE CRIME POLICIES EMERGE IN TIMES OF ECONOMIC STRESS.
"TOUGH ON CRIME" TRIUMPHED AS THE ECONOMY SHIFTED FROM POSTWAR GROWTH TO
THE CURRENT MIX OF VOLATILITY AND INEQUITY.
AS WORKERS FEEL THE PINCH,
POWER ELITES BEGIN TO FEAR REBELLION.
THEY CALL IT "MORAL MALAISE,"
AND CALL FOR HARSHER PUNISHMENTS.
REAGAN SPENT MORE ON THE MILITARY AND CRIME CONTROL,
GIPPER
AT THE EXPENSE OF SOCIAL INVESTING IN COMMUNITIES.

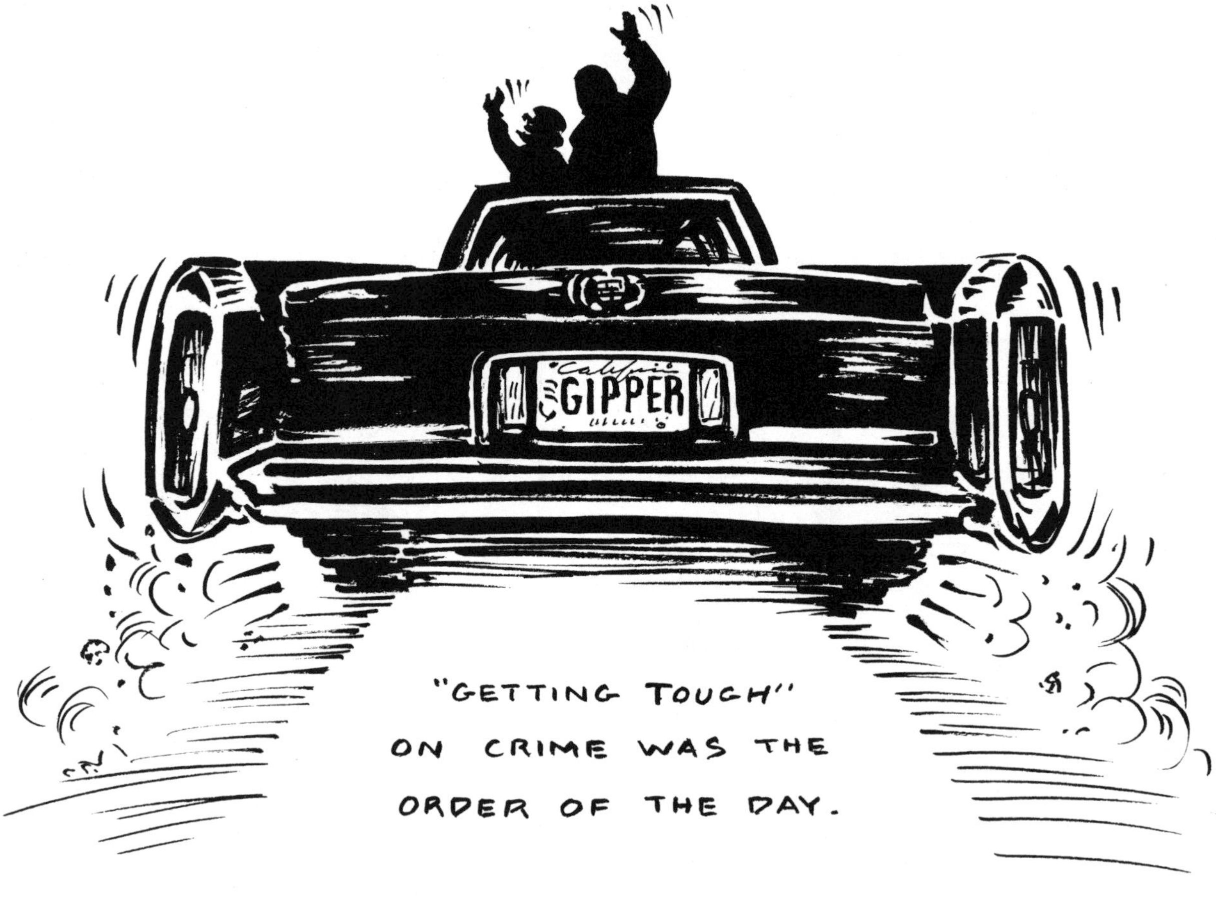
GIPPER
"GETTING TOUGH" ON CRIME WAS THE ORDER OF THE DAY.

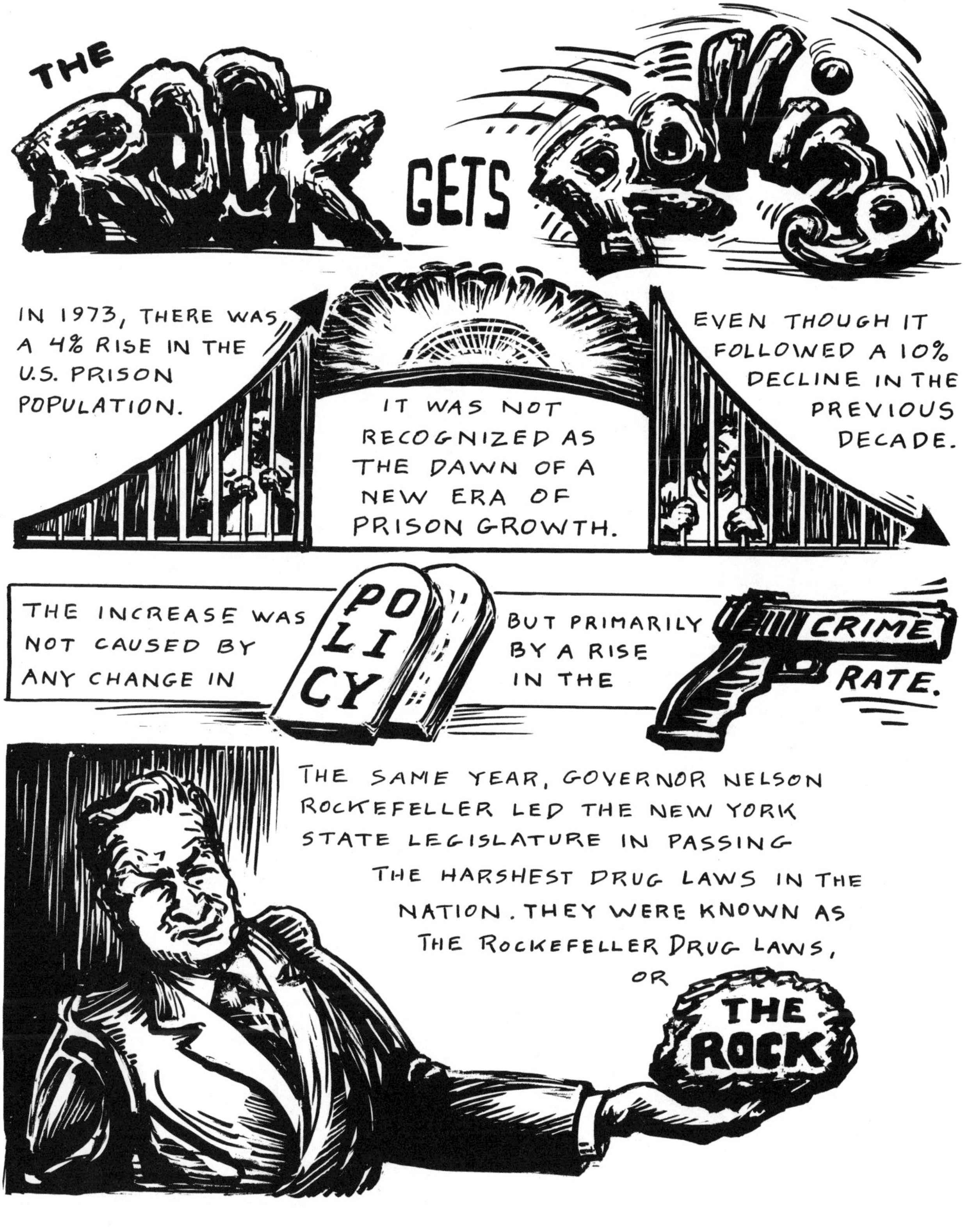
THE ROCK GETS ROLLING
IN 1973, THERE WAS A 4% RISE IN THE U.S. PRISON POPULATION.
IT WAS NOT RECOGNIZED AS THE DAWN OF A NEW ERA OF PRISON GROWTH.
EVEN THOUGH IT FOLLOWED A 10% DECLINE IN THE PREVIOUS DECADE.
THE INCREASE WAS NOT CAUSED BY ANY CHANGE IN
POLICY
BUT PRIMARILY BY A RISE IN THE
CRIME RATE.
THE SAME YEAR, GOVERNOR NELSON ROCKEFELLER LED THE NEW YORK STATE LEGISLATURE IN PASSING THE HARSHEST DRUG LAWS IN THE NATION. THEY WERE KNOWN AS THE ROCKEFELLER DRUG LAWS,
OR
THE ROCK

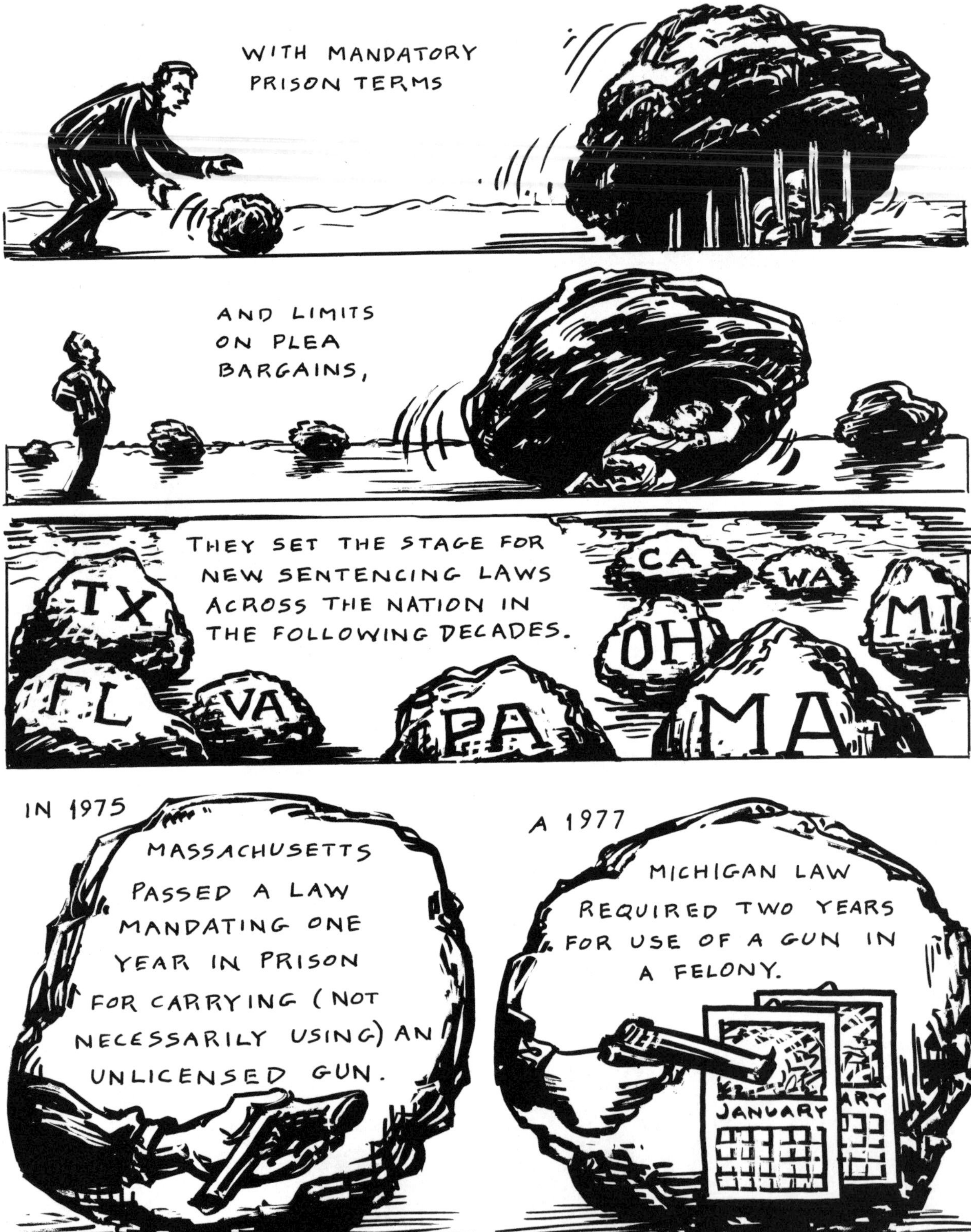
WITH MANDATORY PRISON TERMS
AND LIMITS ON PLEA BARGAINS,
THEY SET THE STAGE FOR NEW SENTENCING LAWS ACROSS THE NATION IN THE FOLLOWING DECADES.
TX
CA
WA
MI
OH
FL
VA
PA
MA
IN 1975
MASSACHUSETTS PASSED A LAW MANDATING ONE YEAR IN PRISON FOR CARRYING (NOT NECESSARILY USING) AN UNLICENSED GUN.
A 1977
MICHIGAN LAW REQUIRED TWO YEARS FOR USE OF A GUN IN A FELONY.
JANUARY

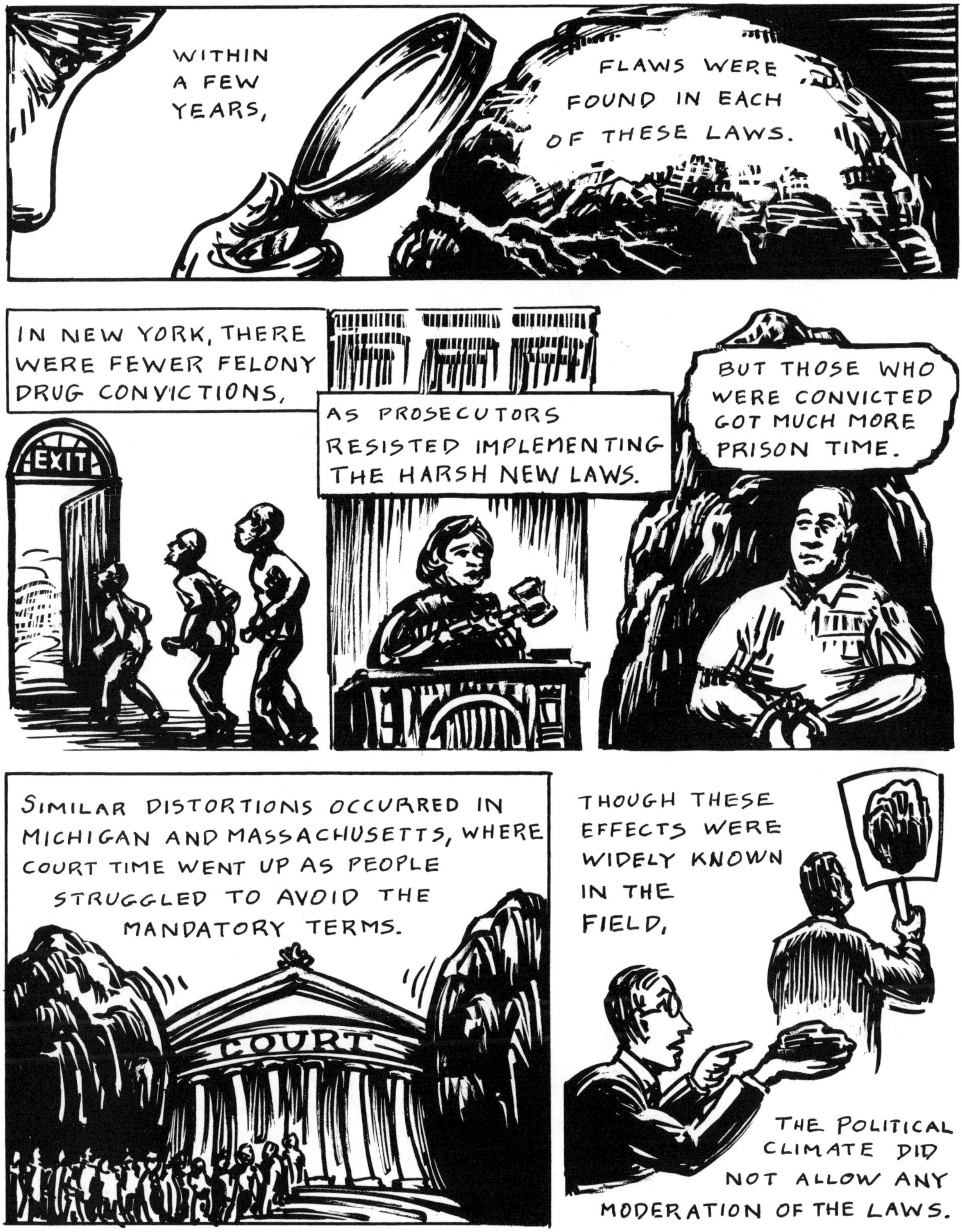
WITHIN A FEW YEARS,
FLAWS WERE FOUND IN EACH OF THESE LAWS.
IN NEW YORK, THERE WERE FEWER FELONY DRUG CONVICTIONS,
EXIT
AS PROSECUTORS RESISTED IMPLEMENTING THE HARSH NEW LAWS.
BUT THOSE WHO WERE CONVICTED GOT MUCH MORE PRISON TIME.
SIMILAR DISTORTIONS OCCURRED IN MICHIGAN AND MASSACHUSETTS, WHERE COURT TIME WENT UP AS PEOPLE STRUGGLED TO AVOID THE MANDATORY TERMS.
COURT
THOUGH THESE EFFECTS WERE WIDELY KNOWN IN THE FIELD,
THE POLITICAL CLIMATE DID NOT ALLOW ANY MODERATION OF THE LAWS.

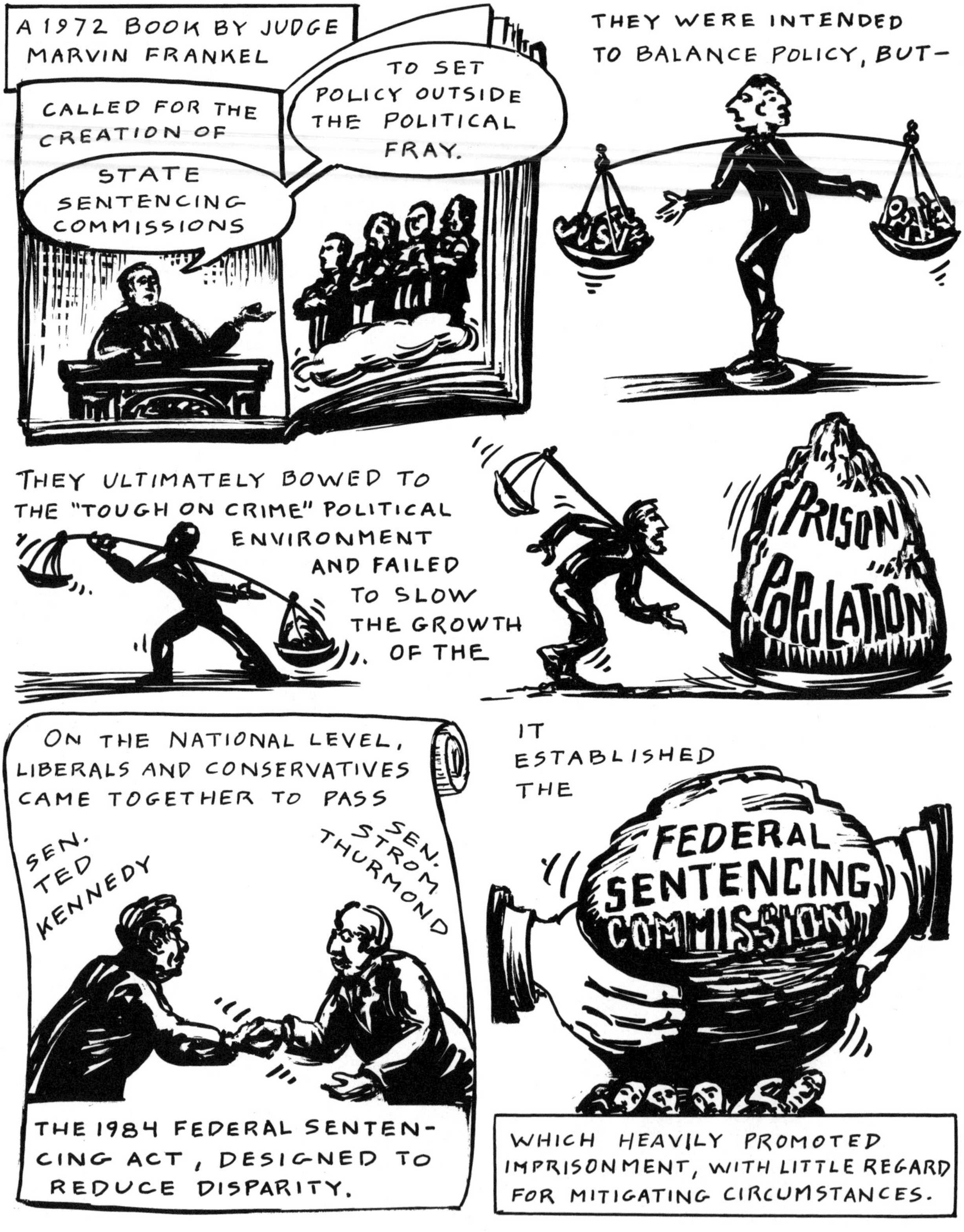

A 1972 BOOK BY JUDGE MARVIN FRANKEL
CALLED FOR THE CREATION OF
STATE SENTENCING COMMISSIONS
TO SET POLICY OUTSIDE THE POLITICAL FRAY.
THEY WERE INTENDED TO BALANCE POLICY, BUT–
THEY ULTIMATELY BOWED TO THE "TOUGH ON CRIME" POLITICAL ENVIRONMENT AND FAILED TO SLOW THE GROWTH OF THE
PRISON POPULATION
ON THE NATIONAL LEVEL, LIBERALS AND CONSERVATIVES CAME TOGETHER TO PASS
SEN. TED KENNEDY
SEN. STROM THURMOND
THE 1984 FEDERAL SENTENCING ACT, DESIGNED TO REDUCE DISPARITY.
IT ESTABLISHED THE
FEDERAL SENTENCING COMMISSION
WHICH HEAVILY PROMOTED IMPRISONMENT, WITH LITTLE REGARD FOR MITIGATING CIRCUMSTANCES.

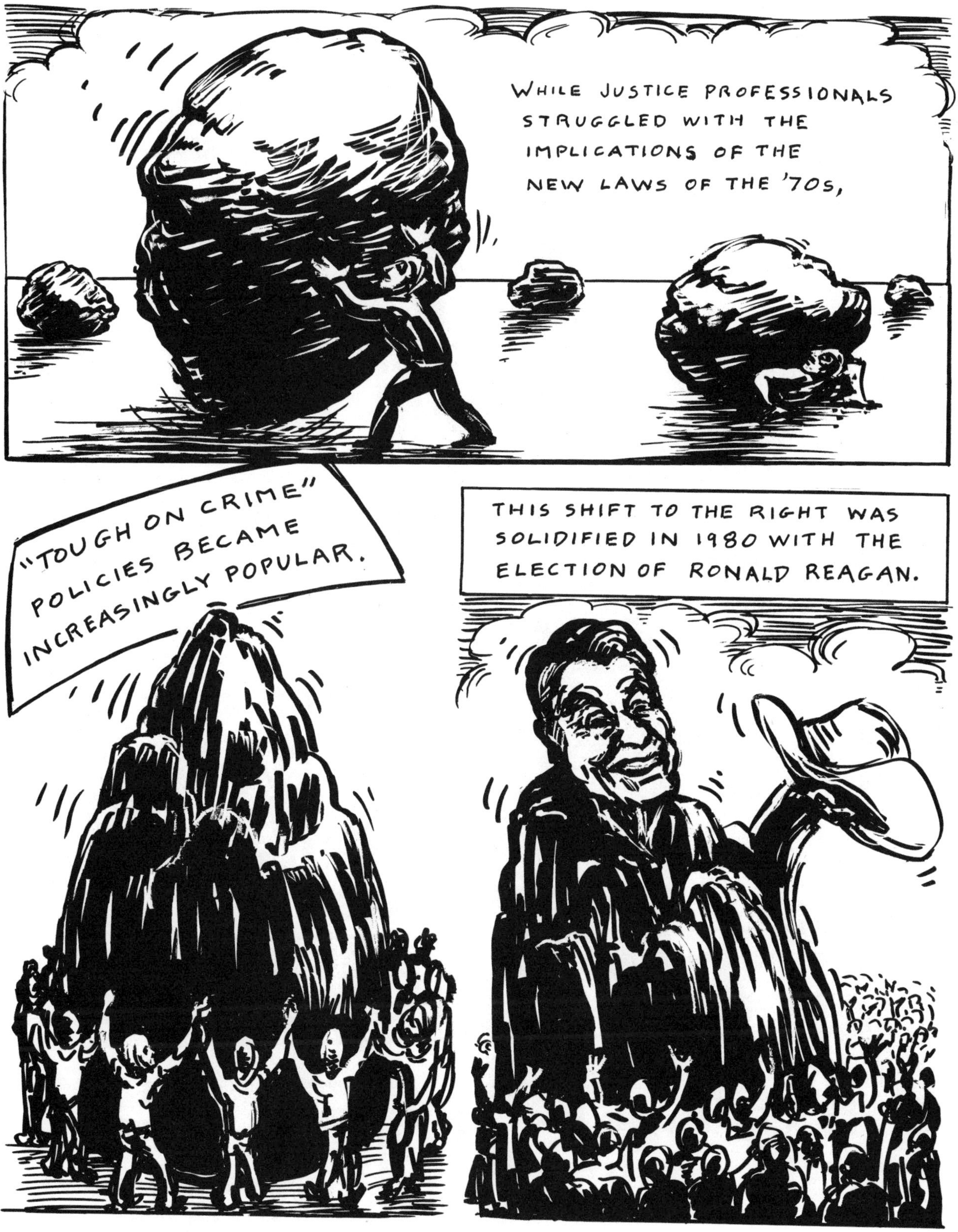
WHILE JUSTICE PROFESSIONALS STRUGGLED WITH THE IMPLICATIONS OF THE NEW LAWS OF THE '70s,
"TOUGH ON CRIME" POLICIES BECAME INCREASINGLY POPULAR.
THIS SHIFT TO THE RIGHT WAS SOLIDIFIED IN 1980 WITH THE ELECTION OF RONALD REAGAN.

CRIME AS POLITICS

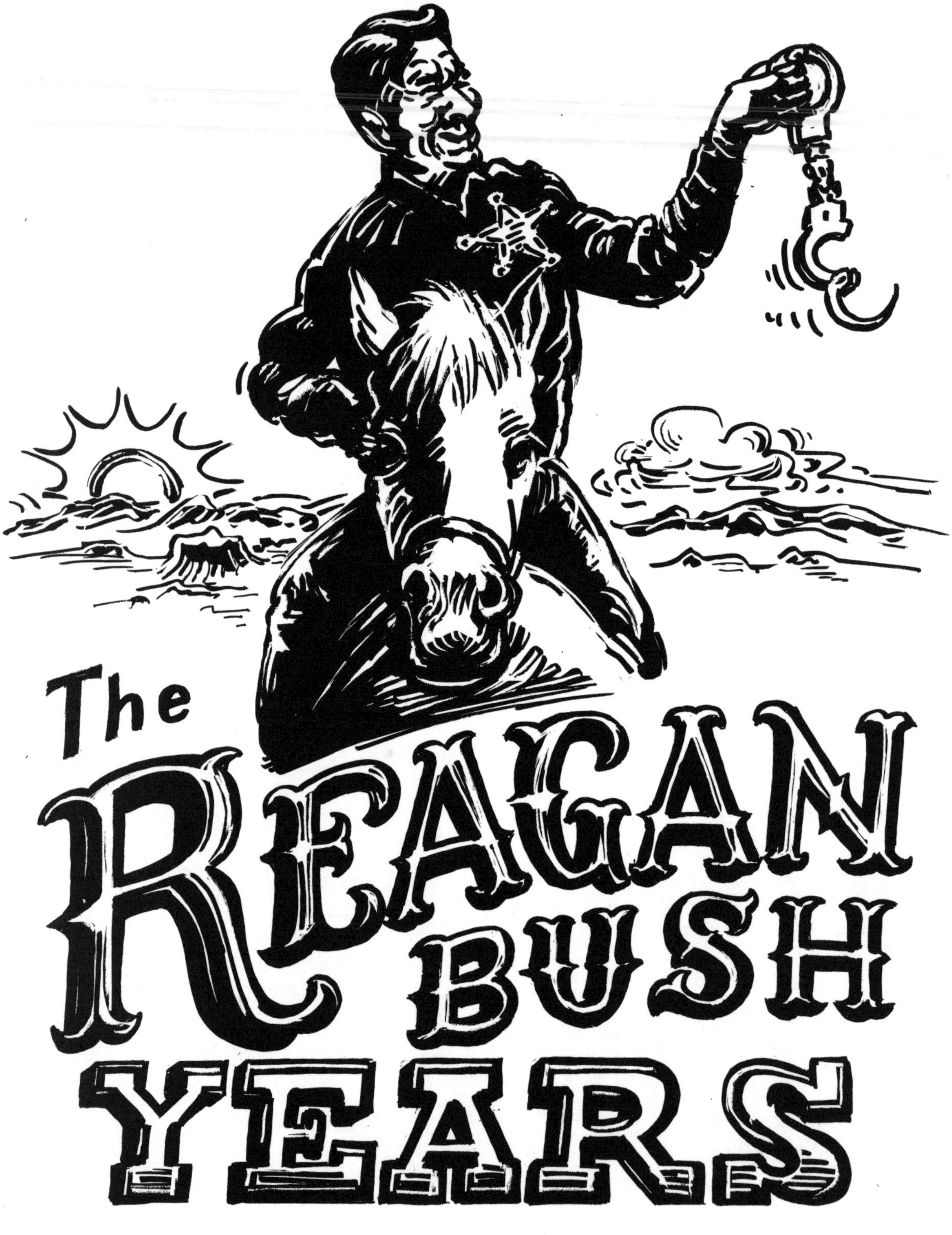
The
REAGAN
BUSH
YEARS

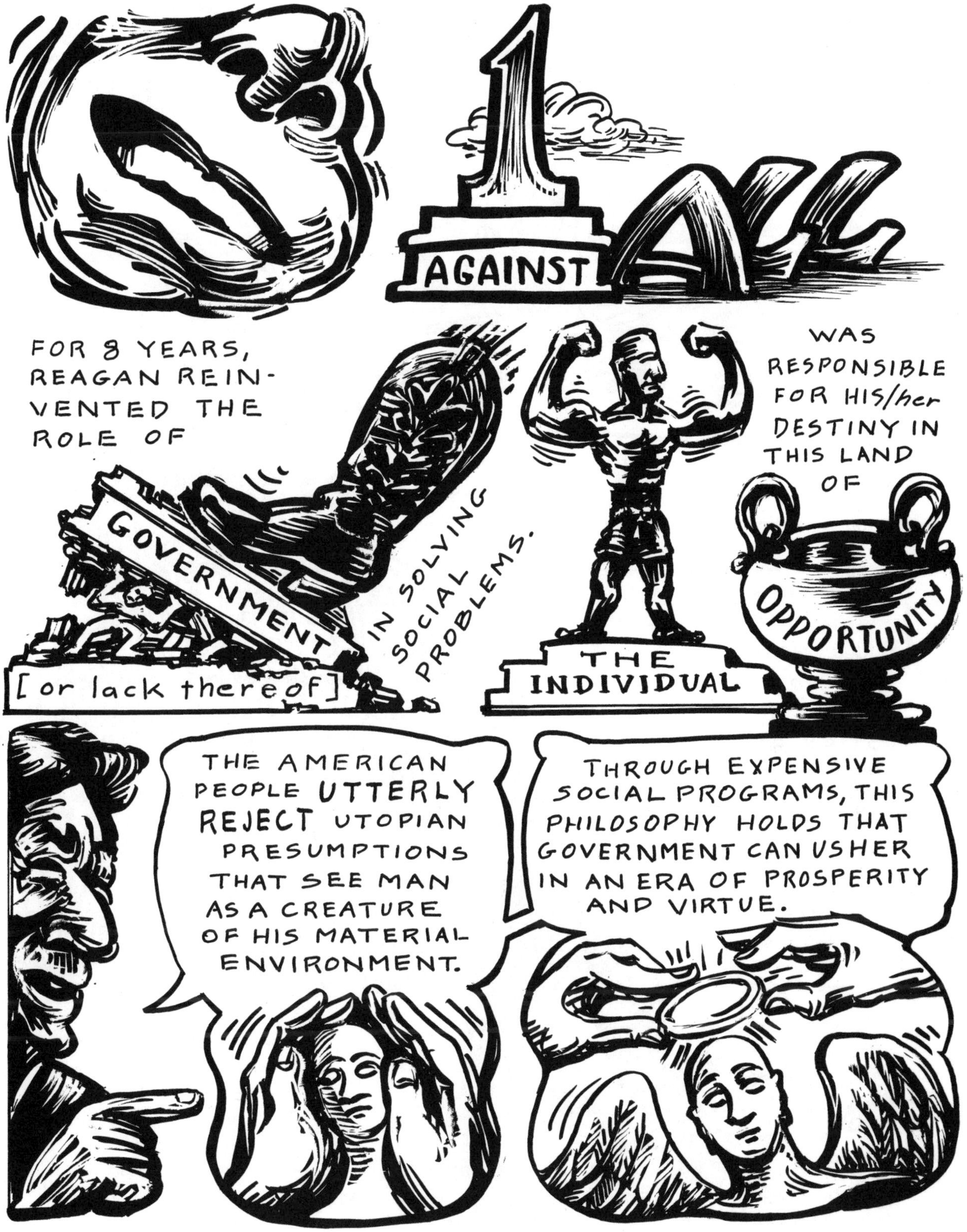

AGAINST
FOR 8 YEARS, REAGAN REINVENTED THE ROLE OF
GOVERNMENT
[or lack thereof]
IN SOLVING SOCIAL PROBLEMS.
THE INDIVIDUAL
WAS RESPONSIBLE FOR HIS/her DESTINY IN THIS LAND OF
OPPORTUNITY
THE AMERICAN PEOPLE UTTERLY REJECT UTOPIAN PRESUMPTIONS THAT SEE MAN AS A CREATURE OF HIS MATERIAL ENVIRONMENT.
THROUGH EXPENSIVE SOCIAL PROGRAMS, THIS PHILOSOPHY HOLDS THAT GOVERNMENT CAN USHER IN AN ERA OF PROSPERITY AND VIRTUE.

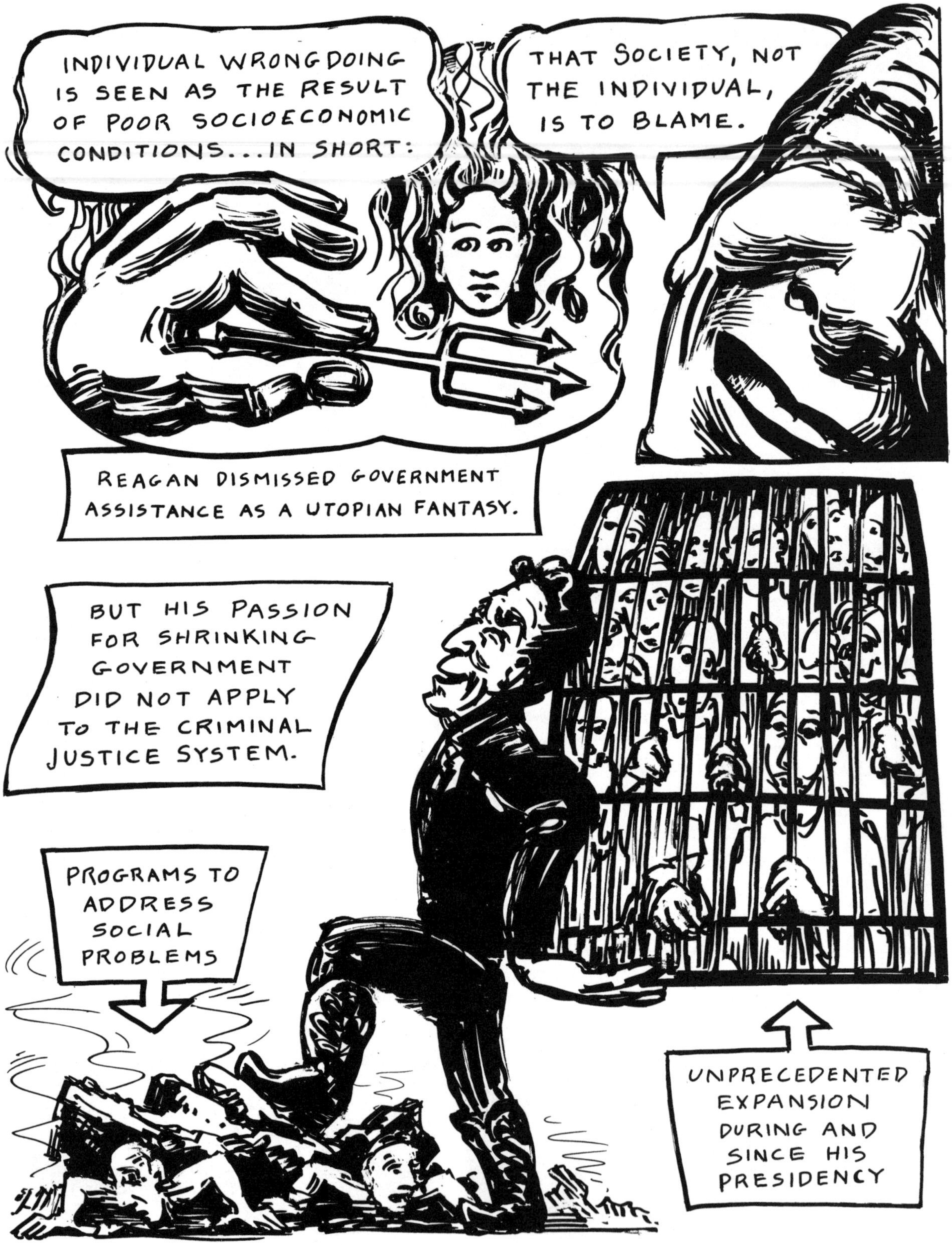

INDIVIDUAL WRONGDOING IS SEEN AS THE RESULT OF POOR SOCIOECONOMIC CONDITIONS...IN SHORT:
THAT SOCIETY, NOT THE INDIVIDUAL, IS TO BLAME.
REAGAN DISMISSED GOVERNMENT ASSISTANCE AS A UTOPIAN FANTASY.
BUT HIS PASSION FOR SHRINKING GOVERNMENT DID NOT APPLY TO THE CRIMINAL JUSTICE SYSTEM.
PROGRAMS TO ADDRESS SOCIAL PROBLEMS
UNPRECEDENTED EXPANSION DURING AND SINCE HIS PRESIDENCY

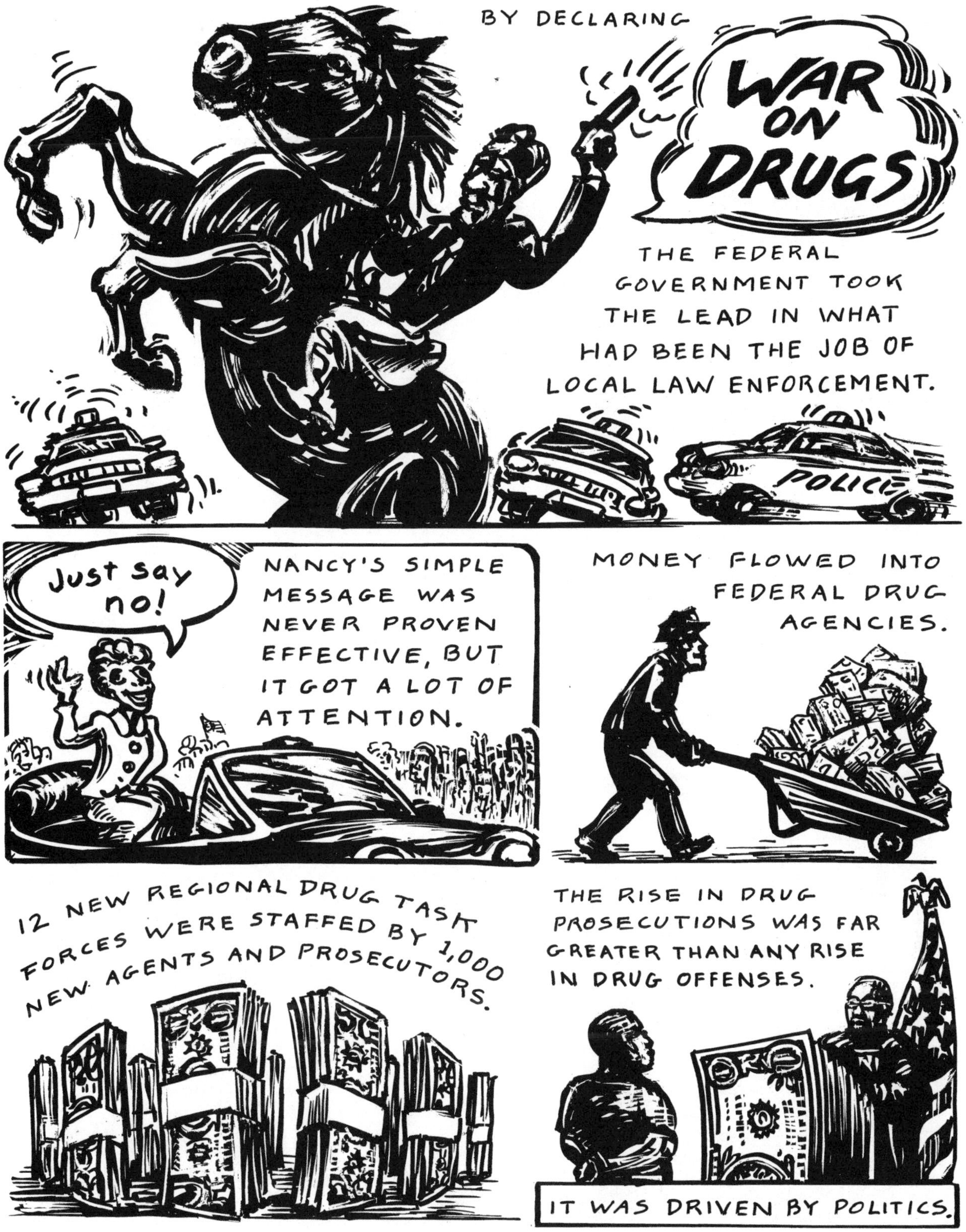
BY DECLARING
WAR ON DRUGS
THE FEDERAL GOVERNMENT TOOK THE LEAD IN WHAT HAD BEEN THE JOB OF LOCAL LAW ENFORCEMENT.
POLICE
Just say no!
NANCY'S SIMPLE MESSAGE WAS NEVER PROVEN EFFECTIVE, BUT IT GOT A LOT OF ATTENTION.
MONEY FLOWED INTO FEDERAL DRUG AGENCIES.
12 NEW REGIONAL DRUG TASK FORCES WERE STAFFED BY 1,000 NEW AGENTS AND PROSECUTORS.
THE RISE IN DRUG PROSECUTIONS WAS FAR GREATER THAN ANY RISE IN DRUG OFFENSES.
IT WAS DRIVEN BY POLITICS.

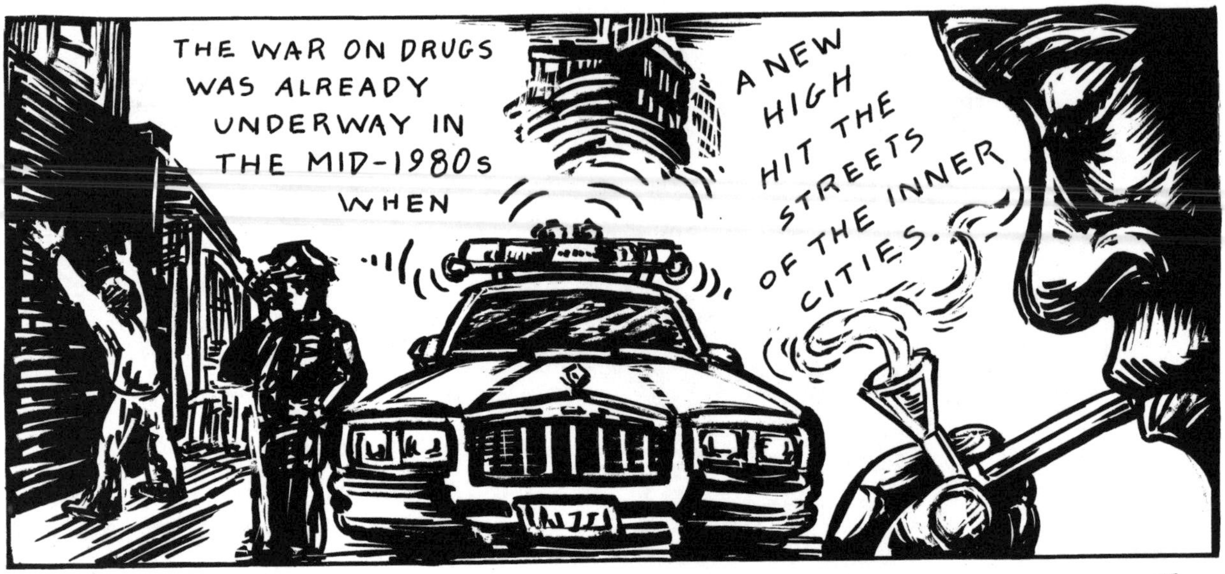
THE WAR ON DRUGS WAS ALREADY UNDERWAY IN THE MID-1980s WHEN
A NEW HIGH HIT THE STREETS OF THE INNER CITIES.

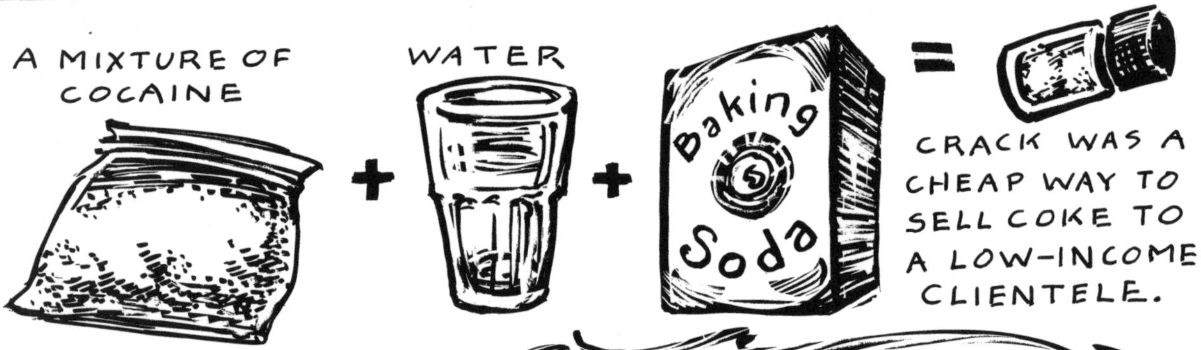
A MIXTURE OF COCAINE
+
WATER
+
Baking Soda
=
CRACK WAS A CHEAP WAY TO SELL COKE TO A LOW-INCOME CLIENTELE.

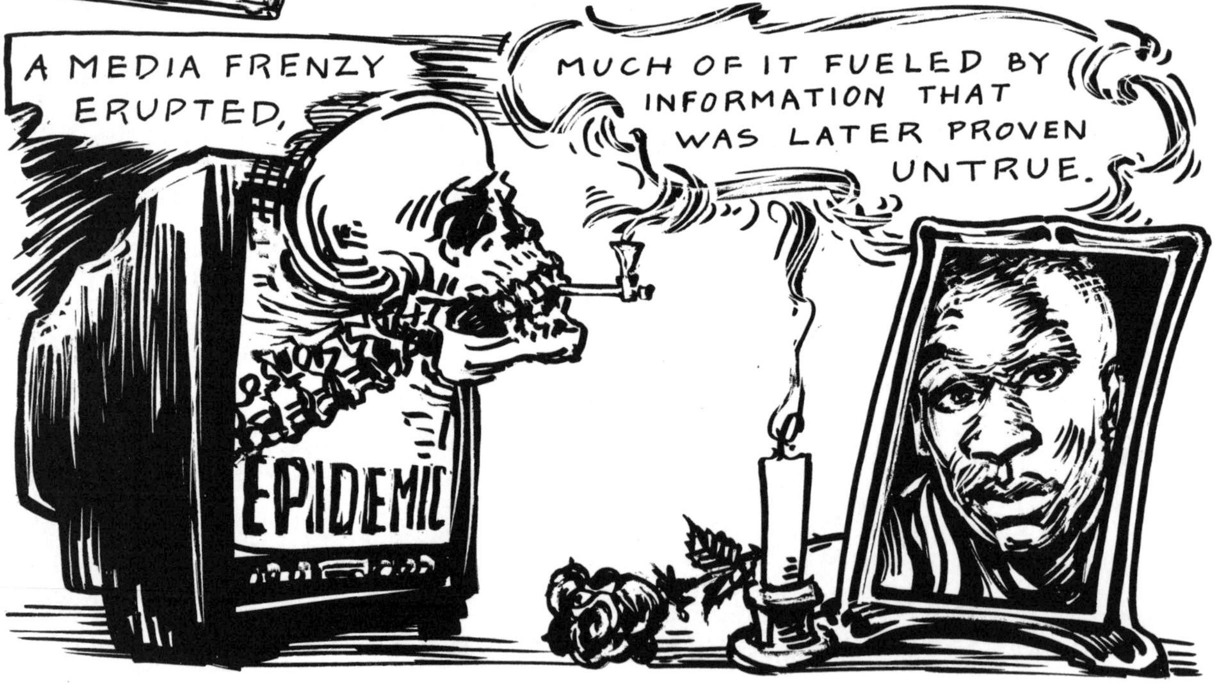
A MEDIA FRENZY ERUPTED,
MUCH OF IT FUELED BY INFORMATION THAT WAS LATER PROVEN UNTRUE.
EPIDEMIC

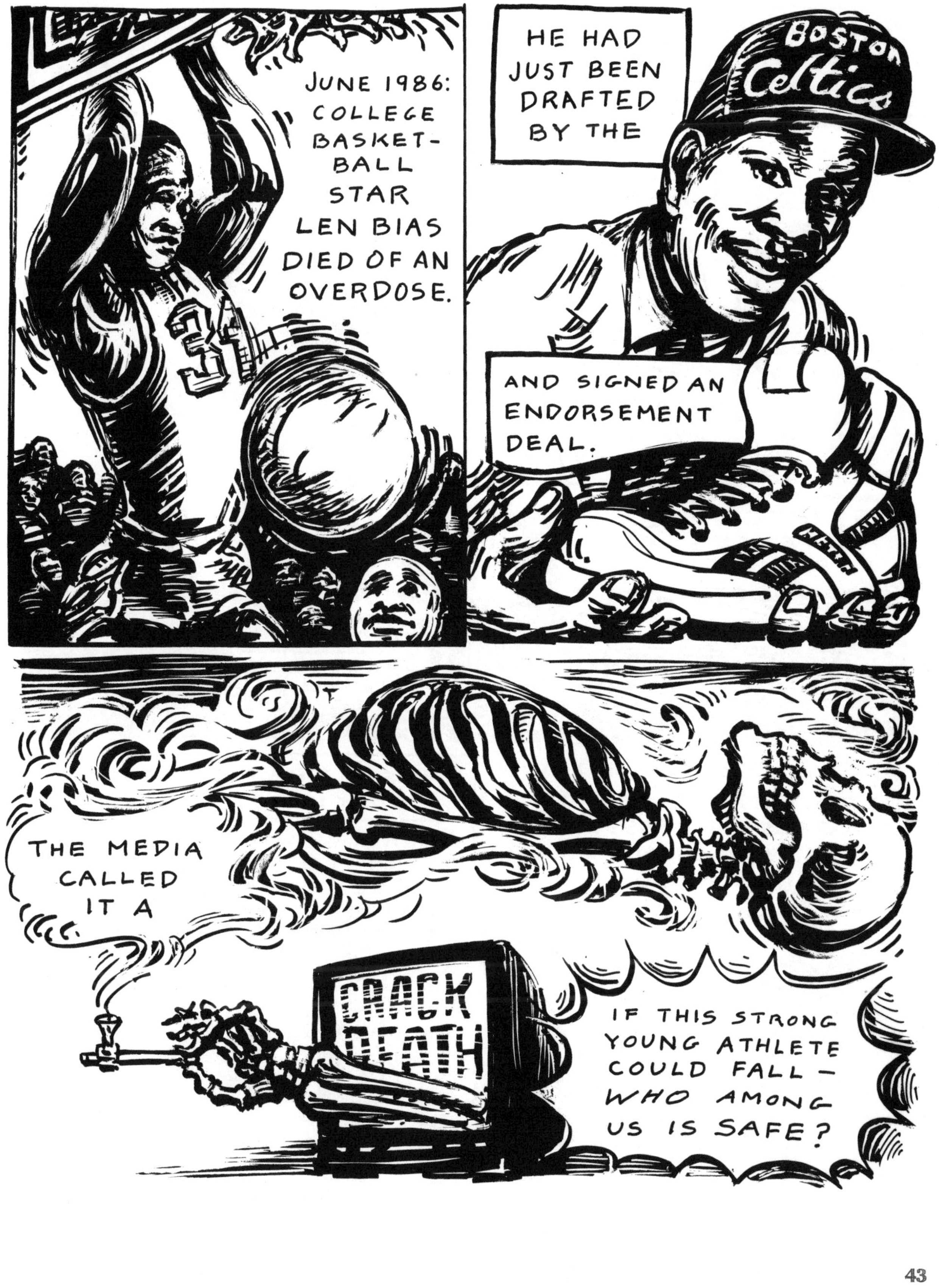
JUNE 1986: COLLEGE BASKET-BALL STAR LEN BIAS DIED OF AN OVERDOSE.
31
HE HAD JUST BEEN DRAFTED BY THE
Boston Celtics
AND SIGNED AN ENDORSEMENT DEAL.
THE MEDIA CALLED IT A
CRACK DEATH
IF THIS STRONG YOUNG ATHLETE COULD FALL — WHO AMONG US IS SAFE?

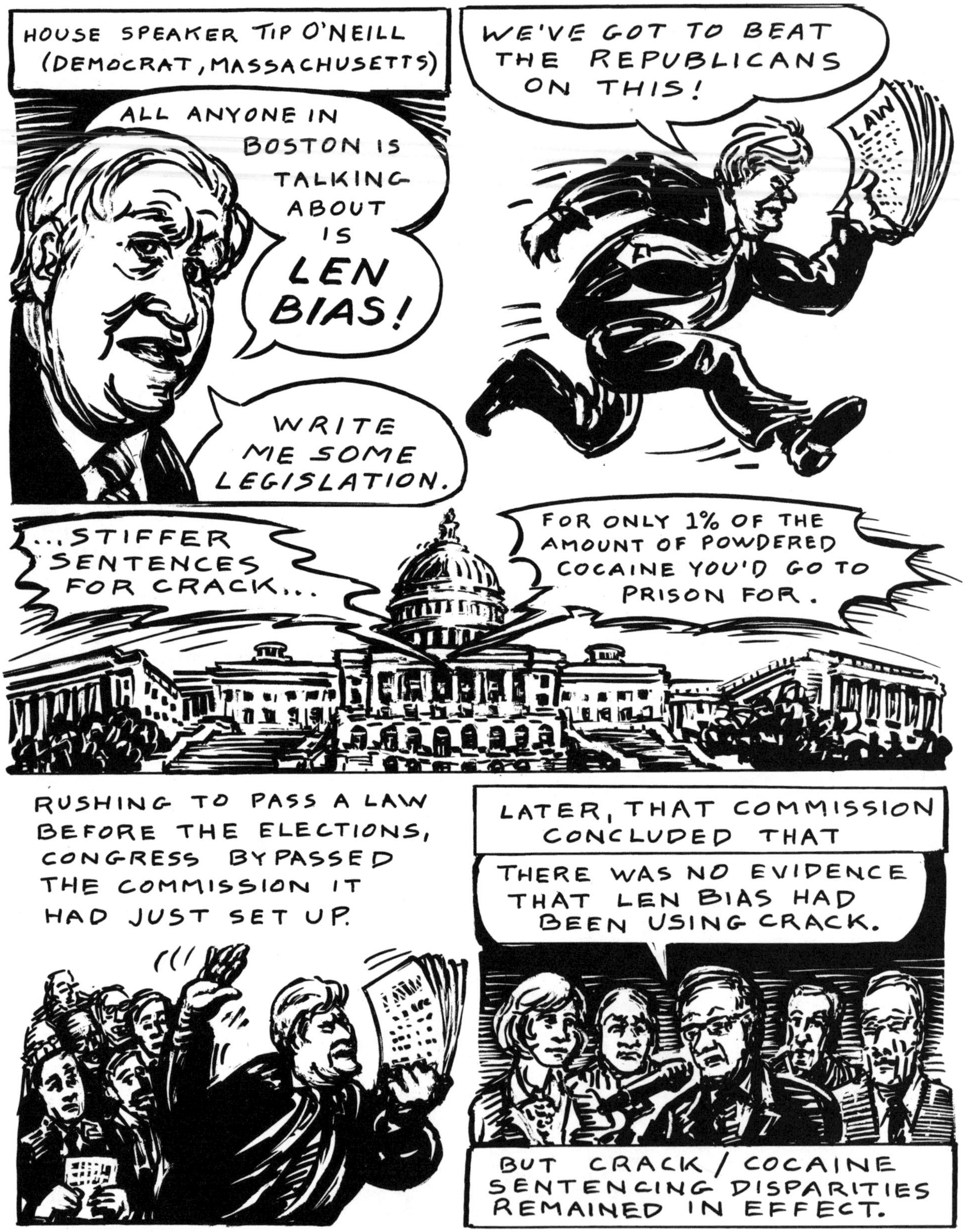
HOUSE SPEAKER TIP O'NEILL (DEMOCRAT, MASSACHUSETTS)
ALL ANYONE IN BOSTON IS TALKING ABOUT IS LEN BIAS!
WRITE ME SOME LEGISLATION.
WE'VE GOT TO BEAT THE REPUBLICANS ON THIS!
LAW
...STIFFER SENTENCES FOR CRACK...
FOR ONLY 1% OF THE AMOUNT OF POWDERED COCAINE YOU'D GO TO PRISON FOR.
RUSHING TO PASS A LAW BEFORE THE ELECTIONS, CONGRESS BYPASSED THE COMMISSION IT HAD JUST SET UP.
LATER, THAT COMMISSION CONCLUDED THAT
THERE WAS NO EVIDENCE THAT LEN BIAS HAD BEEN USING CRACK.
BUT CRACK / COCAINE SENTENCING DISPARITIES REMAINED IN EFFECT.

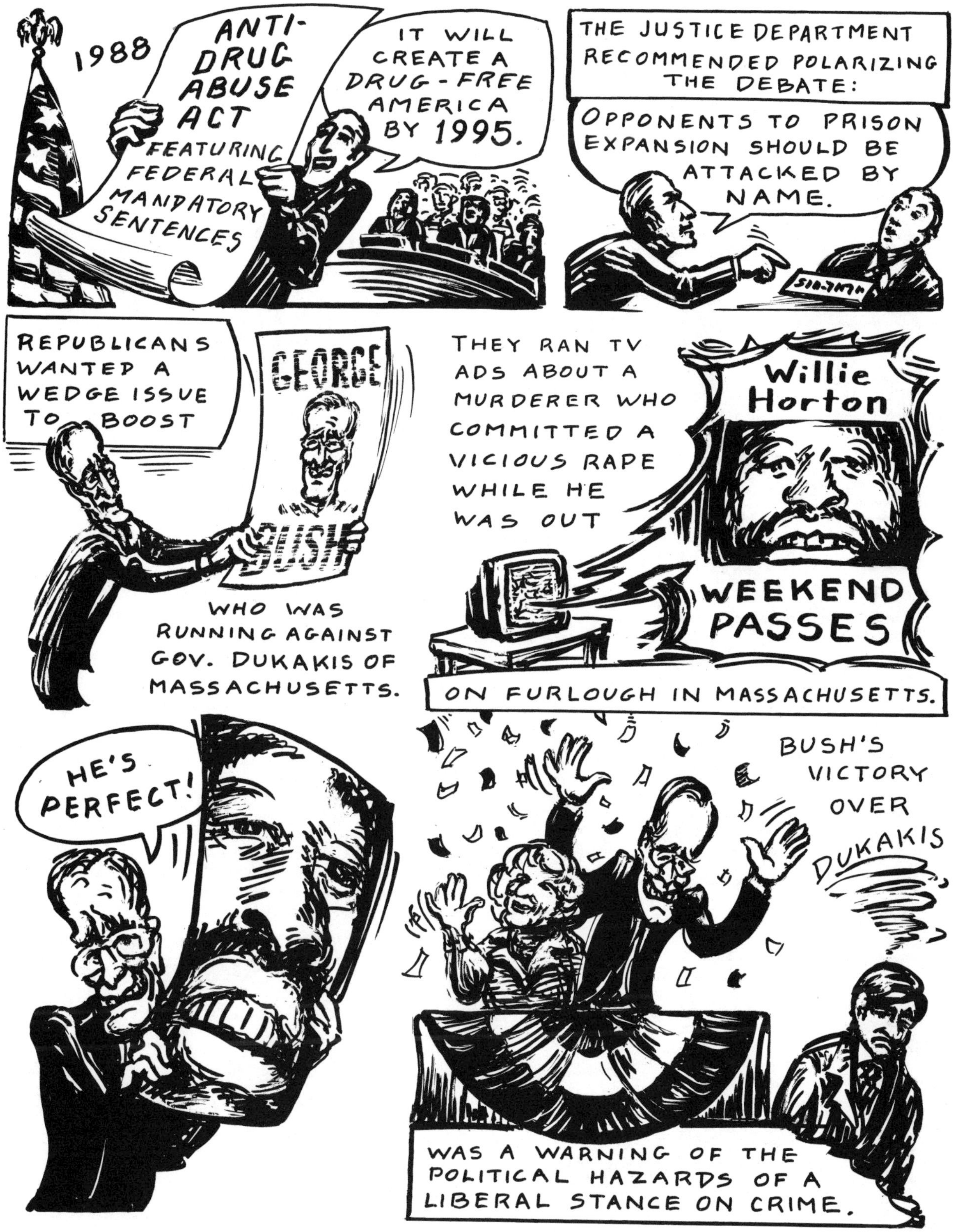
1988
ANTI-DRUG ABUSE ACT FEATURING FEDERAL MANDATORY SENTENCES
IT WILL CREATE A DRUG-FREE AMERICA BY 1995.
THE JUSTICE DEPARTMENT RECOMMENDED POLARIZING THE DEBATE:
OPPONENTS TO PRISON EXPANSION SHOULD BE ATTACKED BY NAME.
REPUBLICANS WANTED A WEDGE ISSUE TO BOOST
GEORGE BUSH
WHO WAS RUNNING AGAINST GOV. DUKAKIS OF MASSACHUSETTS.
THEY RAN TV ADS ABOUT A MURDERER WHO COMMITTED A VICIOUS RAPE WHILE HE WAS OUT
Willie Horton
WEEKEND PASSES
ON FURLOUGH IN MASSACHUSETTS.
HE'S PERFECT!
BUSH'S VICTORY OVER DUKAKIS
DUKAKIS
WAS A WARNING OF THE POLITICAL HAZARDS OF A LIBERAL STANCE ON CRIME.

BUSH INHERITED A JUSTICE DEPARTMENT THAT WAS COMMITTED TO EVER HARSHER POLICIES, DESPITE CHALLENGES TO THEIR EFFECTIVENESS.

"INCAPACITATION DOES **NOT** APPEAR TO ACHIEVE LARGE **REDUCTIONS** IN **CRIME**..." But these policies "CAN CAUSE **ENORMOUS** INCREASES IN THE PRISON **POPULATION**."

THEY IGNORED A 1983 STUDY BY THE REAGAN JUSTICE DEPT.

THEY PREFERRED A 1987 STUDY THAT CLAIMED

INCARCERATING A SINGLE OFFENDER SAVES TAXPAYERS $405,000.

EVEN THOUGH THE ANALYSIS WAS WIDELY CRITICIZED,

"COMPOUND, CATASTROPHIC ERROR"

THE ADMINISTRATION SPREAD THE DISCREDITED NOTION THAT WE WERE

SAVING $405,000 FOR EVERY OFFENDER WHO IS INCARCERATED.

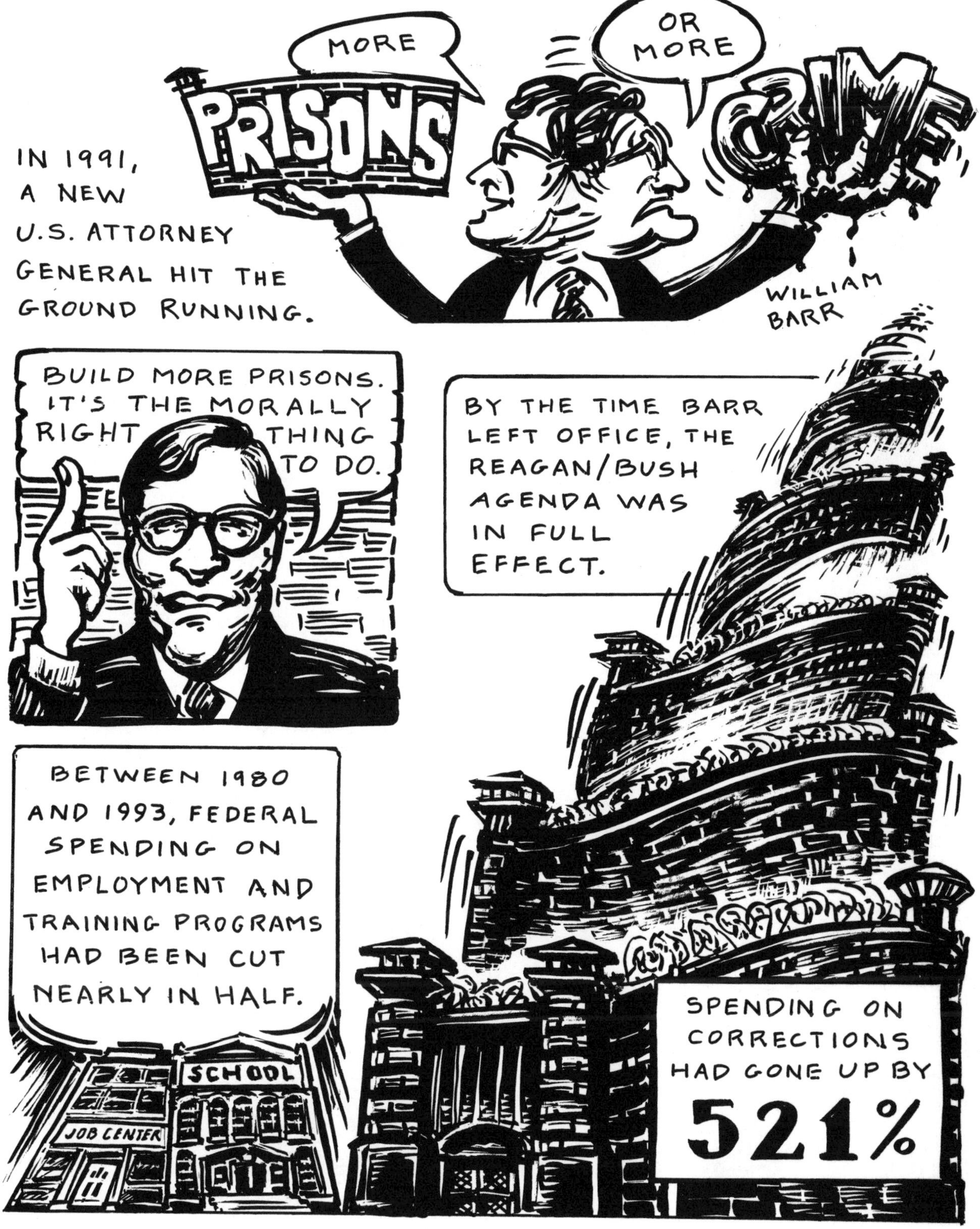
IN 1991, A NEW U.S. ATTORNEY GENERAL HIT THE GROUND RUNNING.
MORE
PRISONS
OR MORE
CRIME
WILLIAM BARR
BUILD MORE PRISONS. IT'S THE MORALLY RIGHT THING TO DO.
BY THE TIME BARR LEFT OFFICE, THE REAGAN/BUSH AGENDA WAS IN FULL EFFECT.
BETWEEN 1980 AND 1993, FEDERAL SPENDING ON EMPLOYMENT AND TRAINING PROGRAMS HAD BEEN CUT NEARLY IN HALF.
SCHOOL
JOB CENTER
SPENDING ON CORRECTIONS HAD GONE UP BY
521%

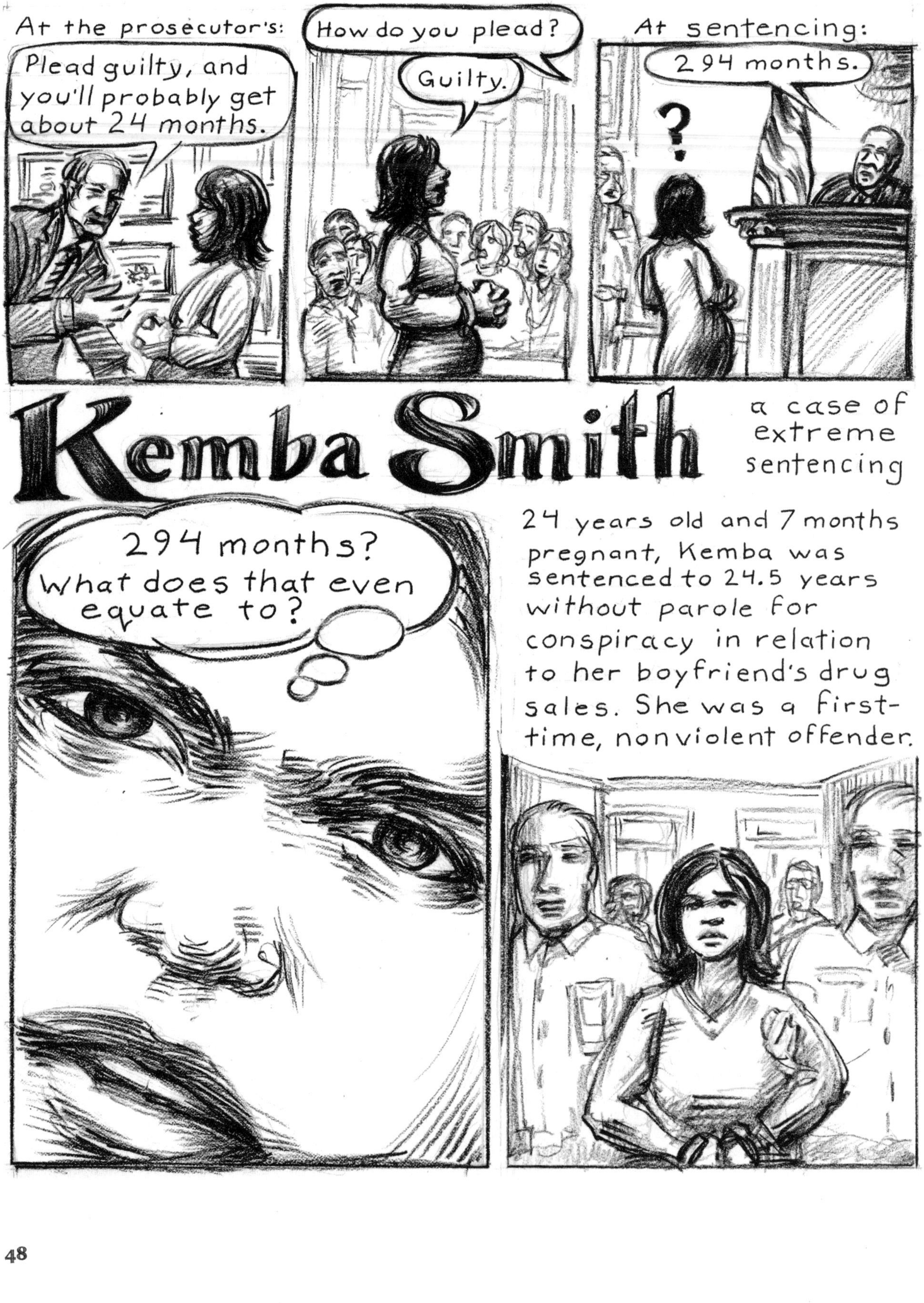
At the prosecutor's:
Plead guilty, and you'll probably get about 24 months.
How do you plead?
Guilty.
At sentencing:
294 months.
?
Kemba Smith
a case of extreme sentencing
294 months? What does that even equate to?
24 years old and 7 months pregnant, Kemba was sentenced to 24.5 years without parole for conspiracy in relation to her boyfriend's drug sales. She was a first-time, nonviolent offender.

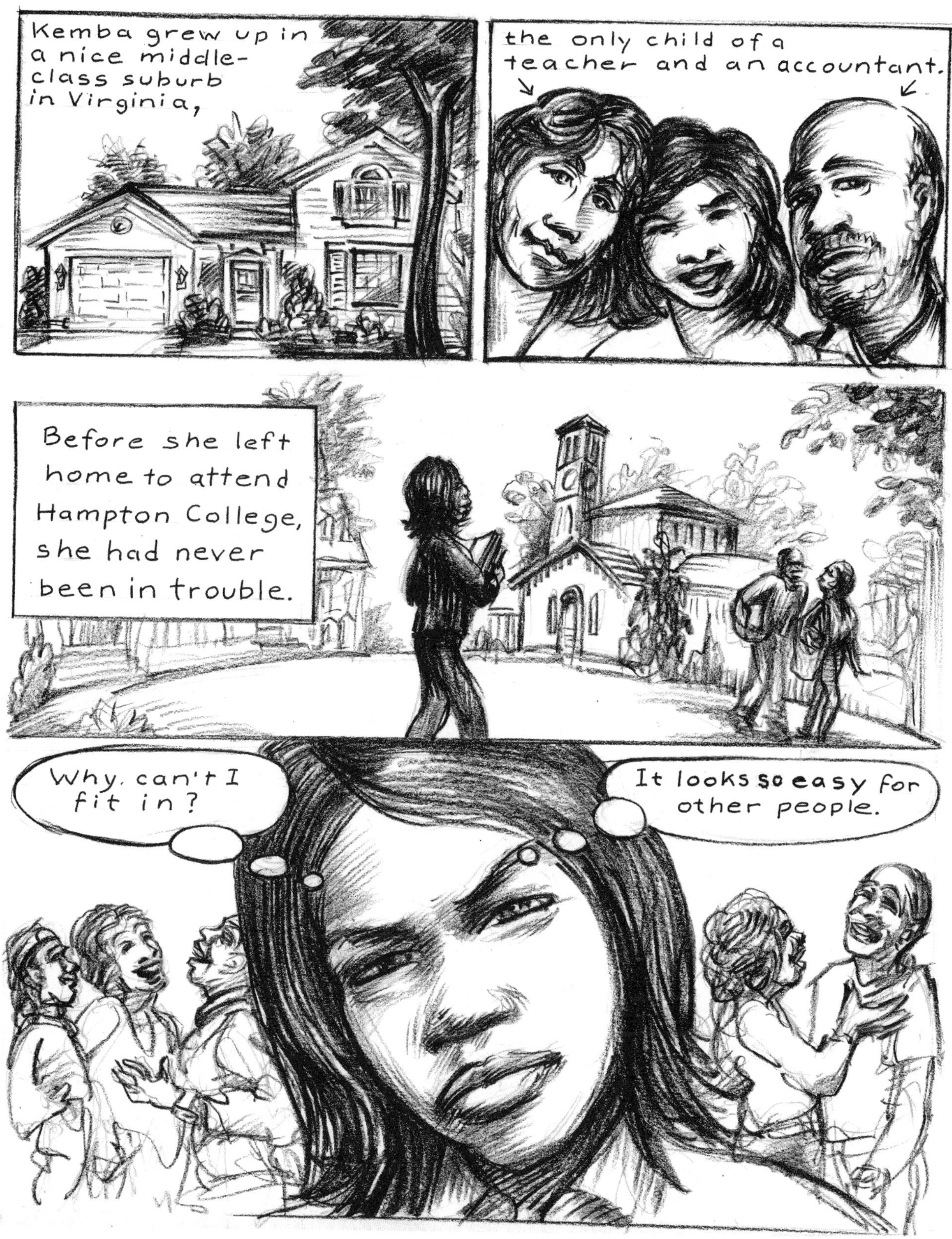
Kemba grew up in a nice middle-class suburb in Virginia,
the only child of a teacher and an accountant.
Before she left home to attend Hampton College, she had never been in trouble.
Why can't I fit in?
It looks so easy for other people.

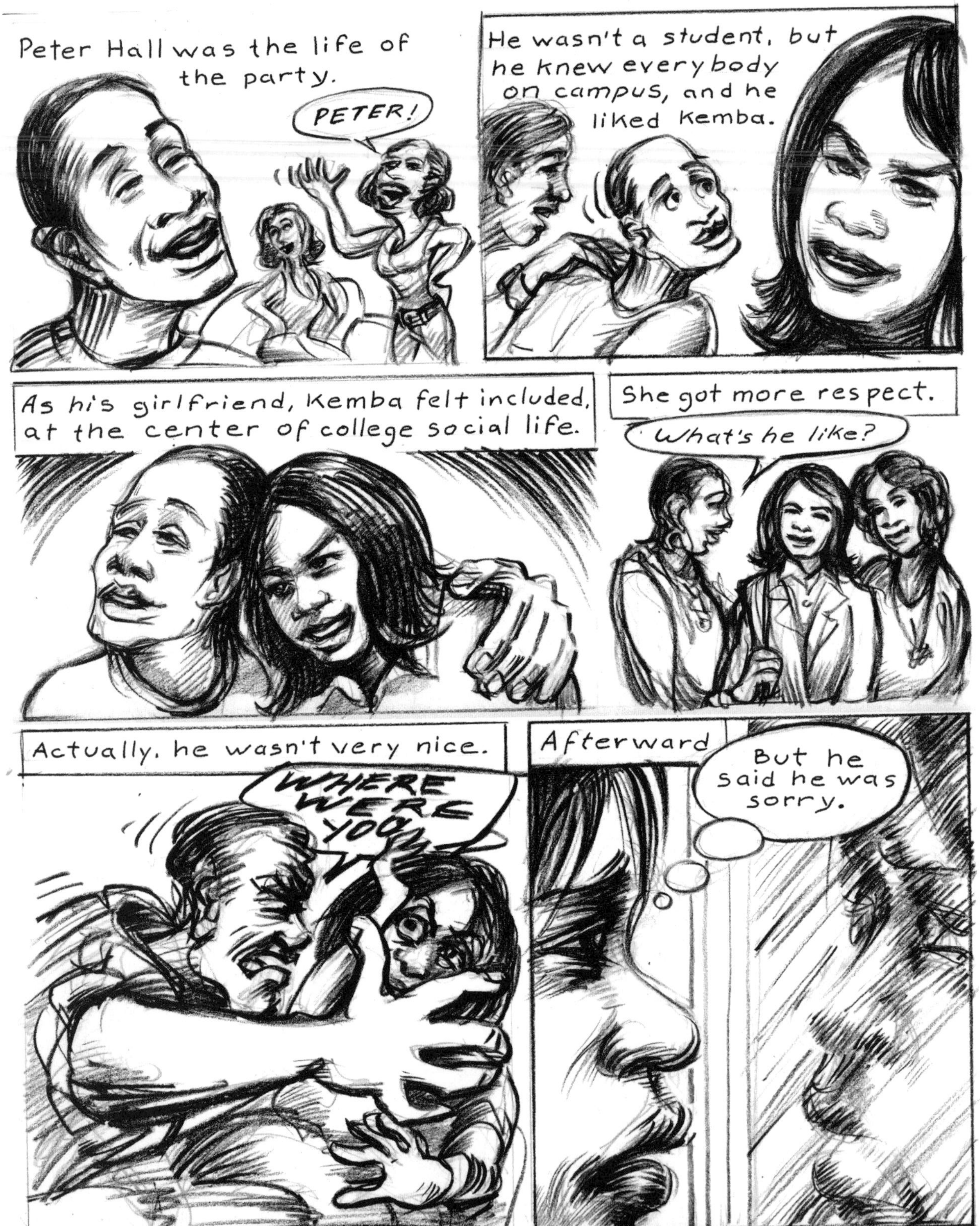
Peter Hall was the life of the party.
PETER!
He wasn't a student, but he knew everybody on campus, and he liked Kemba.
As his girlfriend, Kemba felt included, at the center of college social life.
She got more respect.
What's he like?
Actually, he wasn't very nice.
WHERE WERE YOU
Afterward
But he said he was sorry.

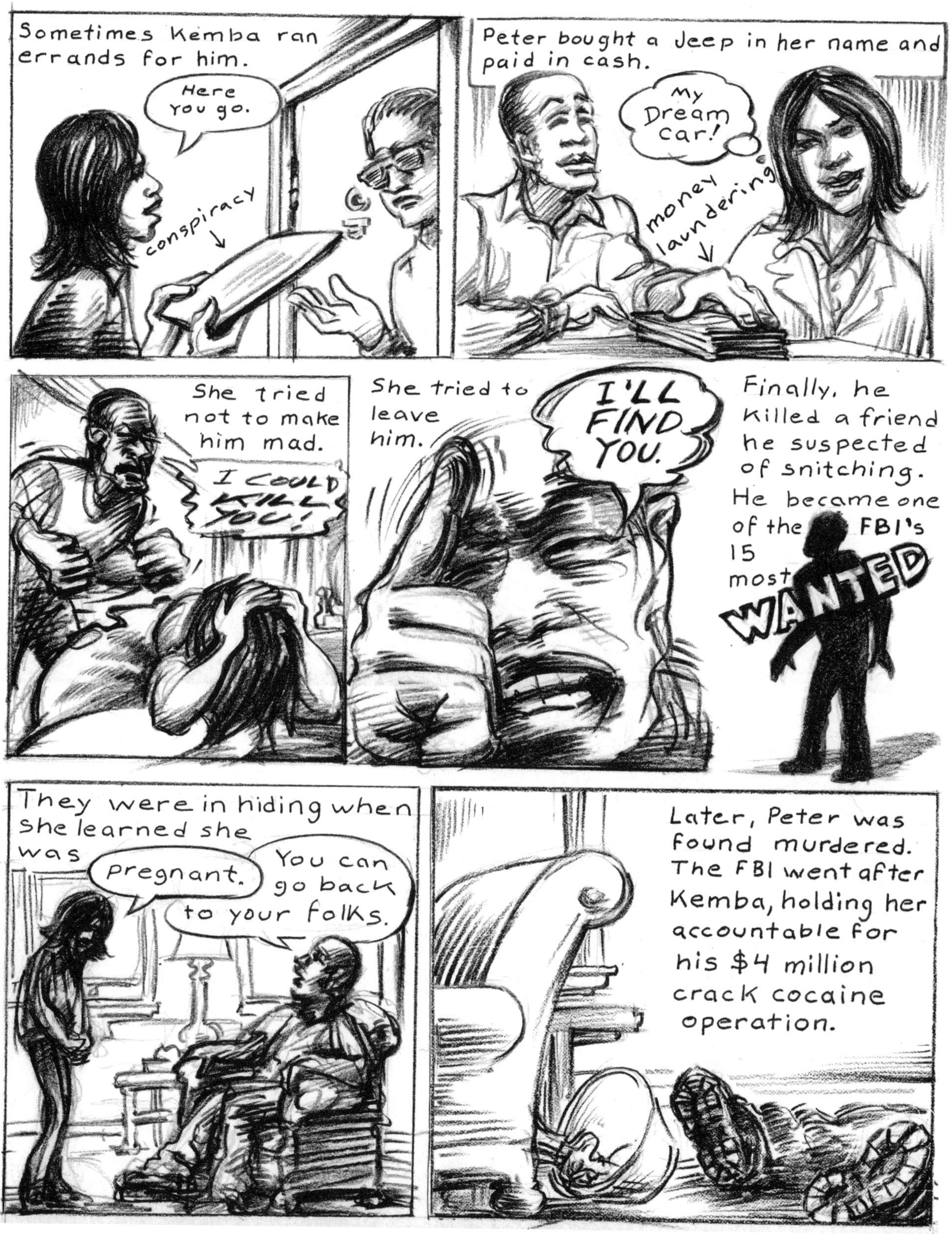
Sometimes Kemba ran errands for him.
Here you go.
conspiracy
Peter bought a Jeep in her name and paid in cash.
My Dream car!
money laundering
She tried not to make him mad.
I COULD KILL YOU!
She tried to leave him.
I'LL FIND YOU.
Finally, he killed a friend he suspected of snitching.
He became one of the FBI's 15 most
WANTED
They were in hiding when she learned she was
pregnant.
You can go back to your folks.
Later, Peter was found murdered. The FBI went after Kemba, holding her accountable for his $4 million crack cocaine operation.

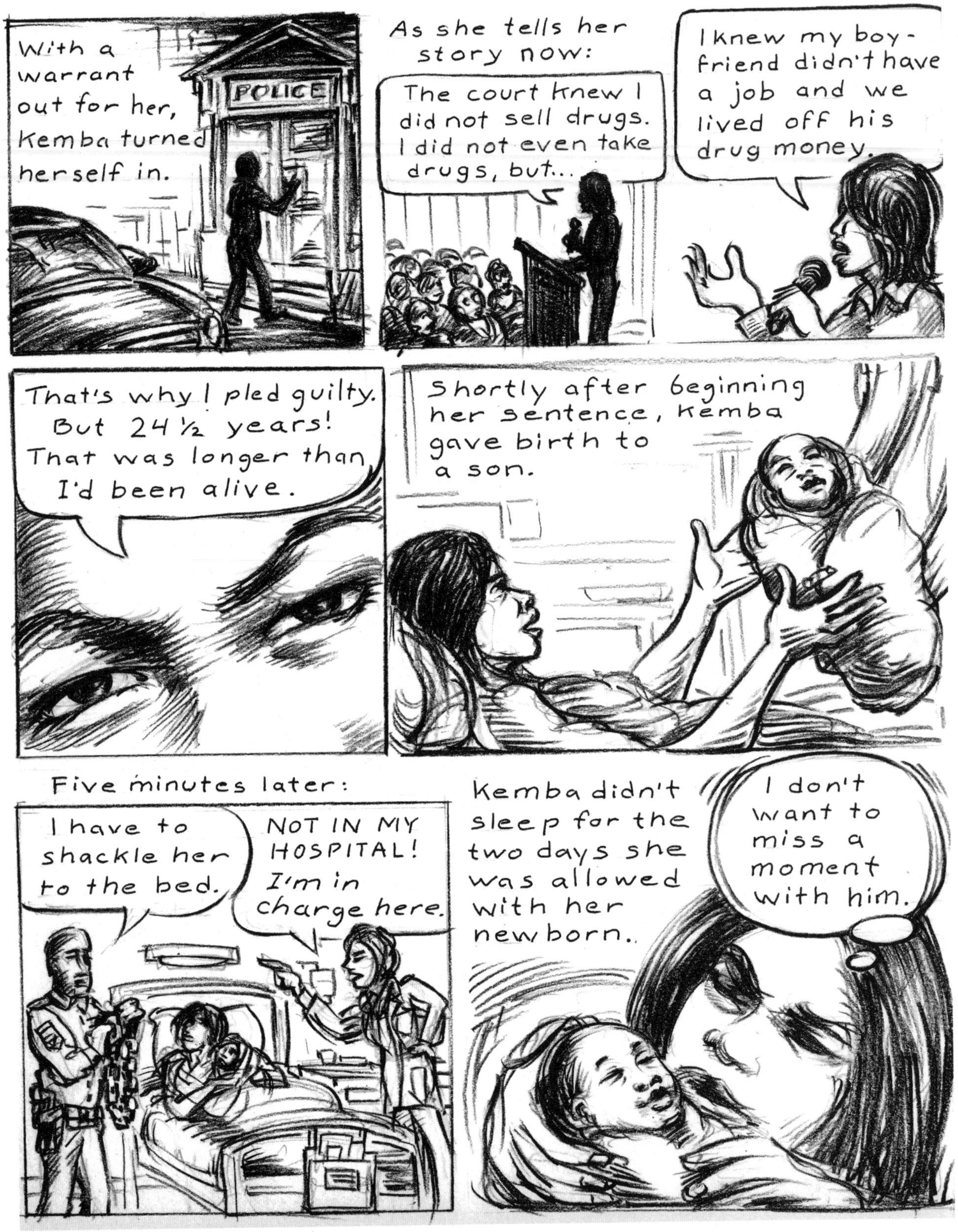
With a warrant out for her, Kemba turned herself in.
POLICE
As she tells her story now:
The court knew I did not sell drugs. I did not even take drugs, but...
I knew my boy-friend didn't have a job and we lived off his drug money.
That's why I pled guilty. But 24½ years! That was longer than I'd been alive.
Shortly after beginning her sentence, Kemba gave birth to a son.
Five minutes later:
I have to shackle her to the bed.
NOT IN MY HOSPITAL! I'm in charge here.
Kemba didn't sleep for the two days she was allowed with her newborn.
I don't want to miss a moment with him.

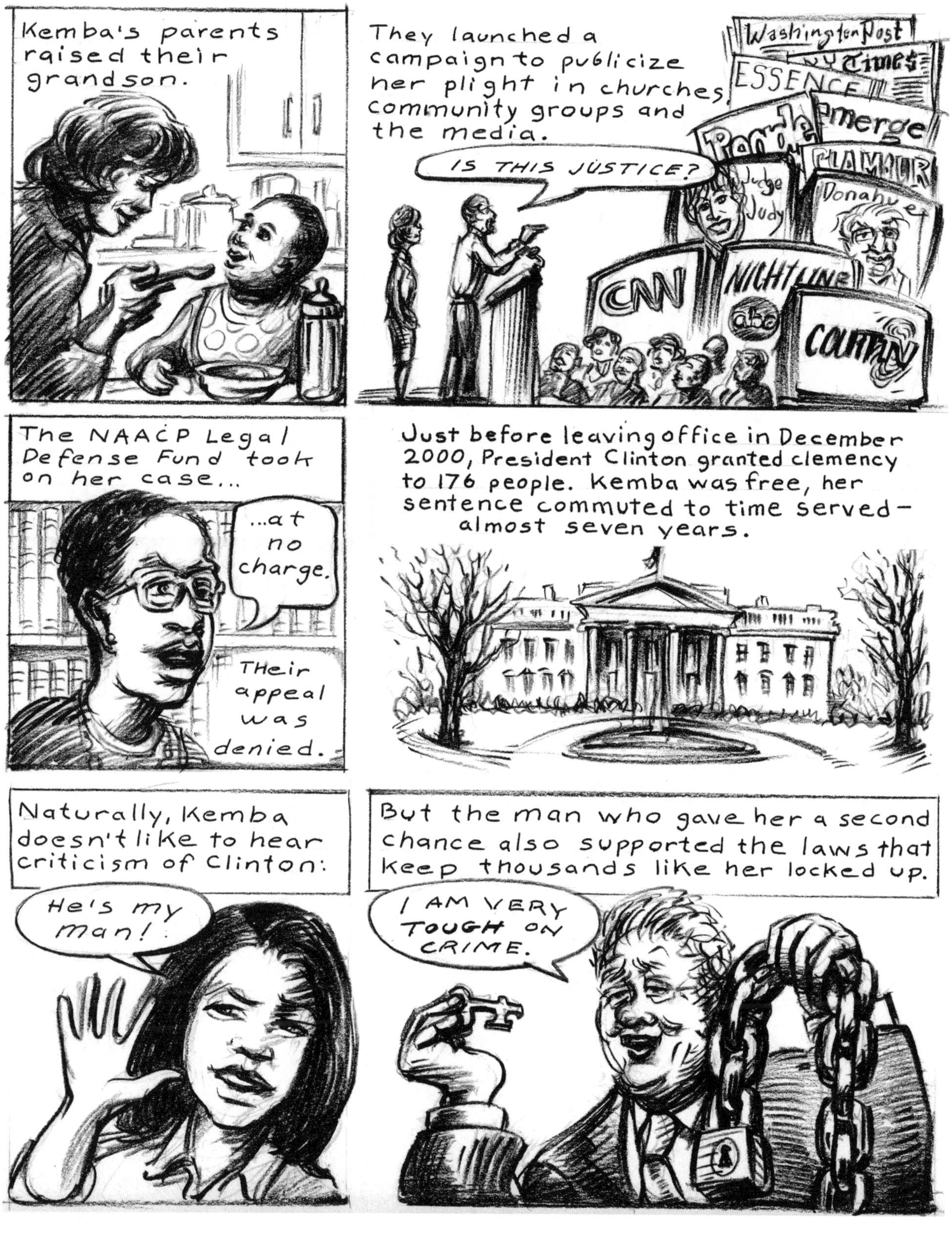
Kemba's parents raised their grandson.
They launched a campaign to publicize her plight in churches, community groups and the media.
Washington Post
ESSENCE
GLAMOUR
Judge Judy
Donahue
CNN
abc
IS THIS JUSTICE?
The NAACP Legal Defense Fund took on her case...
...at no charge.
Their appeal was denied.
Just before leaving office in December 2000, President Clinton granted clemency to 176 people. Kemba was free, her sentence commuted to time served— almost seven years.
Naturally, Kemba doesn't like to hear criticism of Clinton:
He's my man!
But the man who gave her a second chance also supported the laws that keep thousands like her locked up.
I AM VERY TOUGH ON CRIME.

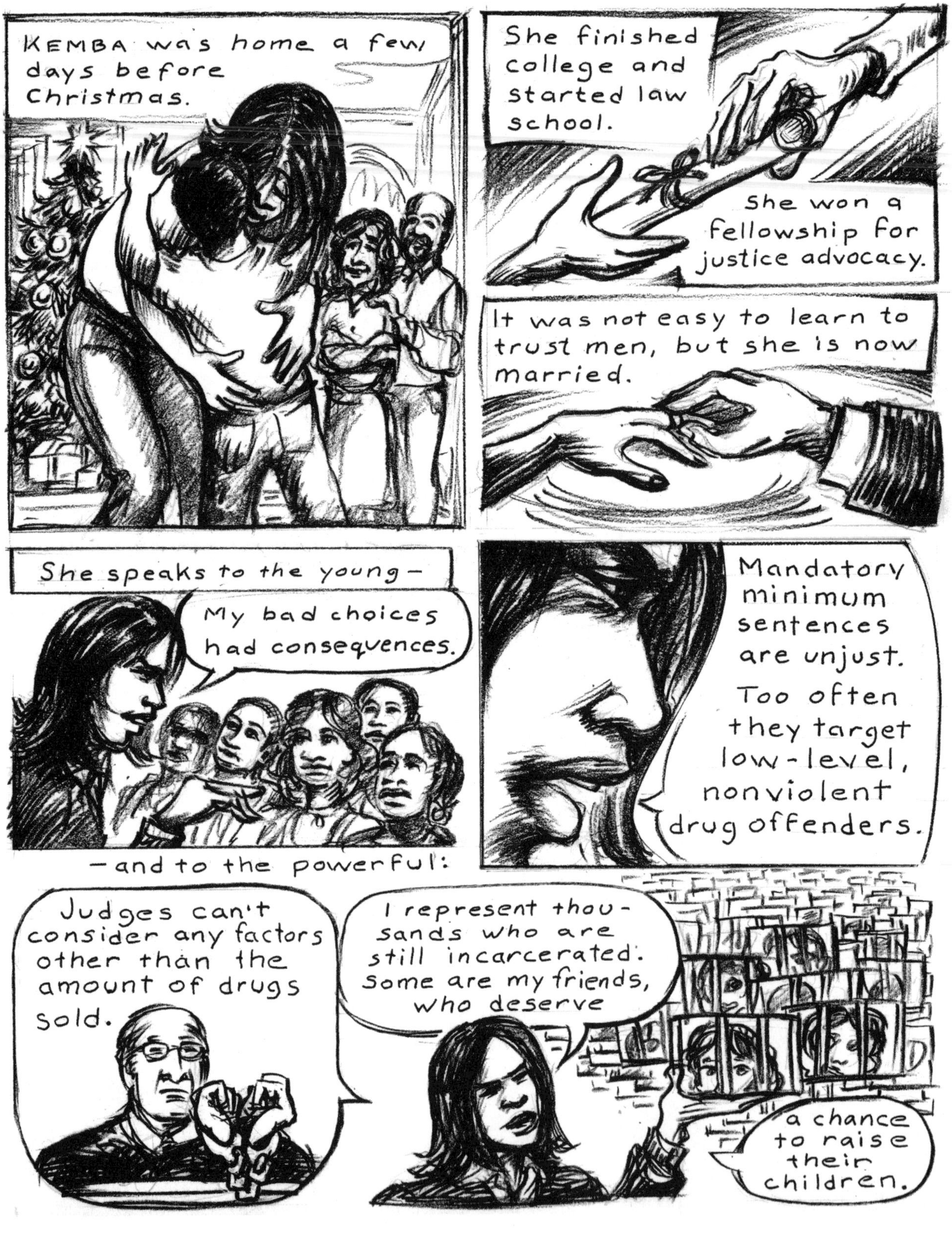
KEMBA was home a few days before Christmas.
She finished college and started law school.
She won a fellowship for justice advocacy.
It was not easy to learn to trust men, but she is now married.
She speaks to the young—
My bad choices had consequences.
Mandatory minimum sentences are unjust.
Too often they target low-level, nonviolent drug offenders.
—and to the powerful:
Judges can't consider any factors other than the amount of drugs sold.
I represent thousands who are still incarcerated. Some are my friends, who deserve
a chance to raise their children.

CRIME AS POLITICS

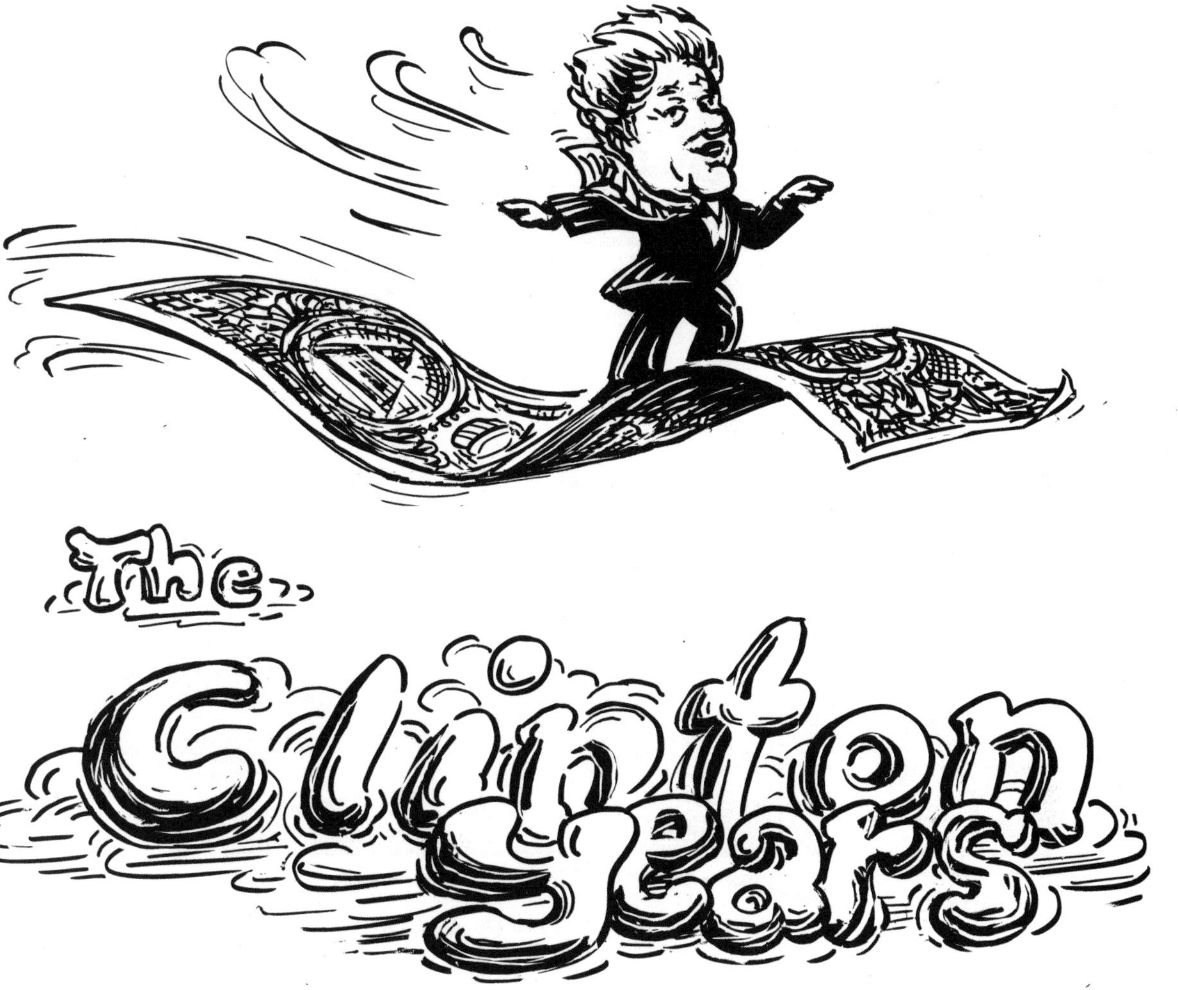

The Clinton Years

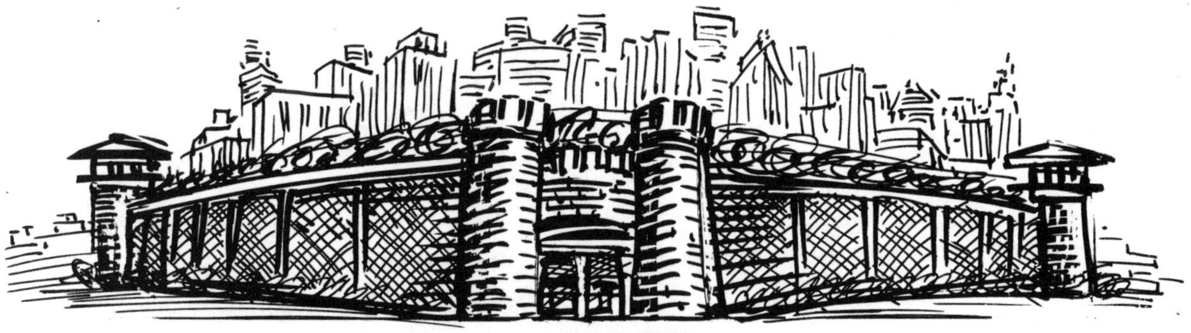

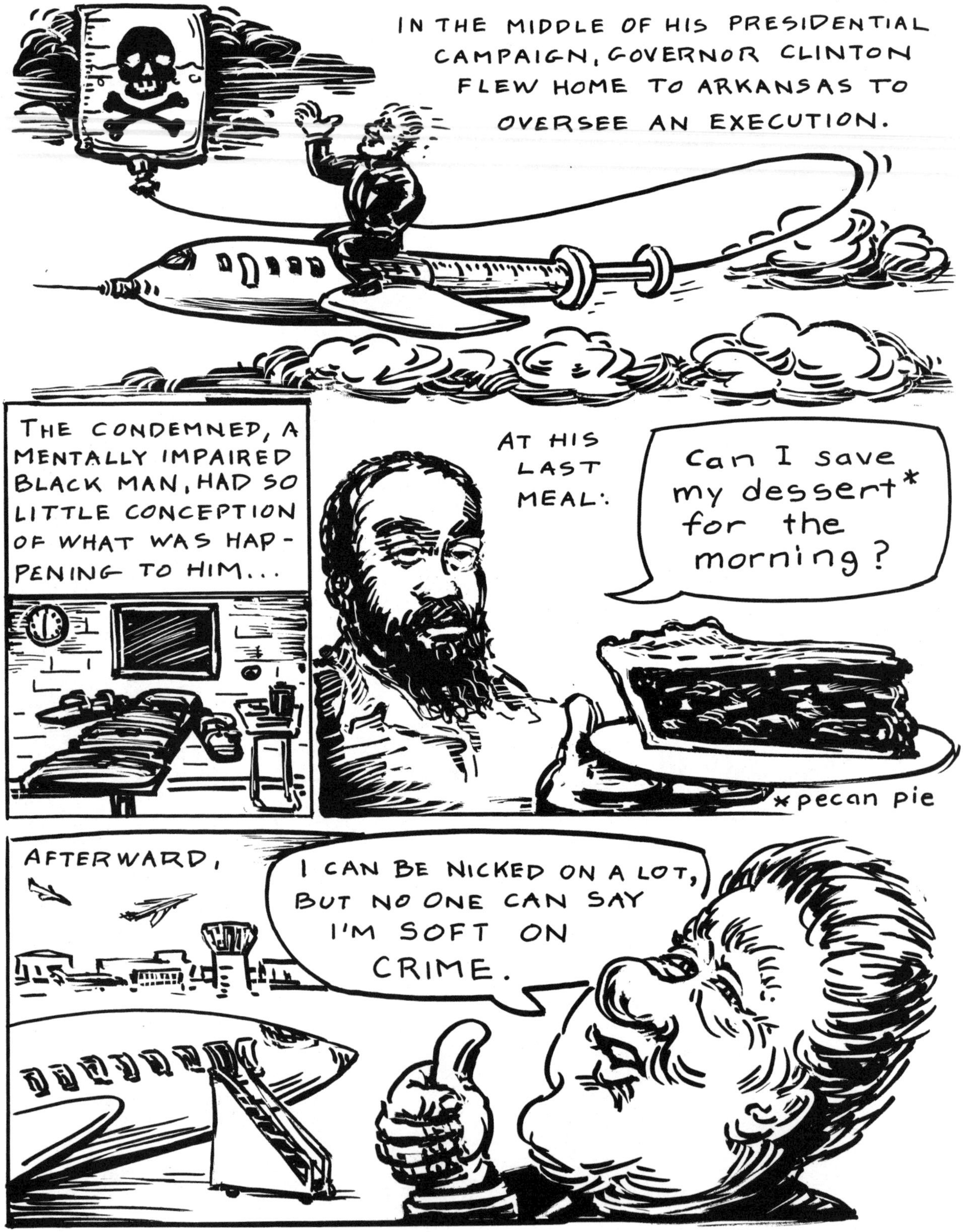
IN THE MIDDLE OF HIS PRESIDENTIAL CAMPAIGN, GOVERNOR CLINTON FLEW HOME TO ARKANSAS TO OVERSEE AN EXECUTION.
THE CONDEMNED, A MENTALLY IMPAIRED BLACK MAN, HAD SO LITTLE CONCEPTION OF WHAT WAS HAPPENING TO HIM...
AT HIS LAST MEAL:
Can I save my dessert* for the morning?
*pecan pie
AFTERWARD,
I CAN BE NICKED ON A LOT, BUT NO ONE CAN SAY I'M SOFT ON CRIME.

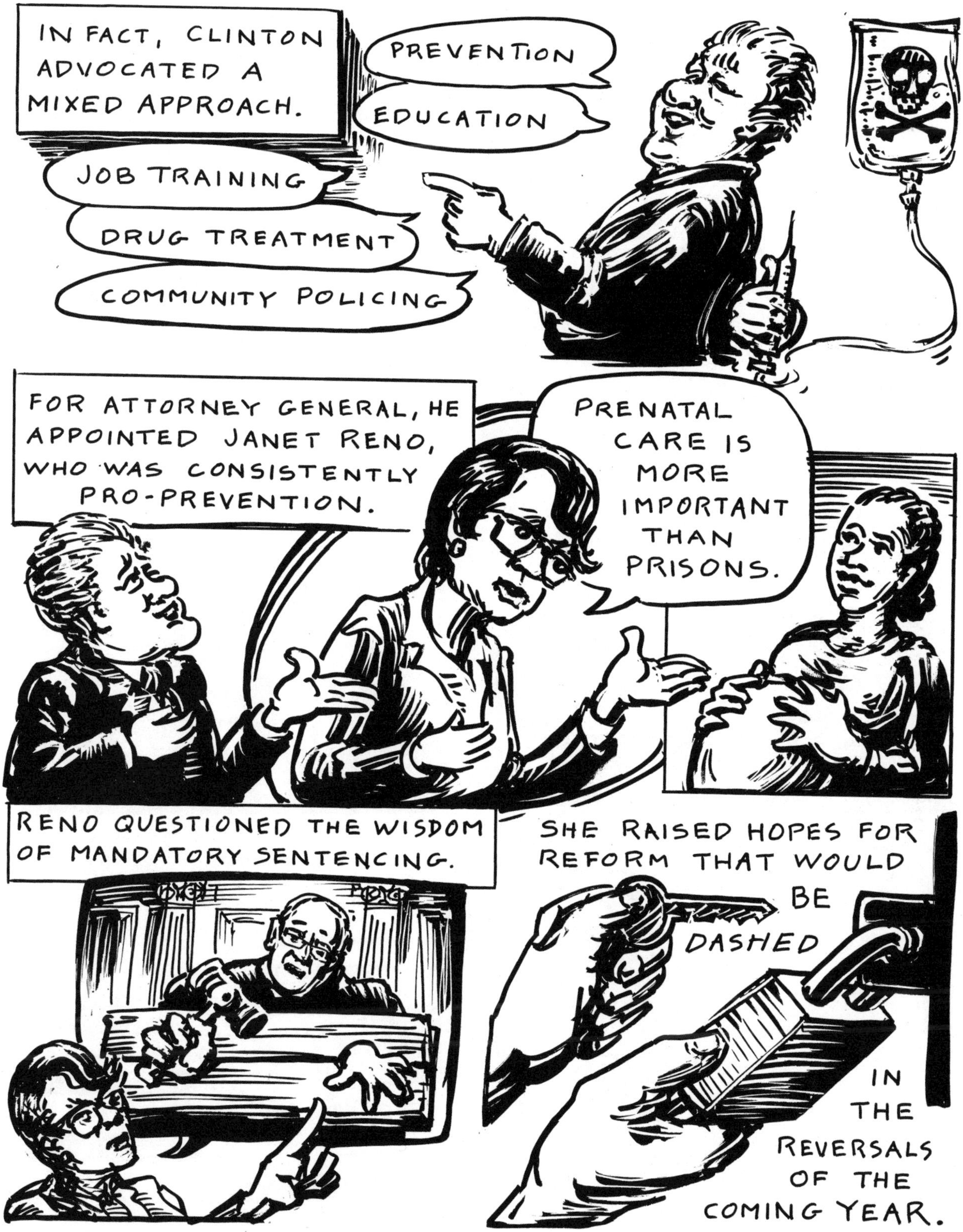

IN FACT, CLINTON ADVOCATED A MIXED APPROACH.
PREVENTION
EDUCATION
JOB TRAINING
DRUG TREATMENT
COMMUNITY POLICING
FOR ATTORNEY GENERAL, HE APPOINTED JANET RENO, WHO WAS CONSISTENTLY PRO-PREVENTION.
PRENATAL CARE IS MORE IMPORTANT THAN PRISONS.
RENO QUESTIONED THE WISDOM OF MANDATORY SENTENCING.
SHE RAISED HOPES FOR REFORM THAT WOULD BE DASHED
IN THE REVERSALS OF THE COMING YEAR.

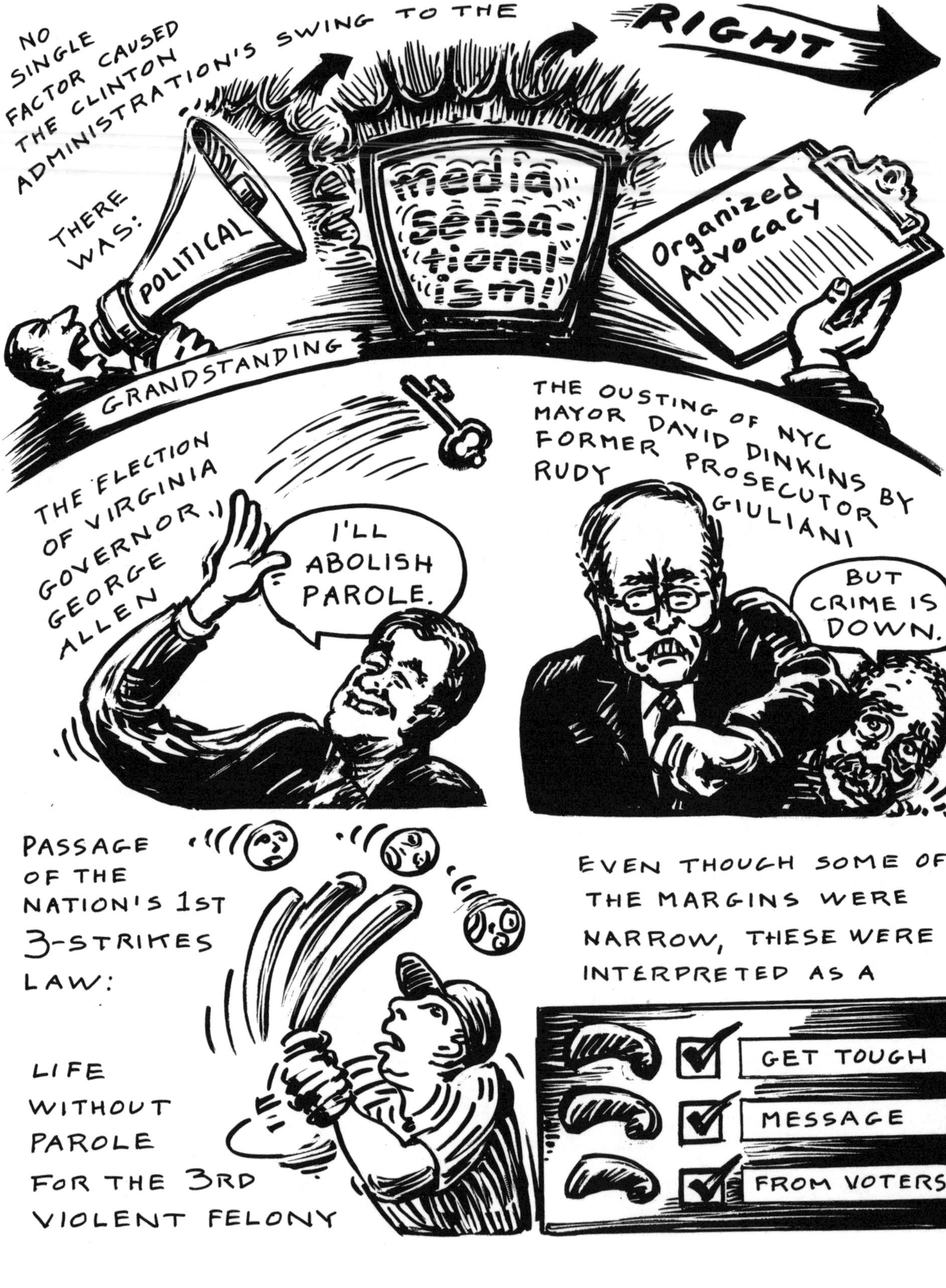
NO SINGLE FACTOR CAUSED THE CLINTON ADMINISTRATION'S SWING TO THE
RIGHT
THERE WAS:
POLITICAL
GRANDSTANDING
media sensa-tional-ism!
Organized Advocacy
THE ELECTION OF VIRGINIA GOVERNOR GEORGE ALLEN
I'LL ABOLISH PAROLE.
THE OUSTING OF NYC MAYOR DAVID DINKINS BY FORMER PROSECUTOR RUDY GIULIANI
BUT CRIME IS DOWN.
PASSAGE OF THE NATION'S 1ST 3-STRIKES LAW:
LIFE WITHOUT PAROLE FOR THE 3RD VIOLENT FELONY
EVEN THOUGH SOME OF THE MARGINS WERE NARROW, THESE WERE INTERPRETED AS A
GET TOUGH
MESSAGE
FROM VOTERS

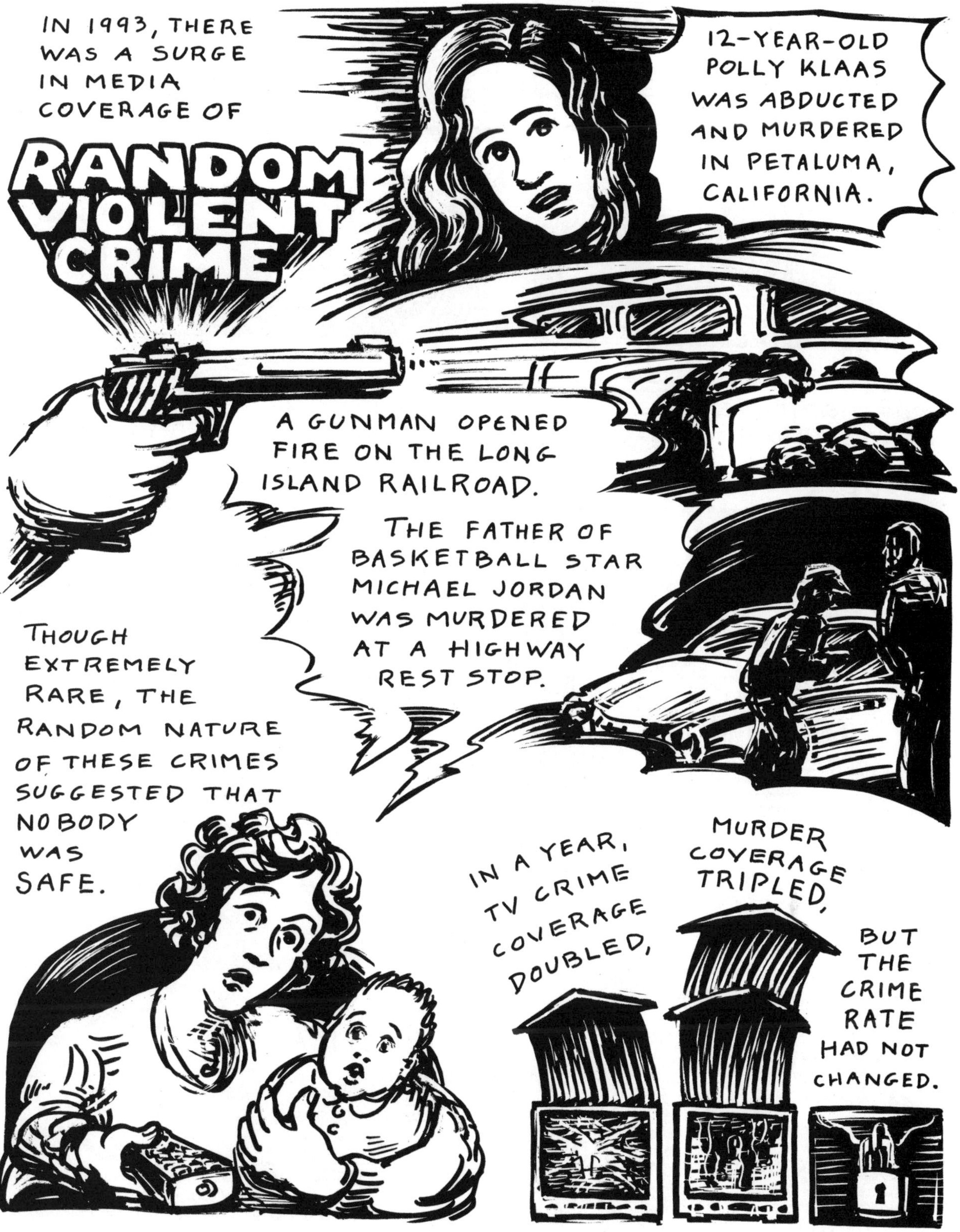
IN 1993, THERE WAS A SURGE IN MEDIA COVERAGE OF
RANDOM VIOLENT CRIME
12-YEAR-OLD POLLY KLAAS WAS ABDUCTED AND MURDERED IN PETALUMA, CALIFORNIA.
A GUNMAN OPENED FIRE ON THE LONG ISLAND RAILROAD.
THE FATHER OF BASKETBALL STAR MICHAEL JORDAN WAS MURDERED AT A HIGHWAY REST STOP.
THOUGH EXTREMELY RARE, THE RANDOM NATURE OF THESE CRIMES SUGGESTED THAT NOBODY WAS SAFE.
IN A YEAR, TV CRIME COVERAGE DOUBLED,
MURDER COVERAGE TRIPLED,
BUT THE CRIME RATE HAD NOT CHANGED.

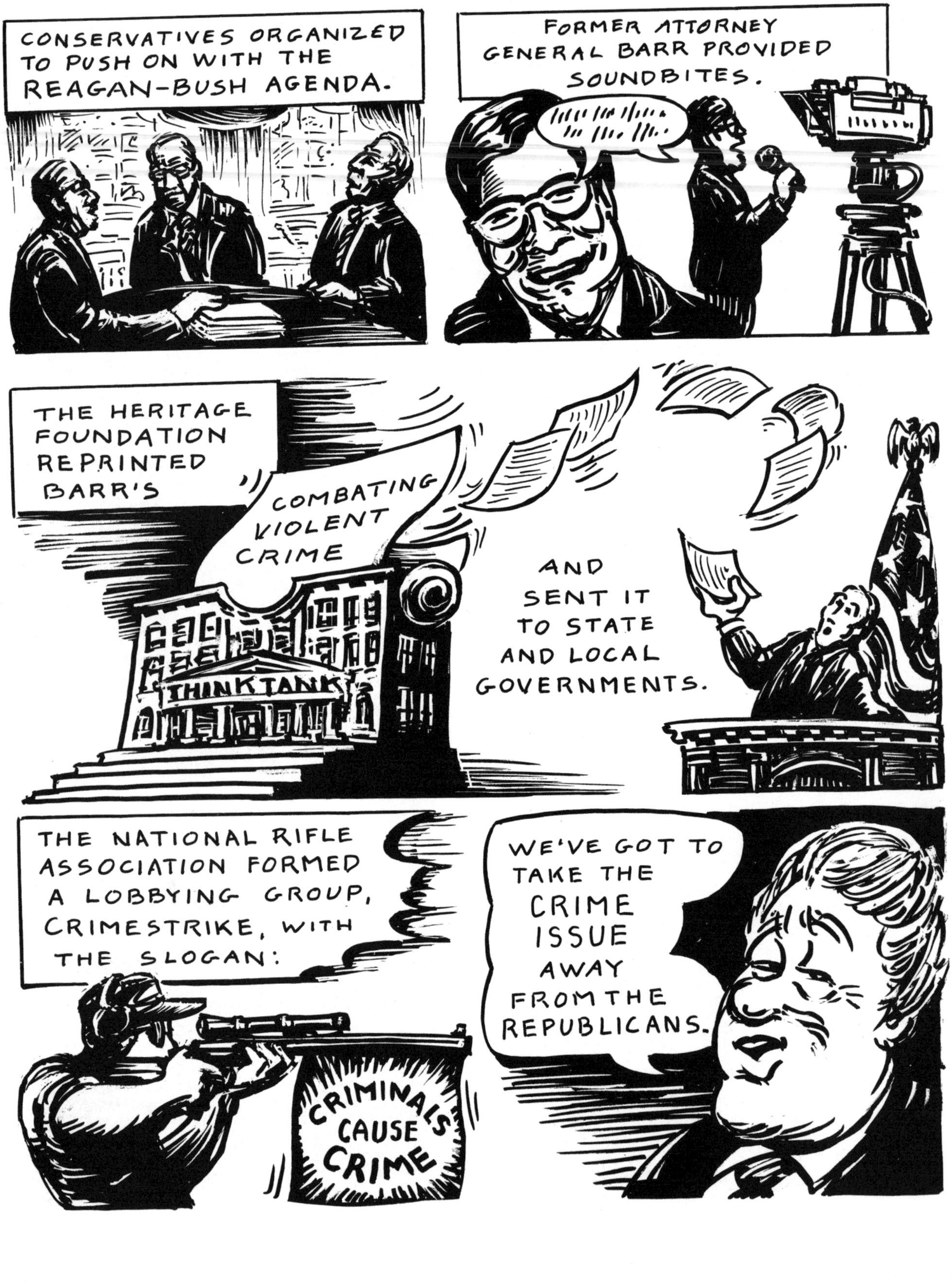
CONSERVATIVES ORGANIZED TO PUSH ON WITH THE REAGAN-BUSH AGENDA.
FORMER ATTORNEY GENERAL BARR PROVIDED SOUNDBITES.
THE HERITAGE FOUNDATION REPRINTED BARR'S
COMBATING VIOLENT CRIME
THINKTANK
AND SENT IT TO STATE AND LOCAL GOVERNMENTS.
THE NATIONAL RIFLE ASSOCIATION FORMED A LOBBYING GROUP, CRIMESTRIKE, WITH THE SLOGAN:
CRIMINALS CAUSE CRIME
WE'VE GOT TO TAKE THE CRIME ISSUE AWAY FROM THE REPUBLICANS.

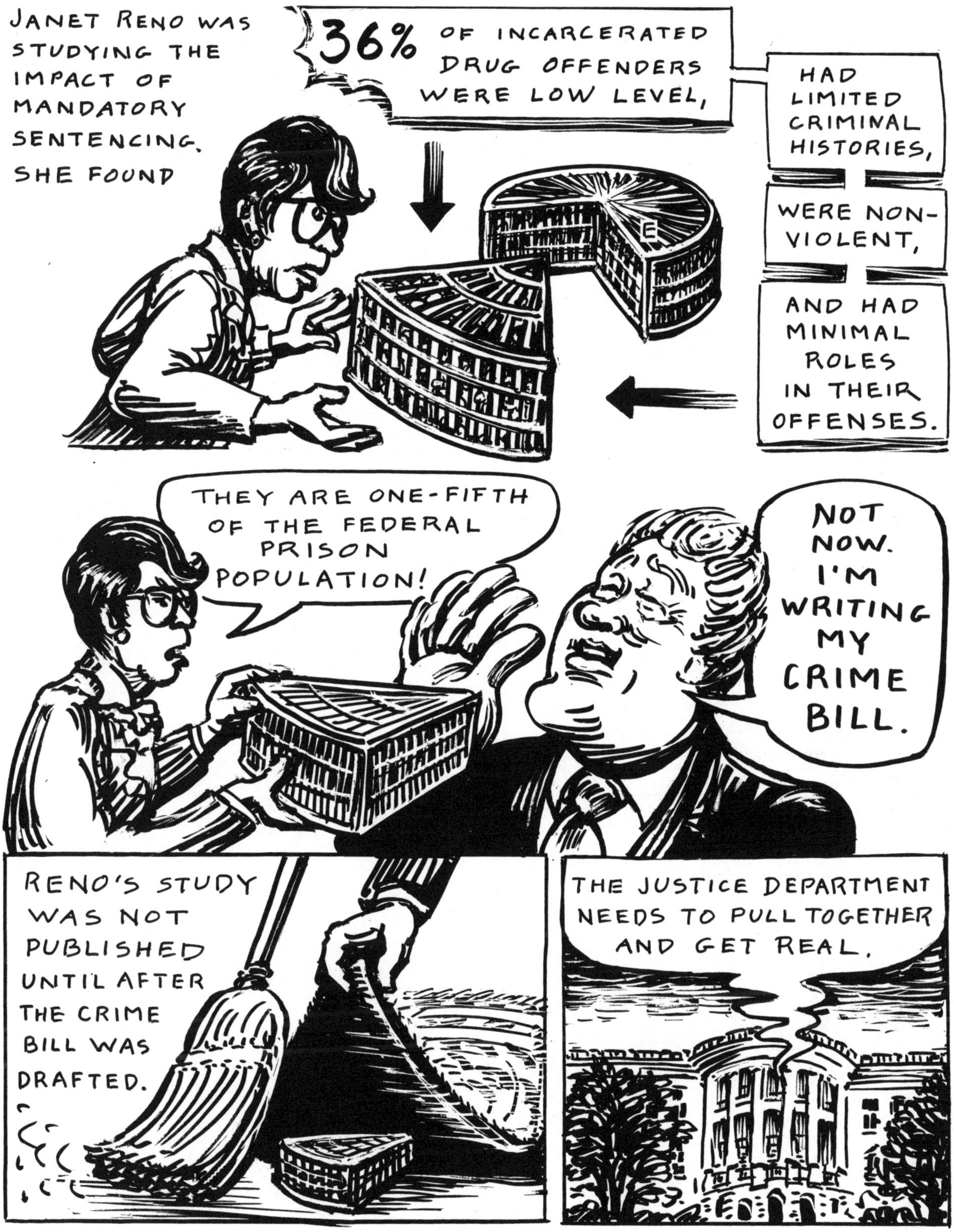
JANET RENO WAS STUDYING THE IMPACT OF MANDATORY SENTENCING. SHE FOUND
36% OF INCARCERATED DRUG OFFENDERS WERE LOW LEVEL,
HAD LIMITED CRIMINAL HISTORIES,
WERE NON-VIOLENT,
AND HAD MINIMAL ROLES IN THEIR OFFENSES.
THEY ARE ONE-FIFTH OF THE FEDERAL PRISON POPULATION!
NOT NOW. I'M WRITING MY CRIME BILL.
RENO'S STUDY WAS NOT PUBLISHED UNTIL AFTER THE CRIME BILL WAS DRAFTED.
THE JUSTICE DEPARTMENT NEEDS TO PULL TOGETHER AND GET REAL.

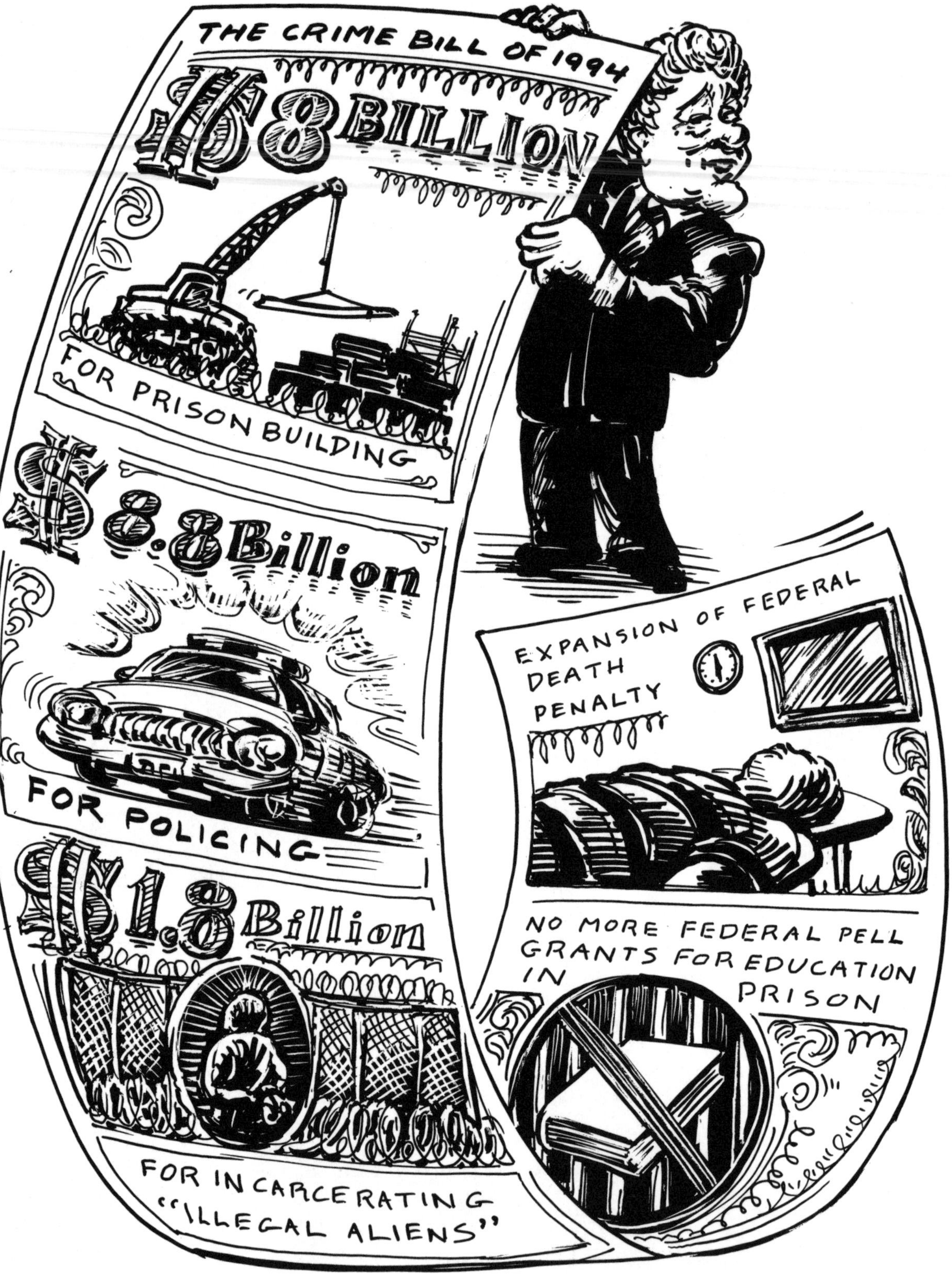
THE CRIME BILL OF 1994
$8 BILLION
FOR PRISON BUILDING
$8.8 Billion
FOR POLICING
$1.8 Billion
FOR INCARCERATING "ILLEGAL ALIENS"
EXPANSION OF FEDERAL DEATH PENALTY
NO MORE FEDERAL PELL GRANTS FOR EDUCATION IN PRISON

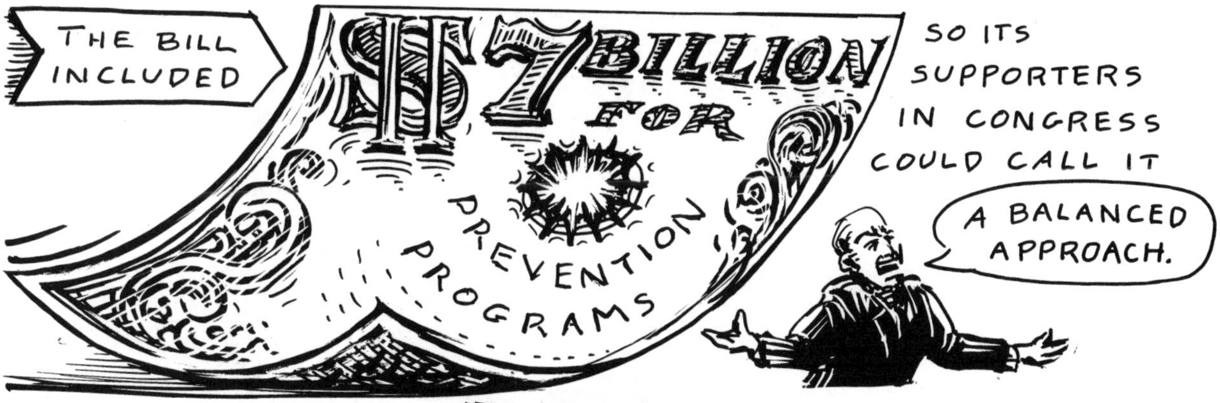
THE BILL INCLUDED
$7 BILLION FOR PREVENTION PROGRAMS
SO ITS SUPPORTERS IN CONGRESS COULD CALL IT
A BALANCED APPROACH.

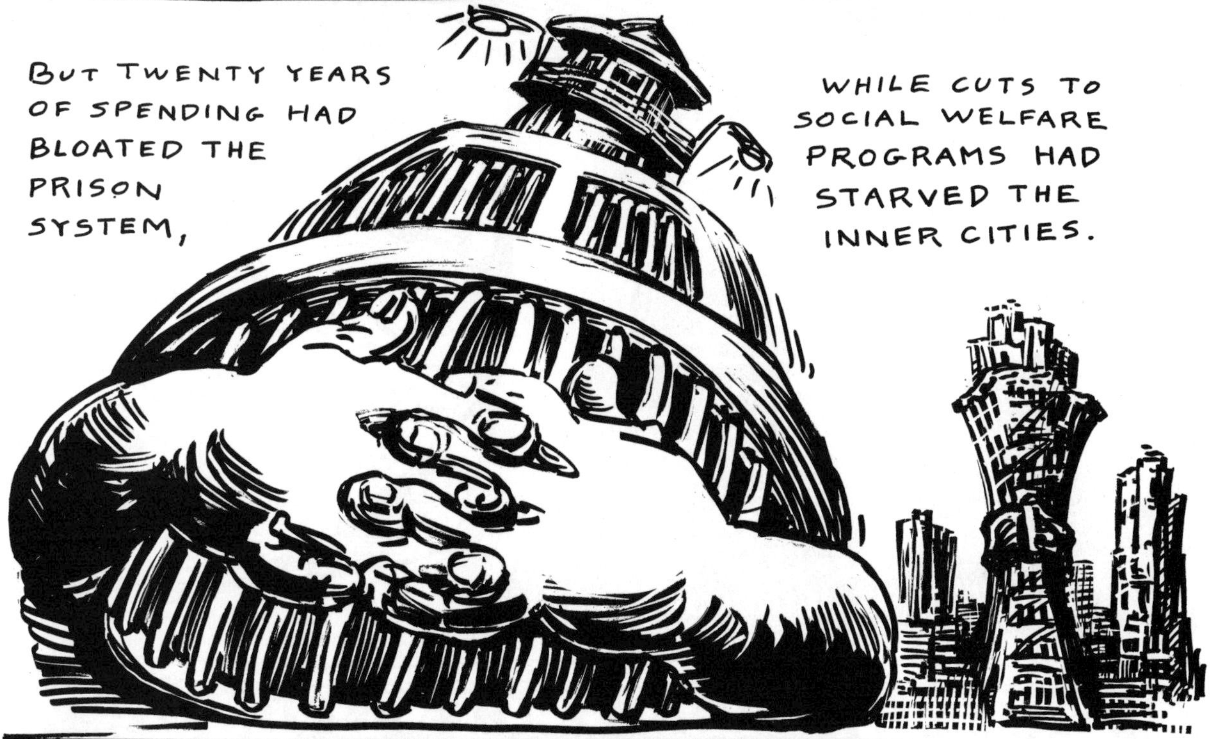
BUT TWENTY YEARS OF SPENDING HAD BLOATED THE PRISON SYSTEM,
WHILE CUTS TO SOCIAL WELFARE PROGRAMS HAD STARVED THE INNER CITIES.

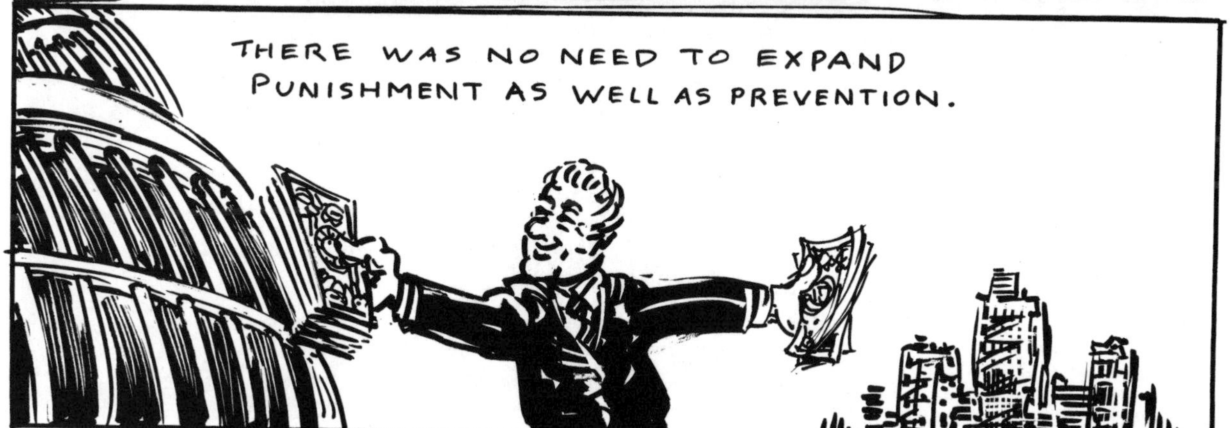
THERE WAS NO NEED TO EXPAND PUNISHMENT AS WELL AS PREVENTION.

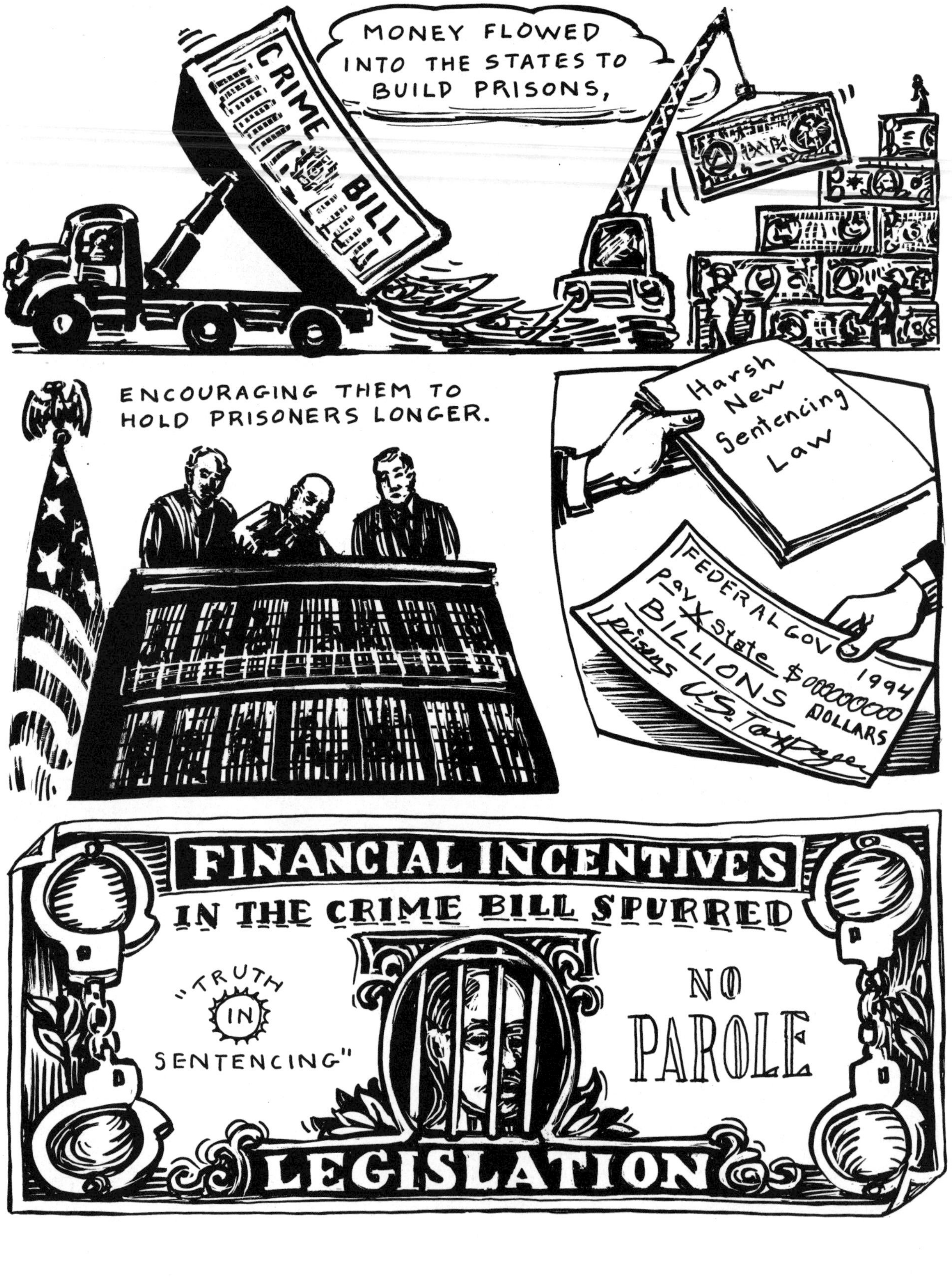
MONEY FLOWED INTO THE STATES TO BUILD PRISONS,
CRIME BILL
ENCOURAGING THEM TO HOLD PRISONERS LONGER.
Harsh New Sentencing Law
FEDERAL GOV
Pay X state
BILLIONS
1994
DOLLARS
prisons
FINANCIAL INCENTIVES
IN THE CRIME BILL SPURRED
"TRUTH IN SENTENCING"
NO PAROLE
LEGISLATION

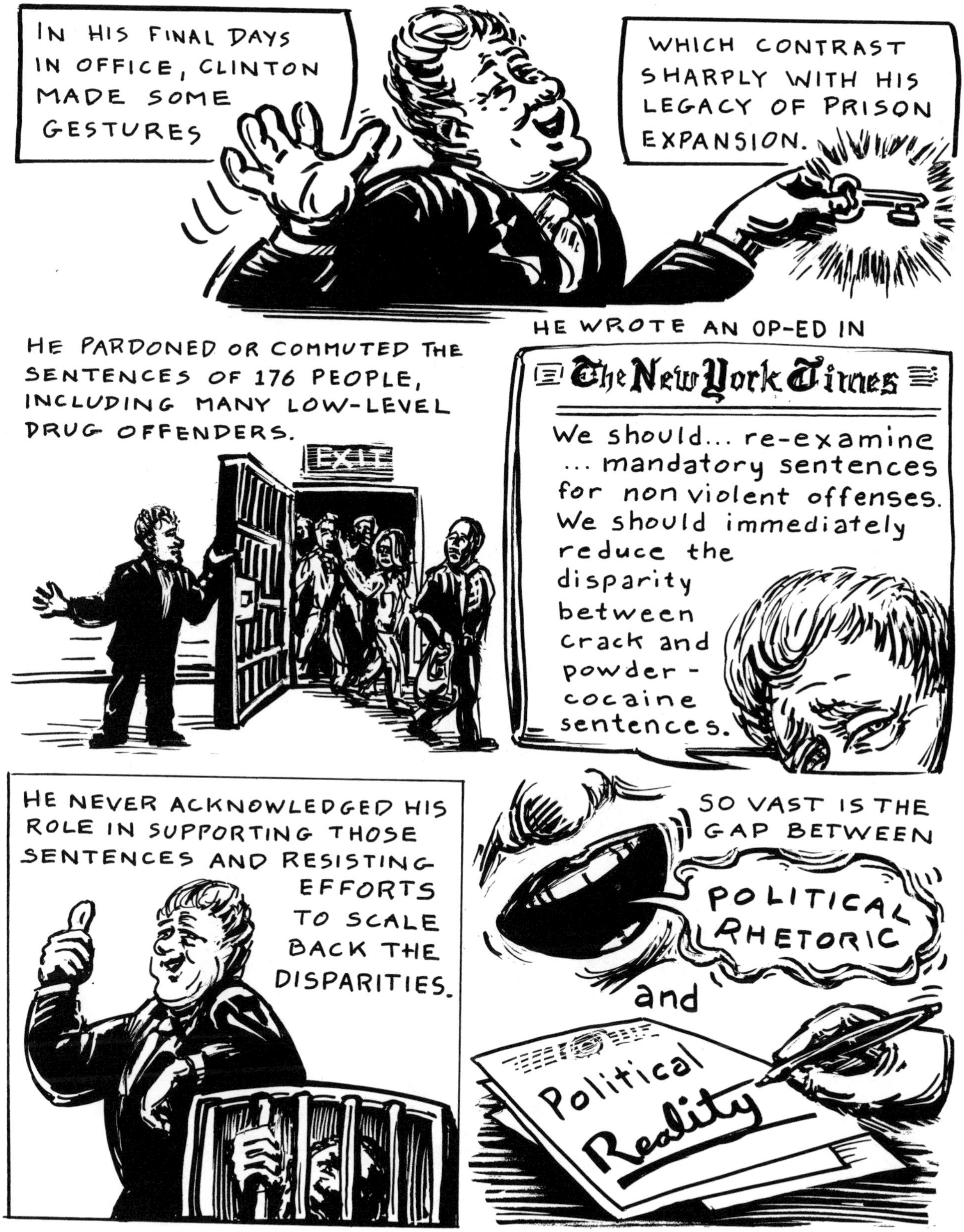
IN HIS FINAL DAYS IN OFFICE, CLINTON MADE SOME GESTURES
WHICH CONTRAST SHARPLY WITH HIS LEGACY OF PRISON EXPANSION.
HE PARDONED OR COMMUTED THE SENTENCES OF 176 PEOPLE, INCLUDING MANY LOW-LEVEL DRUG OFFENDERS.
EXIT
HE WROTE AN OP-ED IN
The New York Times
We should... re-examine ... mandatory sentences for nonviolent offenses. We should immediately reduce the disparity between crack and powder-cocaine sentences.
HE NEVER ACKNOWLEDGED HIS ROLE IN SUPPORTING THOSE SENTENCES AND RESISTING EFFORTS TO SCALE BACK THE DISPARITIES.
SO VAST IS THE GAP BETWEEN
POLITICAL RHETORIC
and
Political Reality

CRIME AS POLITICS
THE
GEORGE
W
BUSH
YEARS

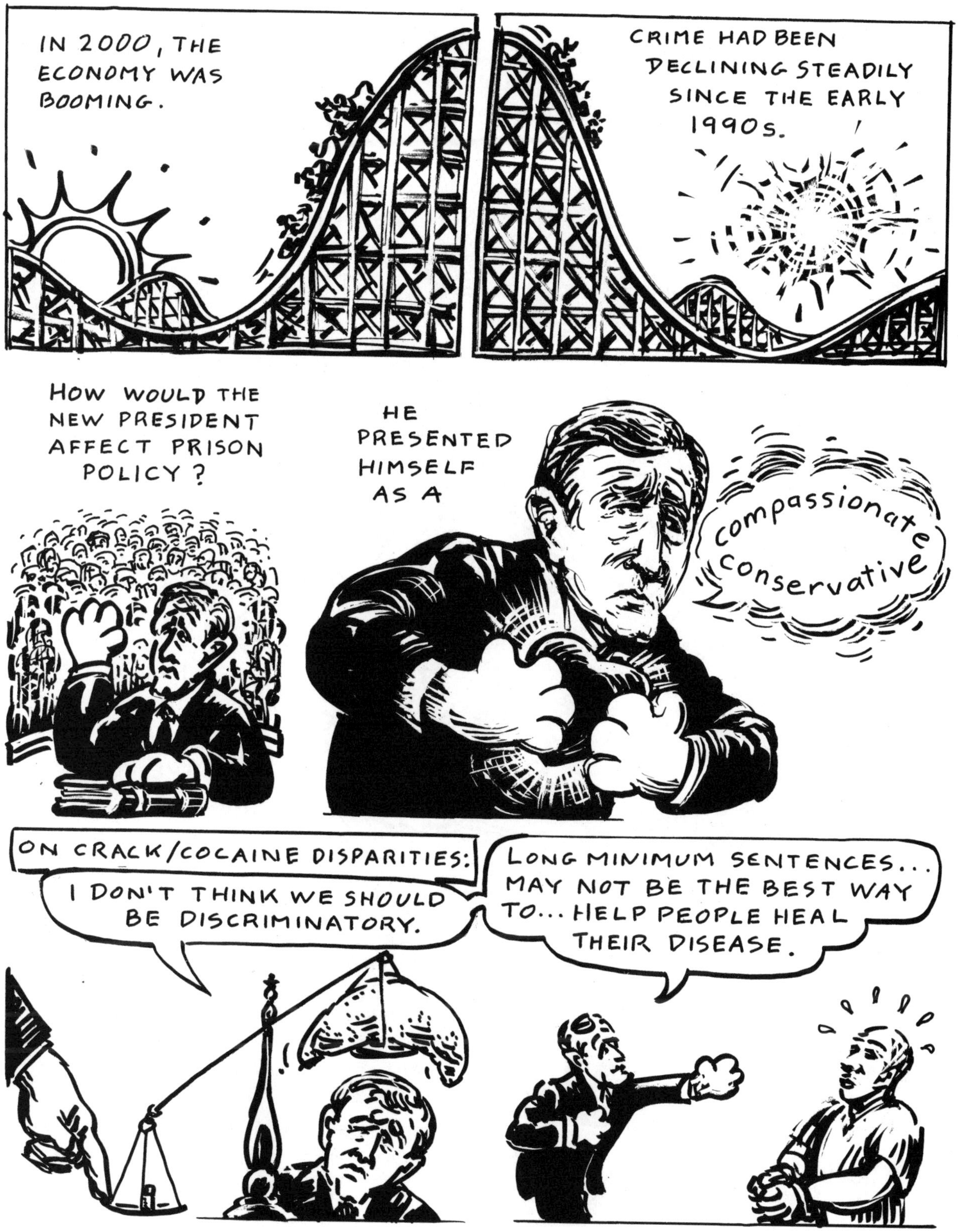
IN 2000, THE ECONOMY WAS BOOMING.
CRIME HAD BEEN DECLINING STEADILY SINCE THE EARLY 1990s.
HOW WOULD THE NEW PRESIDENT AFFECT PRISON POLICY?
HE PRESENTED HIMSELF AS A
compassionate conservative
ON CRACK/COCAINE DISPARITIES:
I DON'T THINK WE SHOULD BE DISCRIMINATORY.
LONG MINIMUM SENTENCES... MAY NOT BE THE BEST WAY TO... HELP PEOPLE HEAL THEIR DISEASE.

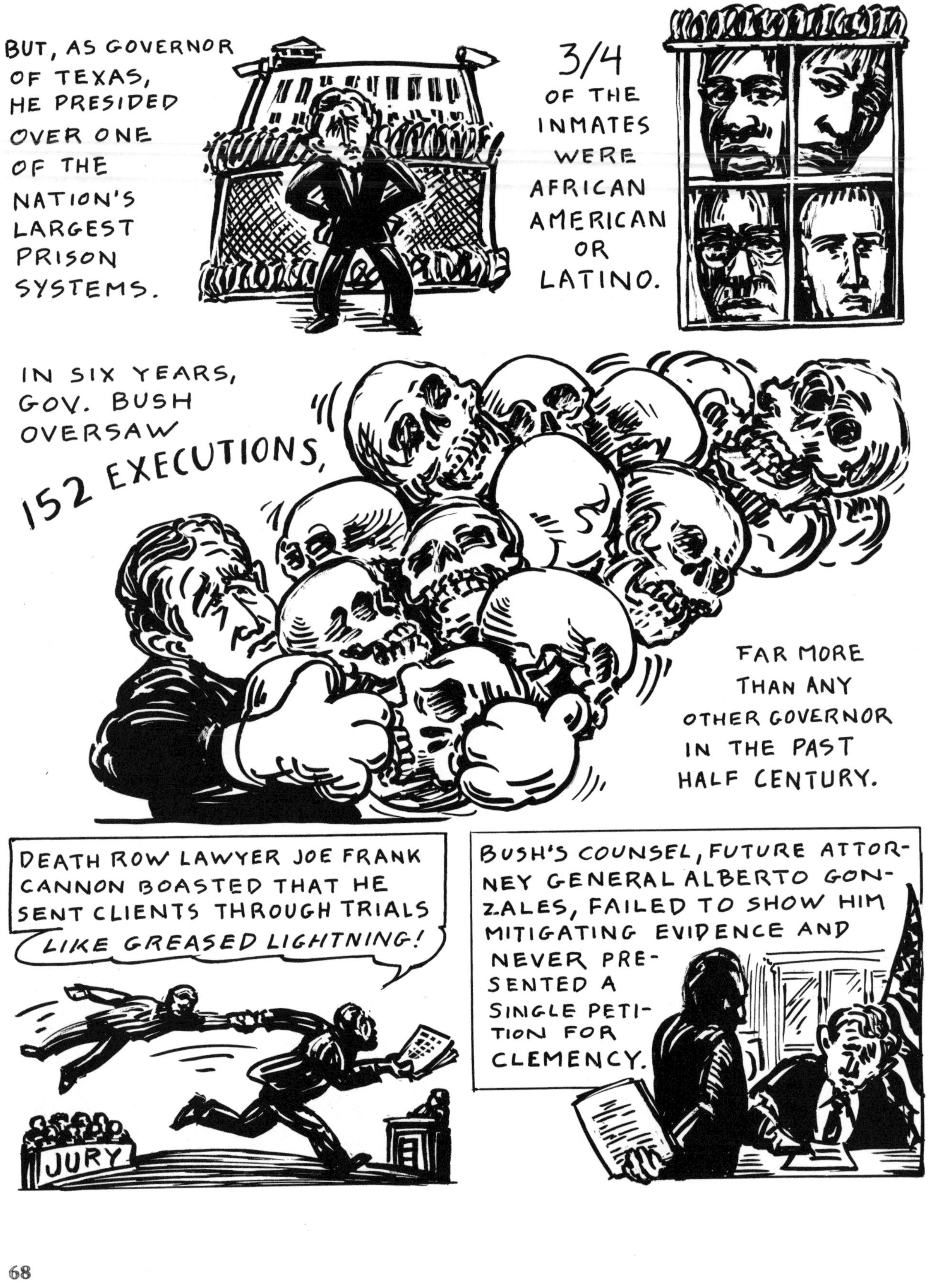

BUT, AS GOVERNOR OF TEXAS, HE PRESIDED OVER ONE OF THE NATION'S LARGEST PRISON SYSTEMS.
3/4 OF THE INMATES WERE AFRICAN AMERICAN OR LATINO.
IN SIX YEARS, GOV. BUSH OVERSAW
152 EXECUTIONS,
FAR MORE THAN ANY OTHER GOVERNOR IN THE PAST HALF CENTURY.
DEATH ROW LAWYER JOE FRANK CANNON BOASTED THAT HE SENT CLIENTS THROUGH TRIALS LIKE GREASED LIGHTNING!
JURY
BUSH'S COUNSEL, FUTURE ATTORNEY GENERAL ALBERTO GONZALES, FAILED TO SHOW HIM MITIGATING EVIDENCE AND NEVER PRESENTED A SINGLE PETITION FOR CLEMENCY.

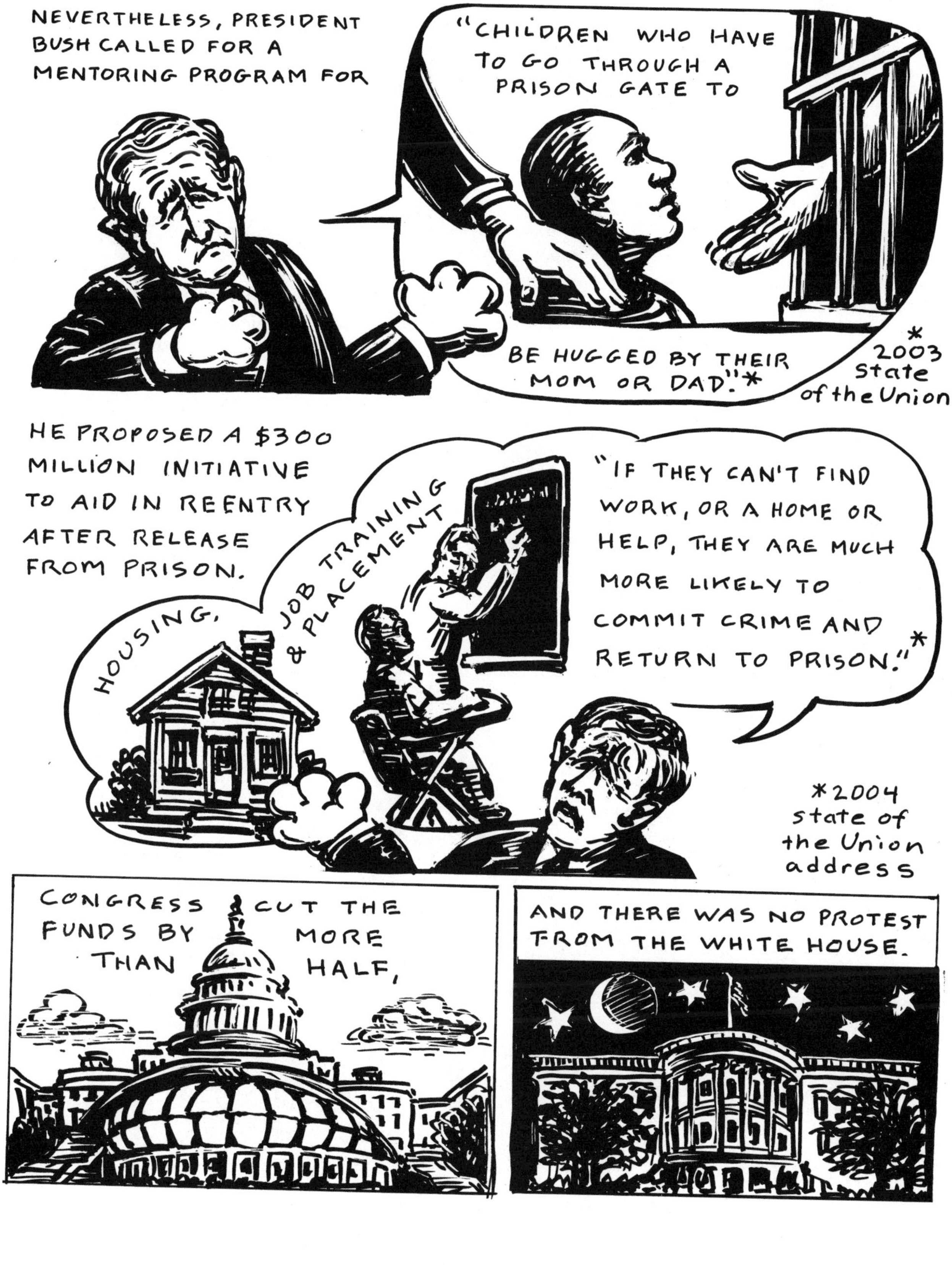
NEVERTHELESS, PRESIDENT BUSH CALLED FOR A MENTORING PROGRAM FOR
"CHILDREN WHO HAVE TO GO THROUGH A PRISON GATE TO
BE HUGGED BY THEIR MOM OR DAD."*
* 2003 State of the Union
HE PROPOSED A $300 MILLION INITIATIVE TO AID IN REENTRY AFTER RELEASE FROM PRISON.
HOUSING,
JOB TRAINING & PLACEMENT
"IF THEY CAN'T FIND WORK, OR A HOME OR HELP, THEY ARE MUCH MORE LIKELY TO COMMIT CRIME AND RETURN TO PRISON."*
*2004 state of the Union address
CONGRESS CUT THE FUNDS BY MORE THAN HALF,
AND THERE WAS NO PROTEST FROM THE WHITE HOUSE.

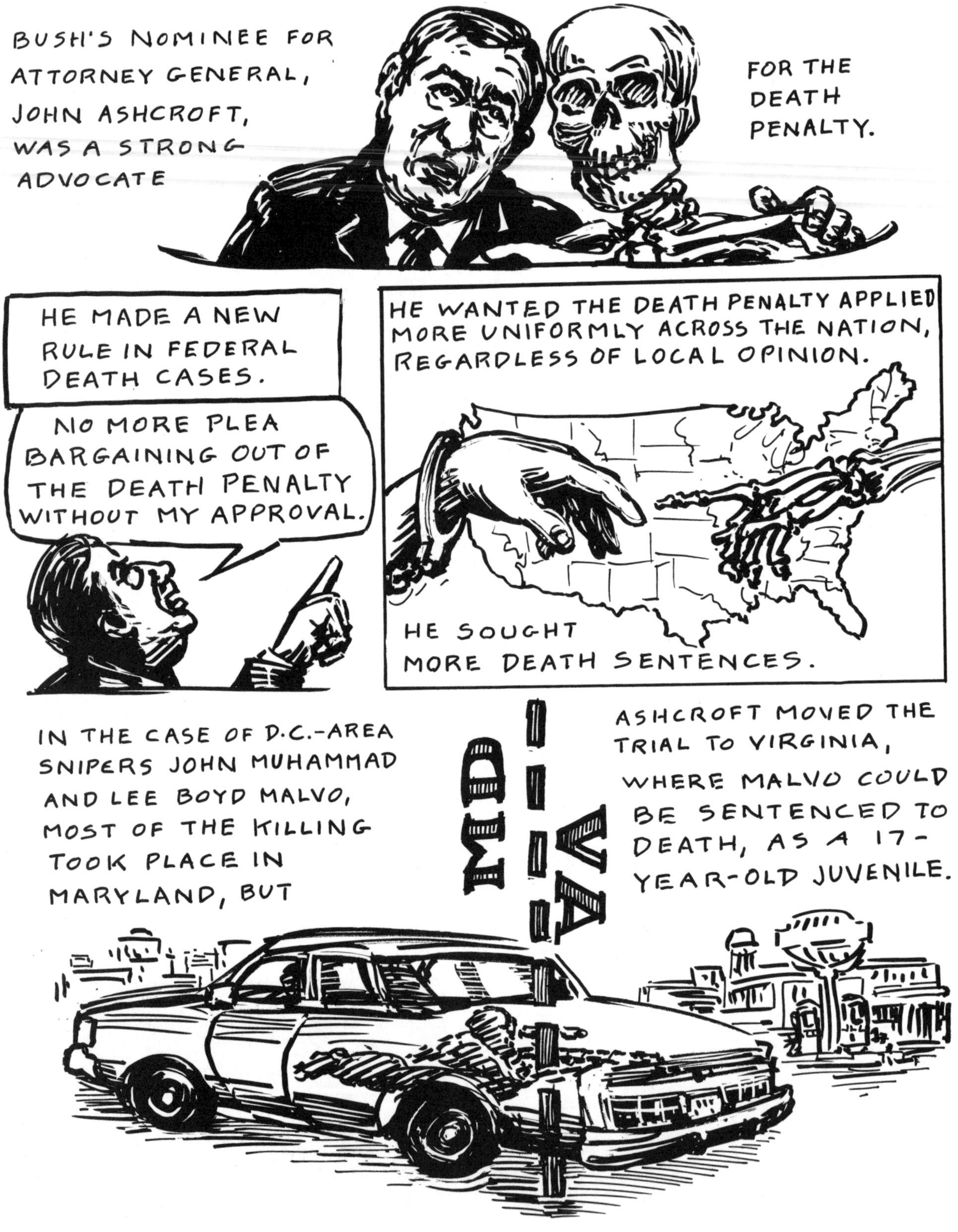
BUSH'S NOMINEE FOR ATTORNEY GENERAL, JOHN ASHCROFT, WAS A STRONG ADVOCATE
FOR THE DEATH PENALTY.
HE MADE A NEW RULE IN FEDERAL DEATH CASES.
NO MORE PLEA BARGAINING OUT OF THE DEATH PENALTY WITHOUT MY APPROVAL.
HE WANTED THE DEATH PENALTY APPLIED MORE UNIFORMLY ACROSS THE NATION, REGARDLESS OF LOCAL OPINION.
HE SOUGHT MORE DEATH SENTENCES.
IN THE CASE OF D.C.-AREA SNIPERS JOHN MUHAMMAD AND LEE BOYD MALVO, MOST OF THE KILLING TOOK PLACE IN MARYLAND, BUT
MD
VA
ASHCROFT MOVED THE TRIAL TO VIRGINIA,
WHERE MALVO COULD BE SENTENCED TO DEATH, AS A 17-YEAR-OLD JUVENILE.

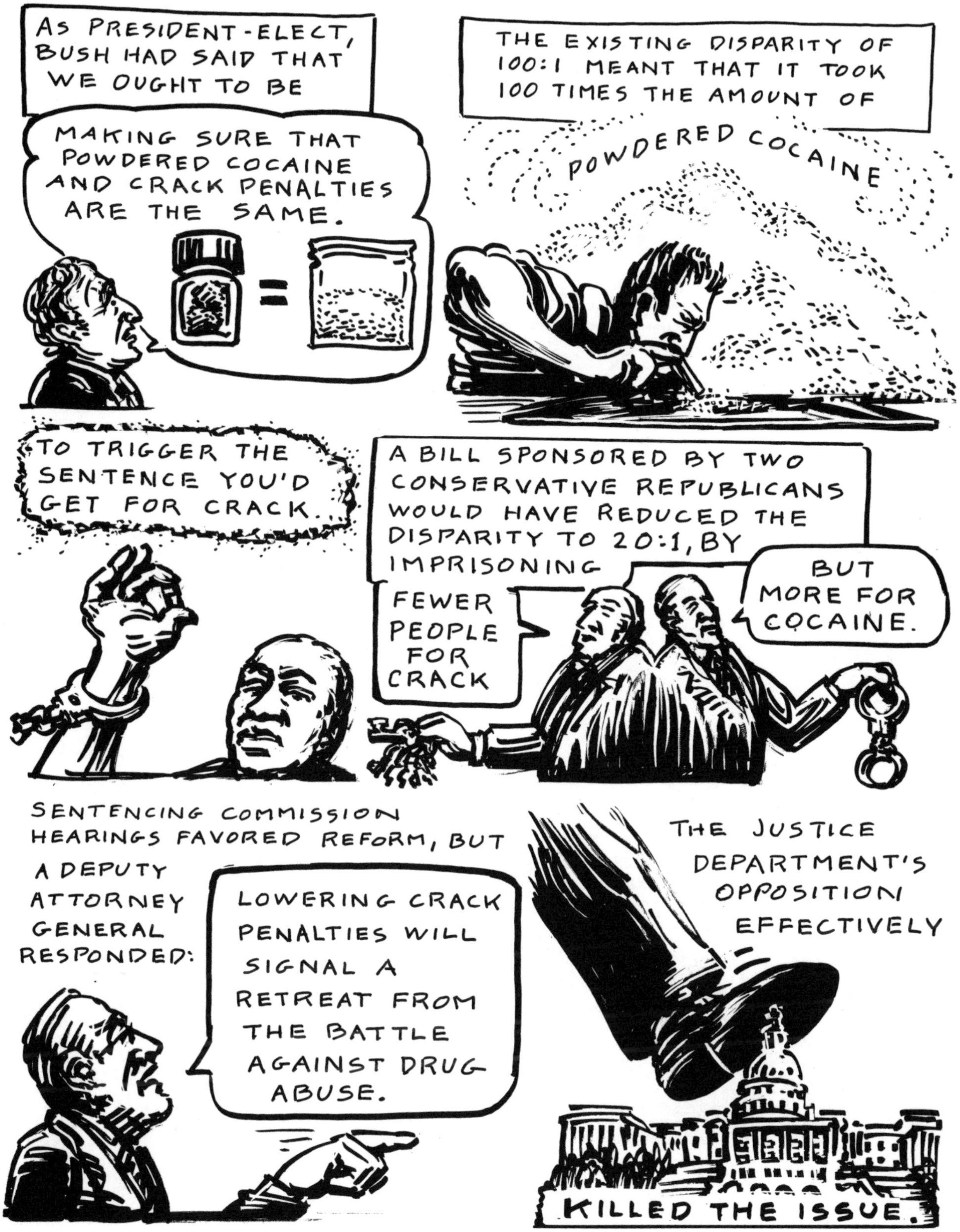

AS PRESIDENT-ELECT, BUSH HAD SAID THAT WE OUGHT TO BE
MAKING SURE THAT POWDERED COCAINE AND CRACK PENALTIES ARE THE SAME.
THE EXISTING DISPARITY OF 100:1 MEANT THAT IT TOOK 100 TIMES THE AMOUNT OF
POWDERED COCAINE
TO TRIGGER THE SENTENCE YOU'D GET FOR CRACK.
A BILL SPONSORED BY TWO CONSERVATIVE REPUBLICANS WOULD HAVE REDUCED THE DISPARITY TO 20:1, BY IMPRISONING
FEWER PEOPLE FOR CRACK
BUT MORE FOR COCAINE.
SENTENCING COMMISSION HEARINGS FAVORED REFORM, BUT
A DEPUTY ATTORNEY GENERAL RESPONDED:
LOWERING CRACK PENALTIES WILL SIGNAL A RETREAT FROM THE BATTLE AGAINST DRUG ABUSE.
THE JUSTICE DEPARTMENT'S OPPOSITION EFFECTIVELY
KILLED THE ISSUE.

THE BUSH ADMINISTRATION CONTINUED TO ASSERT THAT

TOUGH SENTENCES MEAN LESS CRIME.

DURING THE BUSH YEARS, THE FEDERAL PRISON POPULATION GREW AT THREE TIMES THE RATE OF THE STATES.

THE ADMINISTRATION'S POLICIES ON

LAW ENFORCEMENT

PROSECU- TION &

SENTENCING

REMAINED CONSISTENT WITH THE PREVIOUS DECADES.

THE RHETORIC ON CRIME CHANGED SOMEWHAT, BUT THIS WAS LITTLE CONSOLATION TO THE MORE THAN 2 MILLION AMERICANS BEHIND BARS.

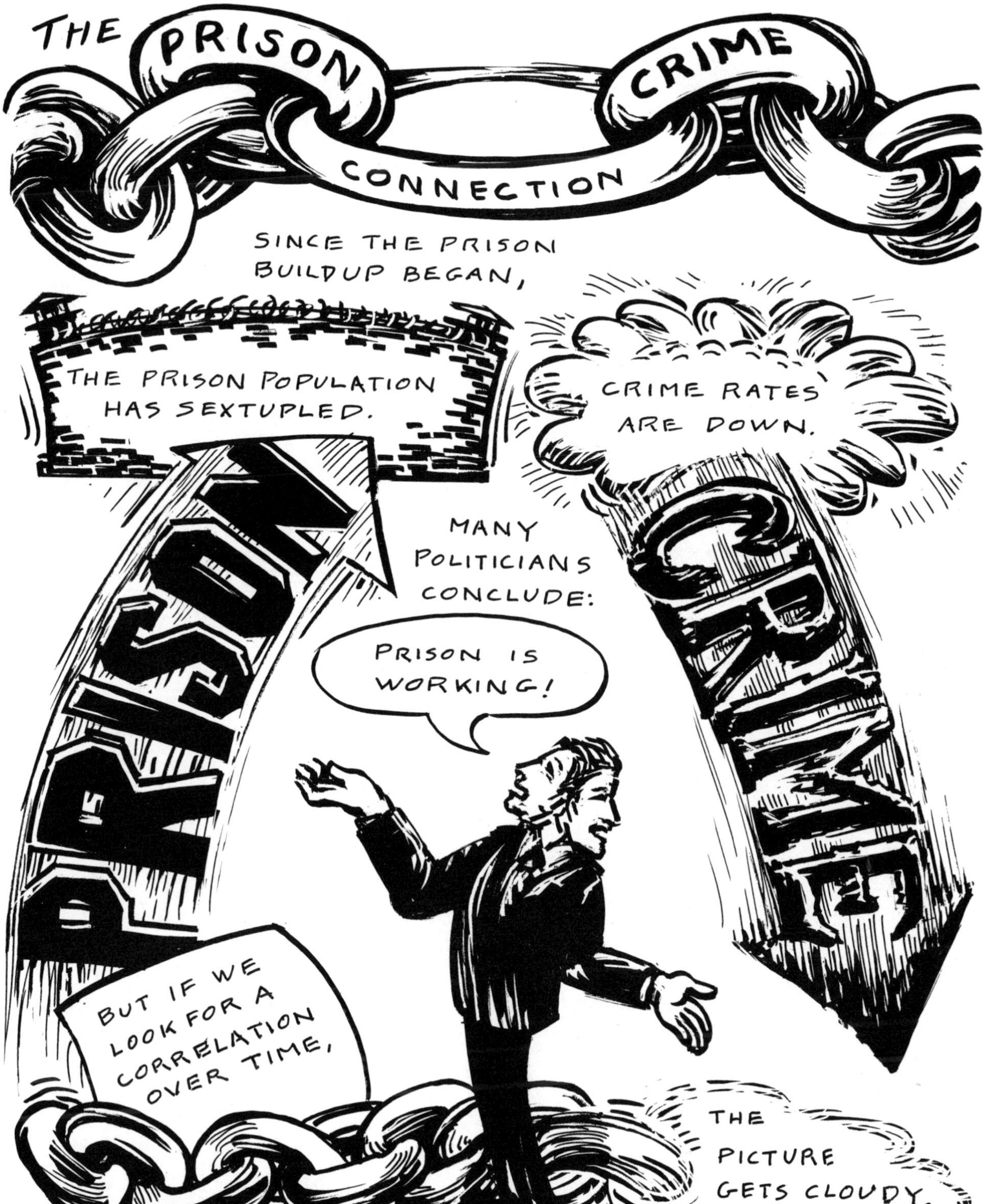
THE PRISON CRIME CONNECTION
SINCE THE PRISON BUILDUP BEGAN,
THE PRISON POPULATION HAS SEXTUPLED.
CRIME RATES ARE DOWN.
PRISON
CRIME
MANY POLITICIANS CONCLUDE:
PRISON IS WORKING!
BUT IF WE LOOK FOR A CORRELATION OVER TIME,
THE PICTURE GETS CLOUDY.

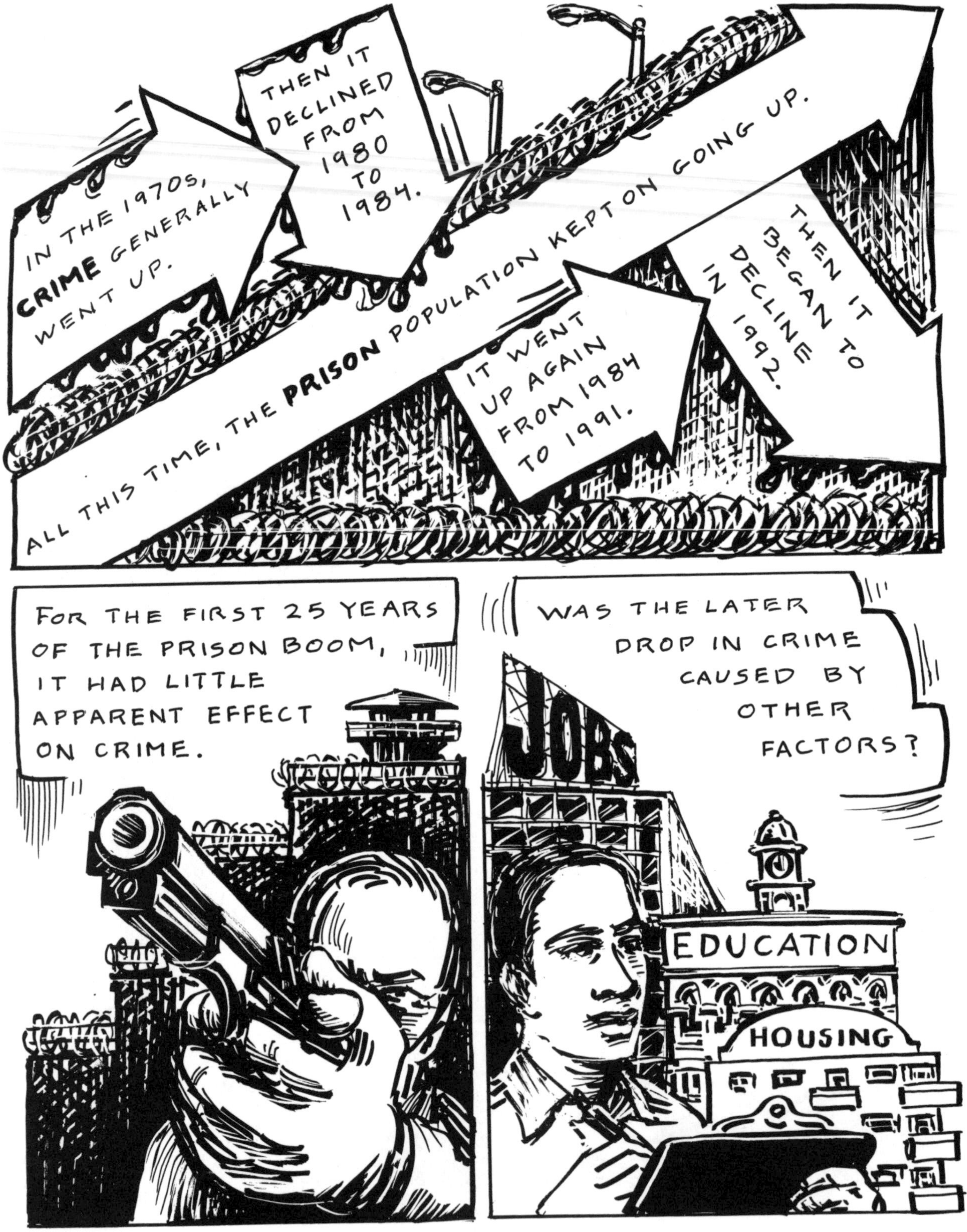
IN THE 1970s, CRIME GENERALLY WENT UP.
THEN IT DECLINED FROM 1980 TO 1984.
ALL THIS TIME, THE PRISON POPULATION KEPT ON GOING UP.
IT WENT UP AGAIN FROM 1984 TO 1991.
THEN IT BEGAN TO DECLINE IN 1992.
FOR THE FIRST 25 YEARS OF THE PRISON BOOM, IT HAD LITTLE APPARENT EFFECT ON CRIME.
WAS THE LATER DROP IN CRIME CAUSED BY OTHER FACTORS?
JOBS
EDUCATION
HOUSING

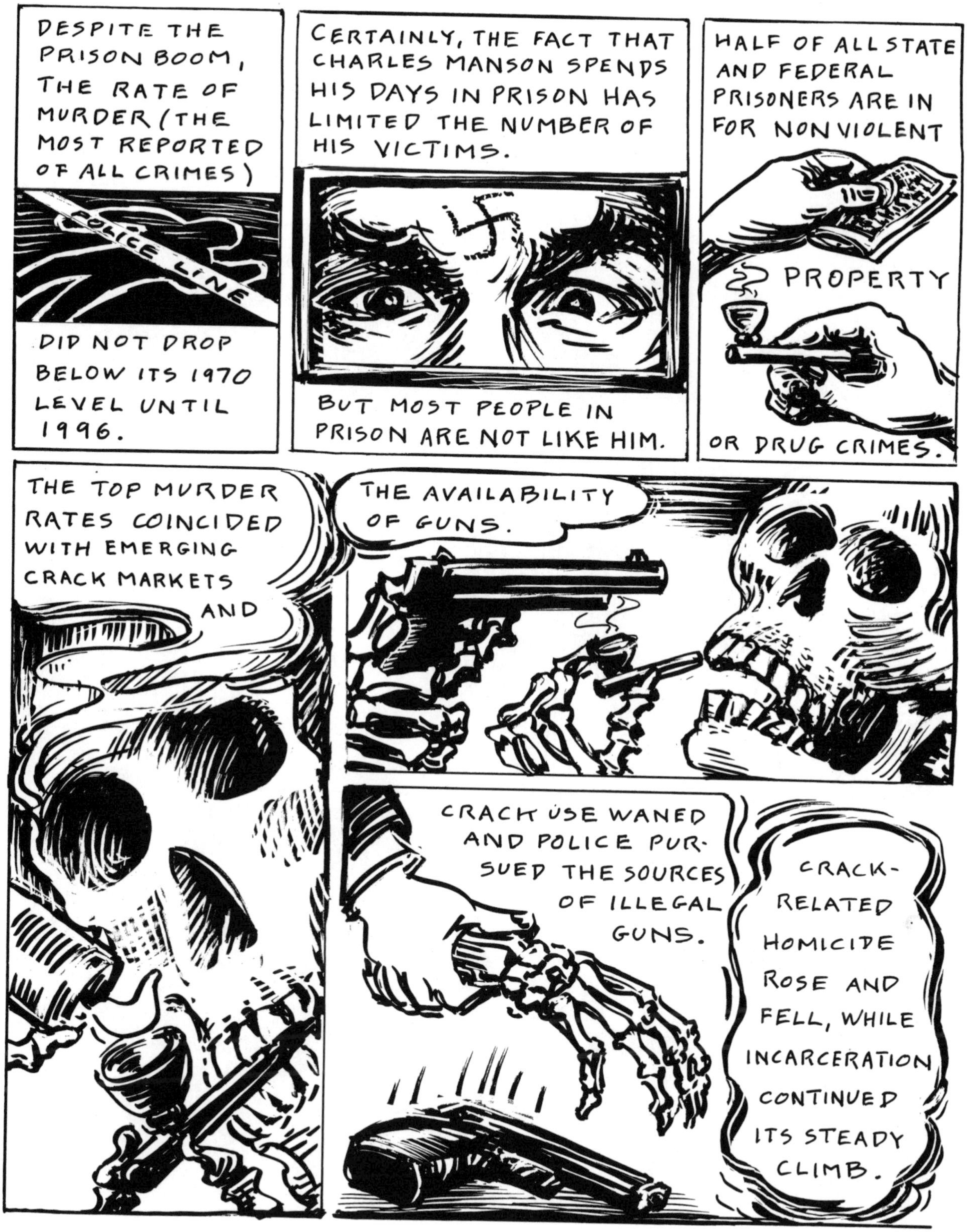
DESPITE THE PRISON BOOM, THE RATE OF MURDER (THE MOST REPORTED OF ALL CRIMES)
POLICE LINE
DID NOT DROP BELOW ITS 1970 LEVEL UNTIL 1996.
CERTAINLY, THE FACT THAT CHARLES MANSON SPENDS HIS DAYS IN PRISON HAS LIMITED THE NUMBER OF HIS VICTIMS.
BUT MOST PEOPLE IN PRISON ARE NOT LIKE HIM.
HALF OF ALL STATE AND FEDERAL PRISONERS ARE IN FOR NON VIOLENT
PROPERTY
OR DRUG CRIMES.
THE TOP MURDER RATES COINCIDED WITH EMERGING CRACK MARKETS
AND
THE AVAILABILITY OF GUNS.
CRACK USE WANED AND POLICE PURSUED THE SOURCES OF ILLEGAL GUNS.
CRACK-RELATED HOMICIDE ROSE AND FELL, WHILE INCARCERATION CONTINUED ITS STEADY CLIMB.

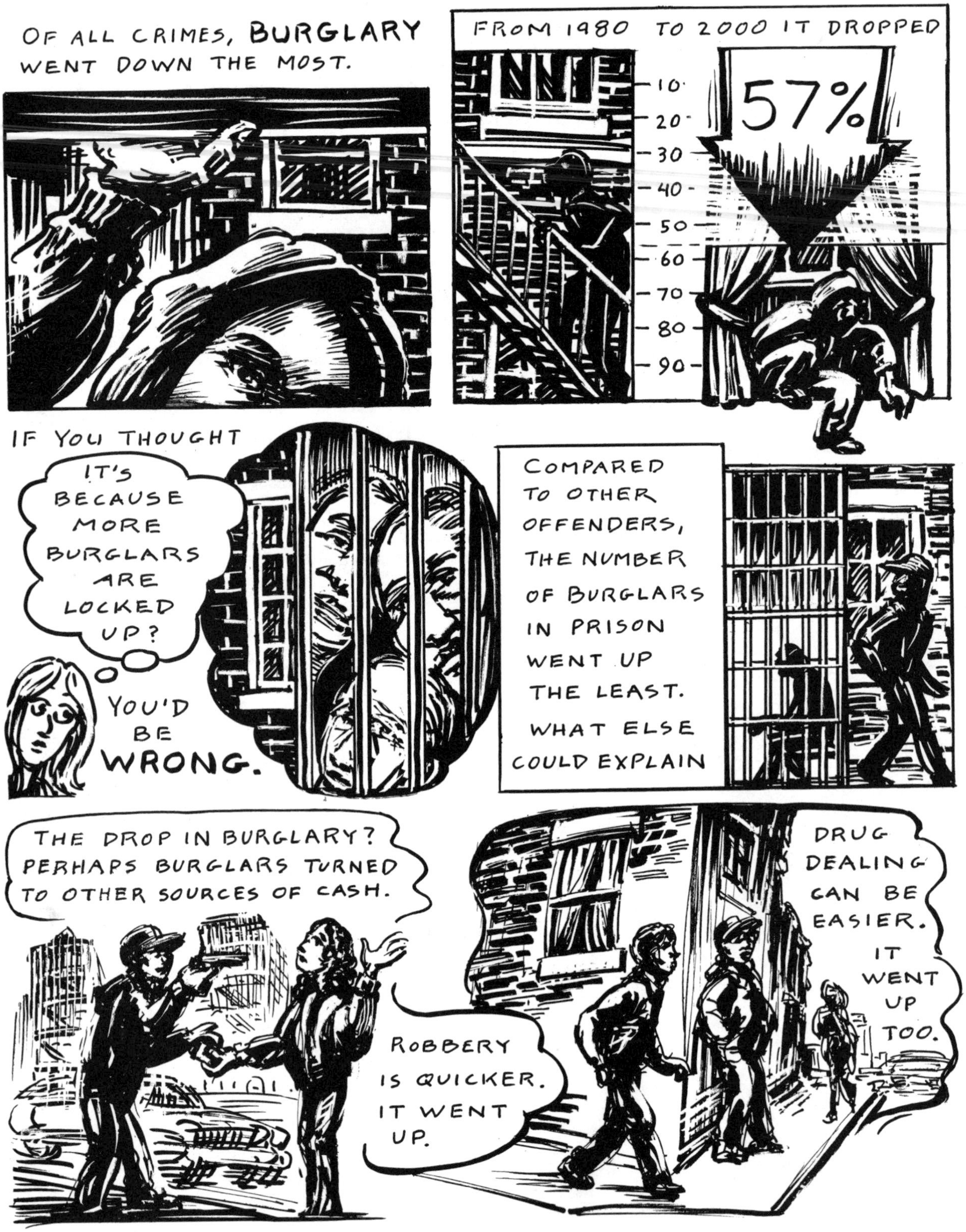
OF ALL CRIMES, BURGLARY WENT DOWN THE MOST.
FROM 1980 TO 2000 IT DROPPED
57%
10
20
30
40
50
60
70
80
90
IF YOU THOUGHT
IT'S BECAUSE MORE BURGLARS ARE LOCKED UP?
YOU'D BE WRONG.
COMPARED TO OTHER OFFENDERS, THE NUMBER OF BURGLARS IN PRISON WENT UP THE LEAST. WHAT ELSE COULD EXPLAIN
THE DROP IN BURGLARY? PERHAPS BURGLARS TURNED TO OTHER SOURCES OF CASH.
ROBBERY IS QUICKER. IT WENT UP.
DRUG DEALING CAN BE EASIER.
IT WENT UP TOO.

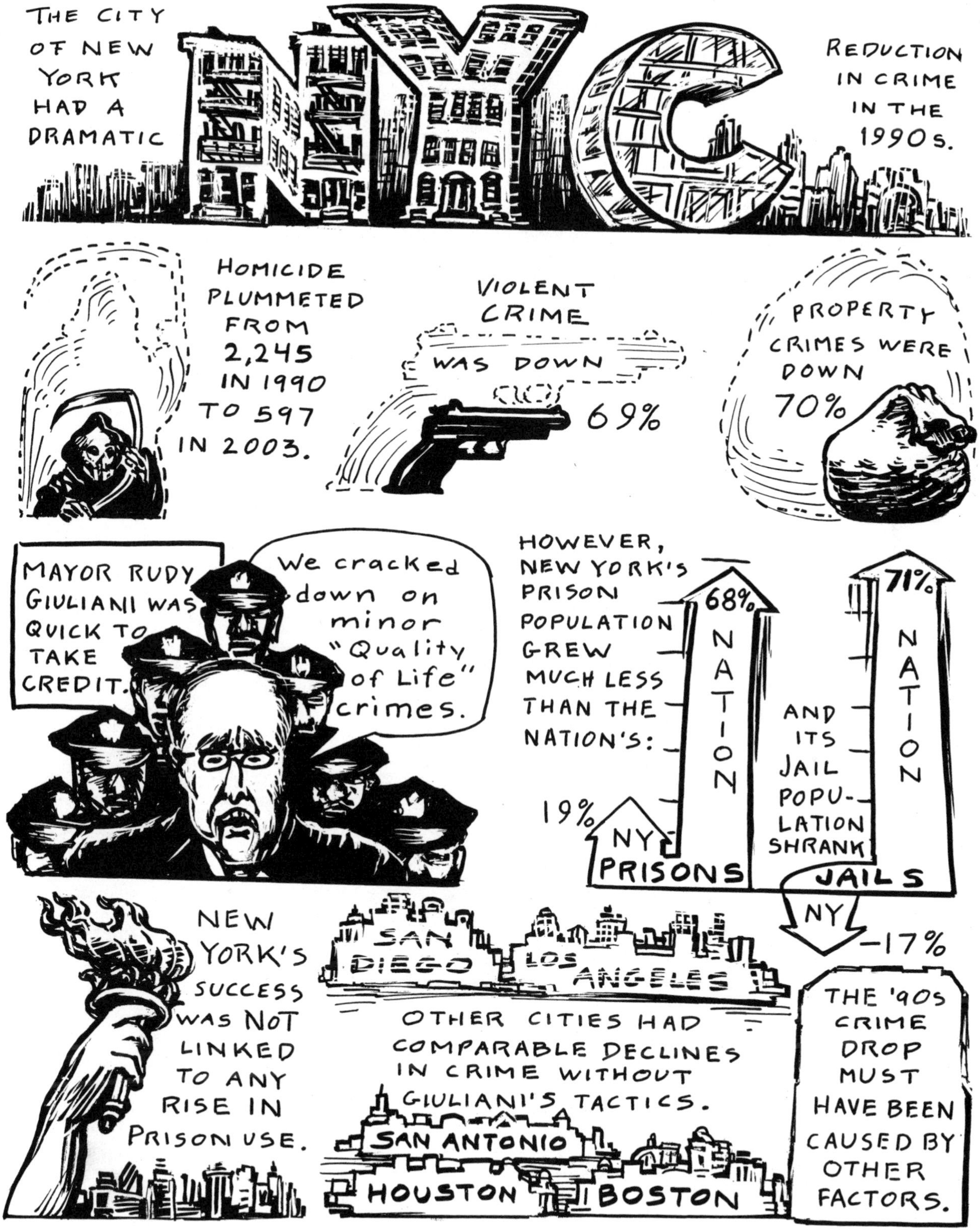
THE CITY OF NEW YORK HAD A DRAMATIC
NYC
REDUCTION IN CRIME IN THE 1990s.
HOMICIDE PLUMMETED FROM 2,245 IN 1990 TO 597 IN 2003.
VIOLENT CRIME WAS DOWN 69%
PROPERTY CRIMES WERE DOWN 70%
MAYOR RUDY GIULIANI WAS QUICK TO TAKE CREDIT.
We cracked down on minor "Quality of Life" crimes.
HOWEVER, NEW YORK'S PRISON POPULATION GREW MUCH LESS THAN THE NATION'S:
68%
NATION
19%
NY
PRISONS
AND ITS JAIL POPULATION SHRANK
71%
NATION
JAILS
NY
−17%
NEW YORK'S SUCCESS WAS NOT LINKED TO ANY RISE IN PRISON USE.
SAN DIEGO
LOS ANGELES
OTHER CITIES HAD COMPARABLE DECLINES IN CRIME WITHOUT GIULIANI'S TACTICS.
SAN ANTONIO
HOUSTON
BOSTON
THE '90s CRIME DROP MUST HAVE BEEN CAUSED BY OTHER FACTORS.

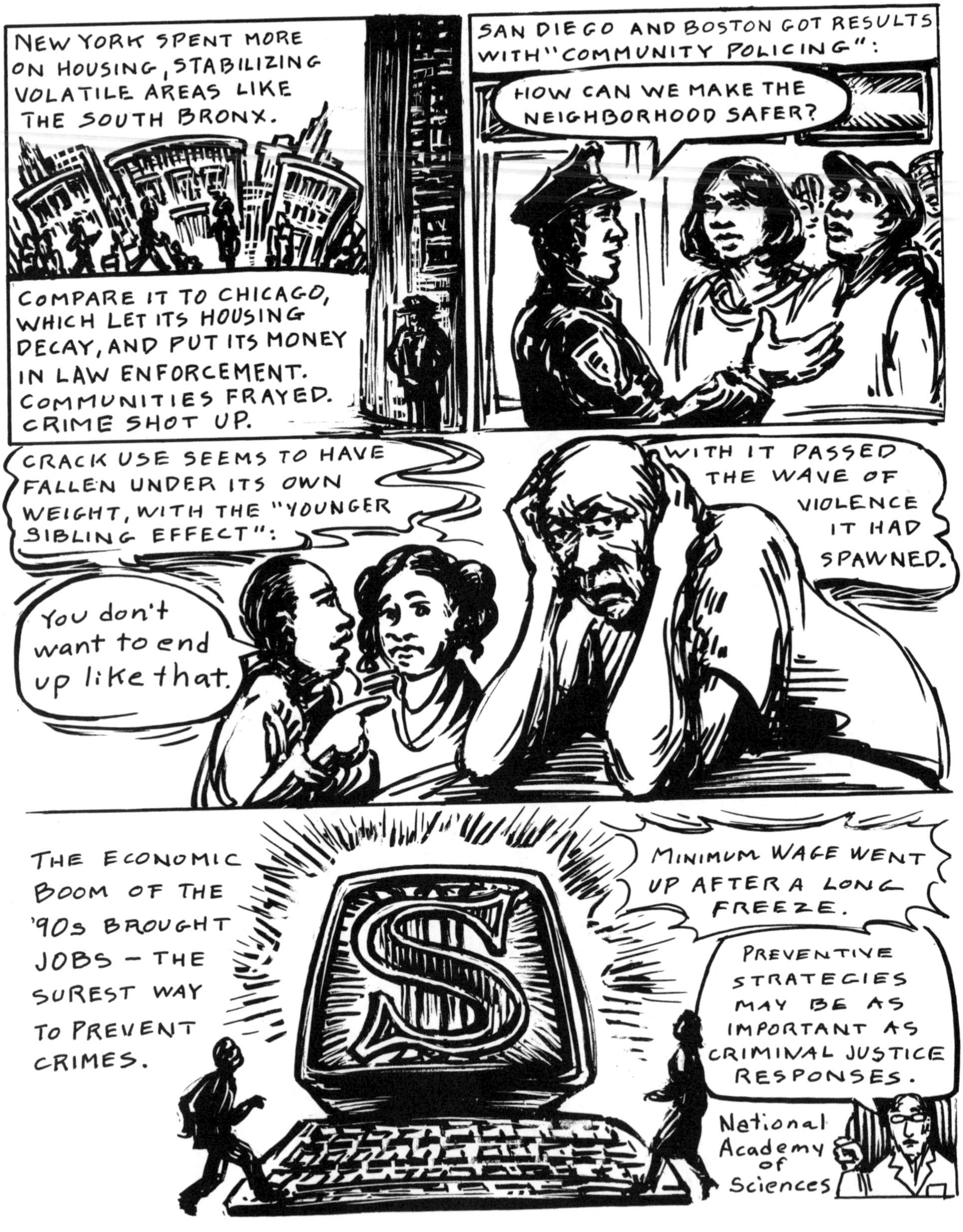
NEW YORK SPENT MORE ON HOUSING, STABILIZING VOLATILE AREAS LIKE THE SOUTH BRONX.
COMPARE IT TO CHICAGO, WHICH LET ITS HOUSING DECAY, AND PUT ITS MONEY IN LAW ENFORCEMENT. COMMUNITIES FRAYED. CRIME SHOT UP.
SAN DIEGO AND BOSTON GOT RESULTS WITH "COMMUNITY POLICING":
HOW CAN WE MAKE THE NEIGHBORHOOD SAFER?
CRACK USE SEEMS TO HAVE FALLEN UNDER ITS OWN WEIGHT, WITH THE "YOUNGER SIBLING EFFECT":
WITH IT PASSED THE WAVE OF VIOLENCE IT HAD SPAWNED.
You don't want to end up like that.
THE ECONOMIC BOOM OF THE '90s BROUGHT JOBS – THE SUREST WAY TO PREVENT CRIMES.
MINIMUM WAGE WENT UP AFTER A LONG FREEZE.
PREVENTIVE STRATEGIES MAY BE AS IMPORTANT AS CRIMINAL JUSTICE RESPONSES.
National Academy of Sciences

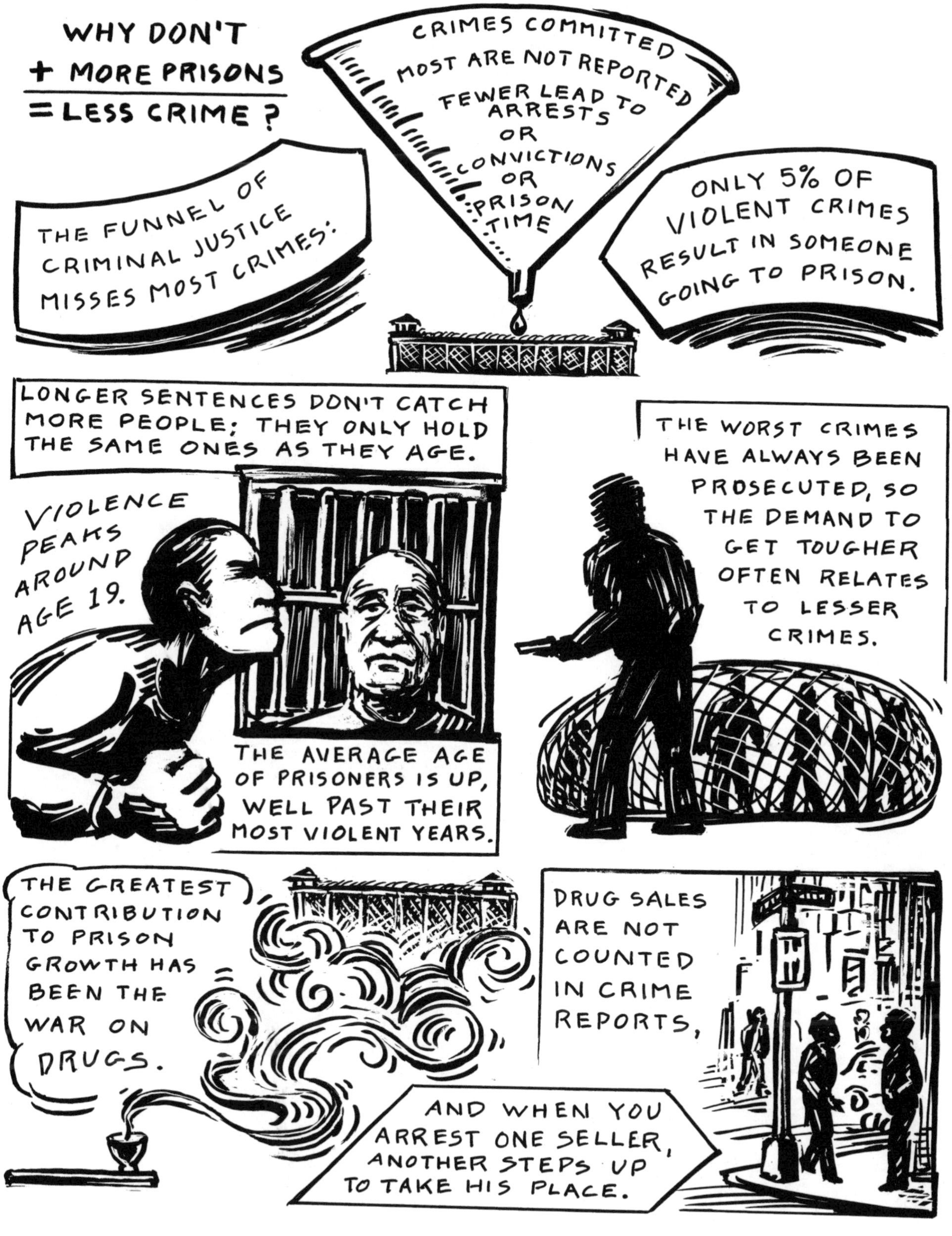

WHY DON'T + MORE PRISONS = LESS CRIME ?
CRIMES COMMITTED
MOST ARE NOT REPORTED
FEWER LEAD TO ARRESTS
OR
CONVICTIONS
OR
PRISON TIME
THE FUNNEL OF CRIMINAL JUSTICE MISSES MOST CRIMES:
ONLY 5% OF VIOLENT CRIMES RESULT IN SOMEONE GOING TO PRISON.
LONGER SENTENCES DON'T CATCH MORE PEOPLE; THEY ONLY HOLD THE SAME ONES AS THEY AGE.
VIOLENCE PEAKS AROUND AGE 19.
THE AVERAGE AGE OF PRISONERS IS UP, WELL PAST THEIR MOST VIOLENT YEARS.
THE WORST CRIMES HAVE ALWAYS BEEN PROSECUTED, SO THE DEMAND TO GET TOUGHER OFTEN RELATES TO LESSER CRIMES.
THE GREATEST CONTRIBUTION TO PRISON GROWTH HAS BEEN THE WAR ON DRUGS.
DRUG SALES ARE NOT COUNTED IN CRIME REPORTS,
AND WHEN YOU ARREST ONE SELLER, ANOTHER STEPS UP TO TAKE HIS PLACE.

COLOR-CODED JUSTICE

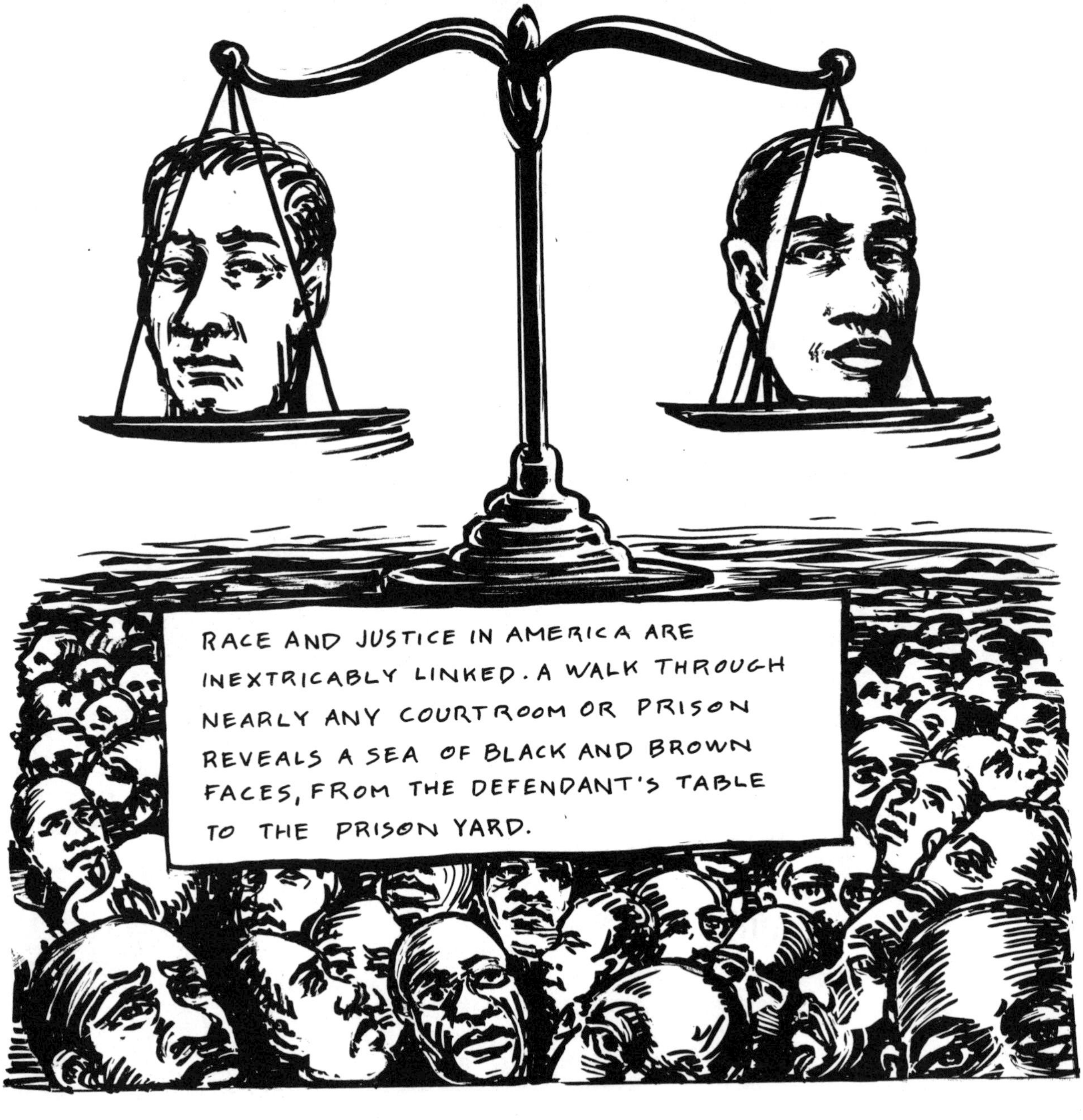
RACE AND JUSTICE IN AMERICA ARE INEXTRICABLY LINKED. A WALK THROUGH NEARLY ANY COURTROOM OR PRISON REVEALS A SEA OF BLACK AND BROWN FACES, FROM THE DEFENDANT'S TABLE TO THE PRISON YARD.

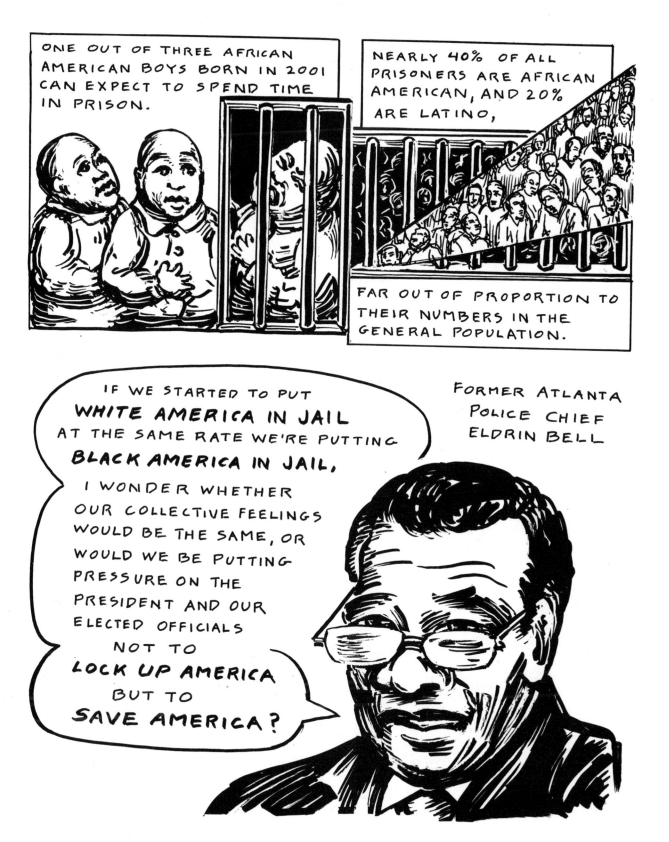

ONE OUT OF THREE AFRICAN AMERICAN BOYS BORN IN 2001 CAN EXPECT TO SPEND TIME IN PRISON.

NEARLY 40% OF ALL PRISONERS ARE AFRICAN AMERICAN, AND 20% ARE LATINO,

FAR OUT OF PROPORTION TO THEIR NUMBERS IN THE GENERAL POPULATION.

IF WE STARTED TO PUT **WHITE AMERICA IN JAIL** AT THE SAME RATE WE'RE PUTTING **BLACK AMERICA IN JAIL**, I WONDER WHETHER OUR COLLECTIVE FEELINGS WOULD BE THE SAME, OR WOULD WE BE PUTTING PRESSURE ON THE PRESIDENT AND OUR ELECTED OFFICIALS NOT TO **LOCK UP AMERICA** BUT TO **SAVE AMERICA?**

FORMER ATLANTA POLICE CHIEF ELDRIN BELL

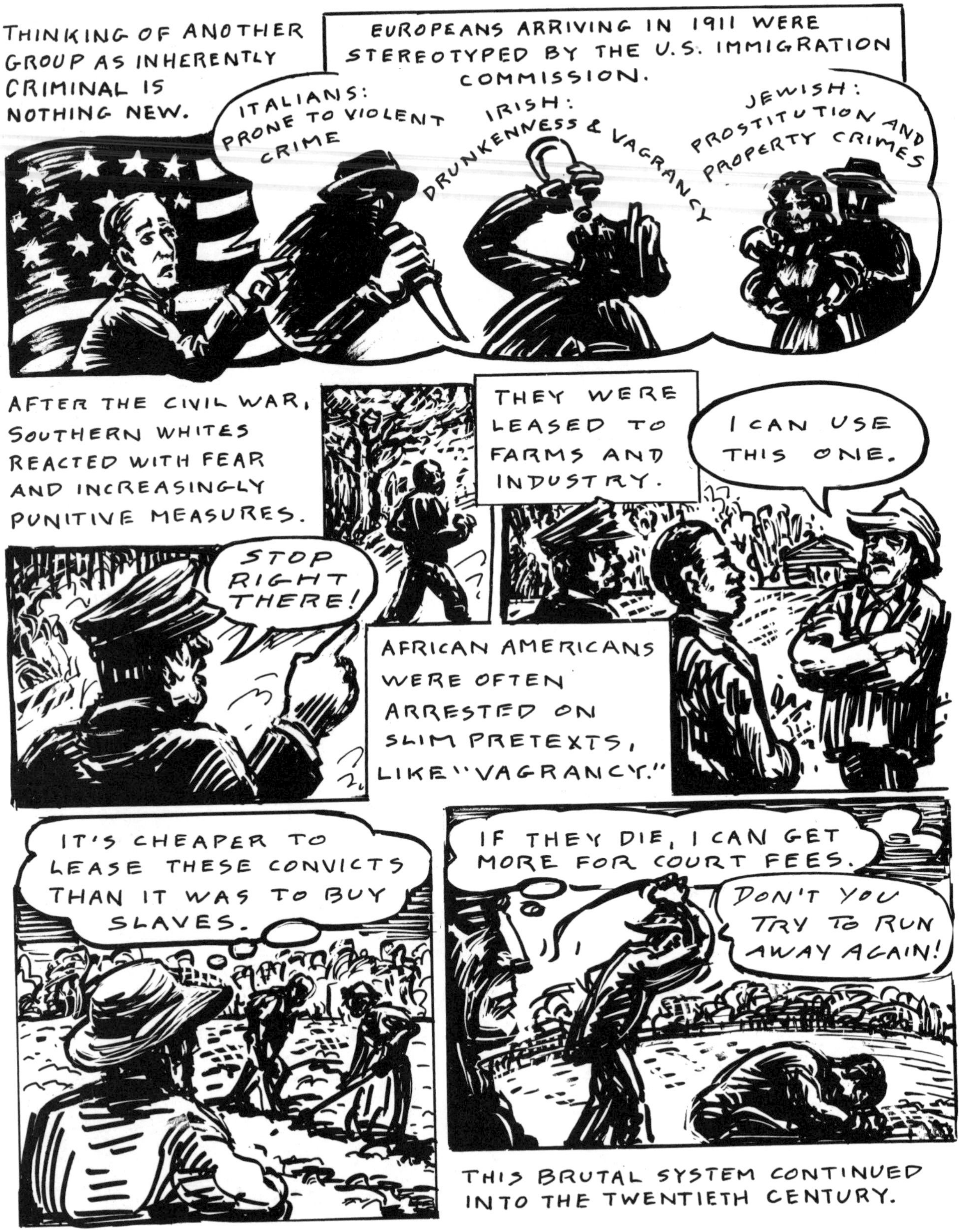
THINKING OF ANOTHER GROUP AS INHERENTLY CRIMINAL IS NOTHING NEW.
EUROPEANS ARRIVING IN 1911 WERE STEREOTYPED BY THE U.S. IMMIGRATION COMMISSION.
ITALIANS: PRONE TO VIOLENT CRIME
IRISH: DRUNKENNESS & VAGRANCY
JEWISH: PROSTITUTION AND PROPERTY CRIMES
AFTER THE CIVIL WAR, SOUTHERN WHITES REACTED WITH FEAR AND INCREASINGLY PUNITIVE MEASURES.
STOP RIGHT THERE!
AFRICAN AMERICANS WERE OFTEN ARRESTED ON SLIM PRETEXTS, LIKE "VAGRANCY."
THEY WERE LEASED TO FARMS AND INDUSTRY.
I CAN USE THIS ONE.
IT'S CHEAPER TO LEASE THESE CONVICTS THAN IT WAS TO BUY SLAVES.
IF THEY DIE, I CAN GET MORE FOR COURT FEES.
DON'T YOU TRY TO RUN AWAY AGAIN!
THIS BRUTAL SYSTEM CONTINUED INTO THE TWENTIETH CENTURY.

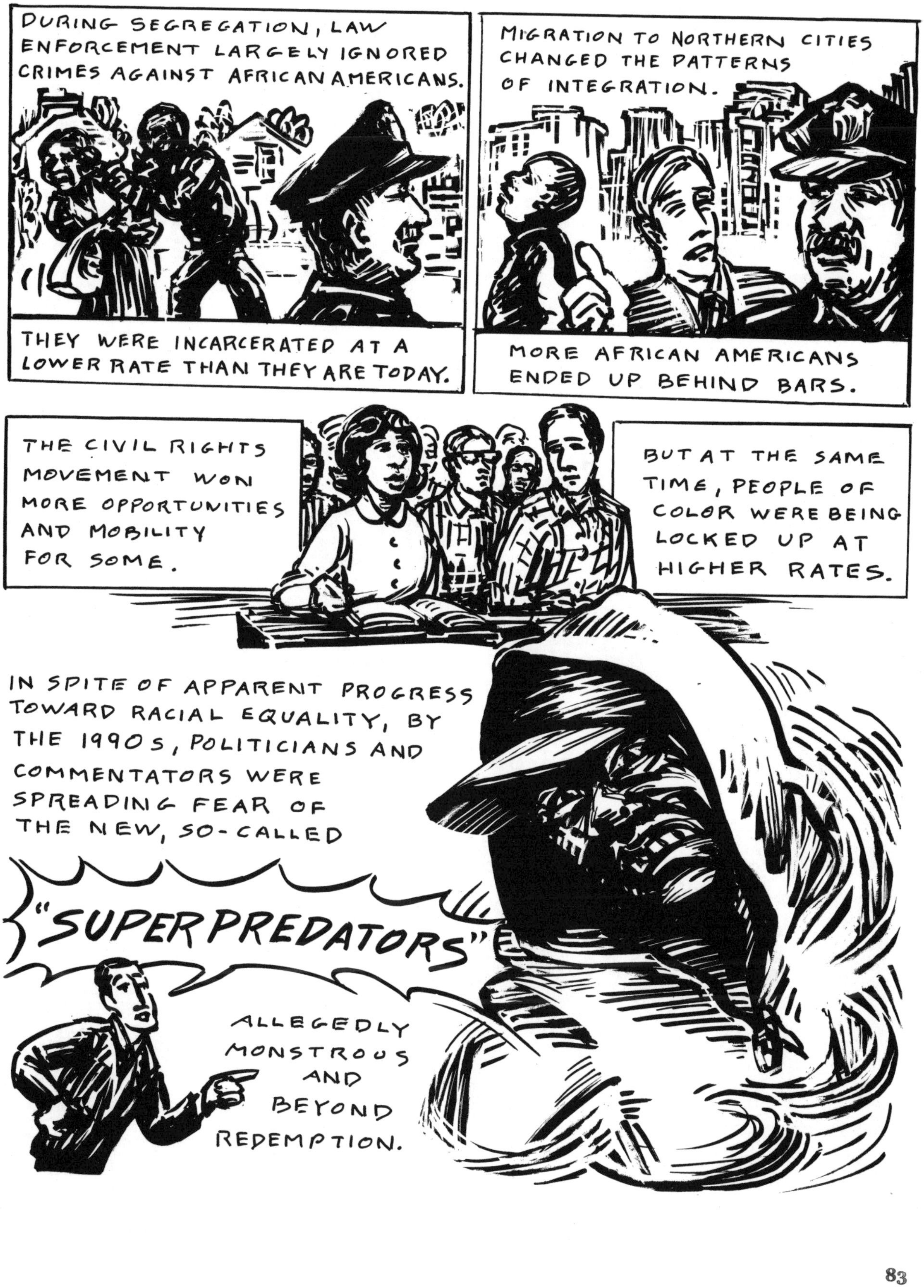
DURING SEGREGATION, LAW ENFORCEMENT LARGELY IGNORED CRIMES AGAINST AFRICAN AMERICANS.
THEY WERE INCARCERATED AT A LOWER RATE THAN THEY ARE TODAY.
MIGRATION TO NORTHERN CITIES CHANGED THE PATTERNS OF INTEGRATION.
MORE AFRICAN AMERICANS ENDED UP BEHIND BARS.
THE CIVIL RIGHTS MOVEMENT WON MORE OPPORTUNITIES AND MOBILITY FOR SOME.
BUT AT THE SAME TIME, PEOPLE OF COLOR WERE BEING LOCKED UP AT HIGHER RATES.
IN SPITE OF APPARENT PROGRESS TOWARD RACIAL EQUALITY, BY THE 1990S, POLITICIANS AND COMMENTATORS WERE SPREADING FEAR OF THE NEW, SO-CALLED
"SUPERPREDATORS"
ALLEGEDLY MONSTROUS AND BEYOND REDEMPTION.

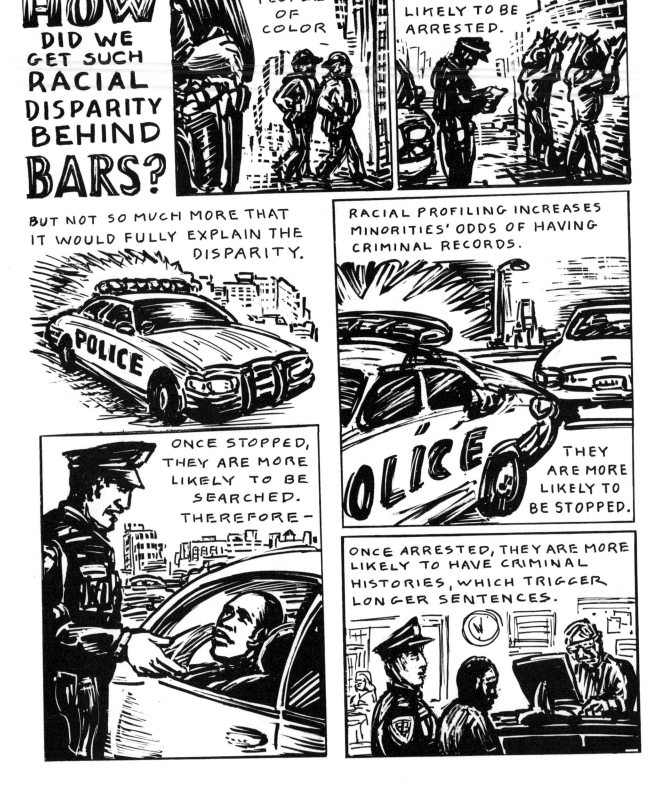

HOW DID WE GET SUCH RACIAL DISPARITY BEHIND BARS?

PEOPLE OF COLOR ARE MORE LIKELY TO BE ARRESTED.

BUT NOT SO MUCH MORE THAT IT WOULD FULLY EXPLAIN THE DISPARITY.

RACIAL PROFILING INCREASES MINORITIES' ODDS OF HAVING CRIMINAL RECORDS.

POLICE

ONCE STOPPED, THEY ARE MORE LIKELY TO BE SEARCHED. THEREFORE—

THEY ARE MORE LIKELY TO BE STOPPED.

ONCE ARRESTED, THEY ARE MORE LIKELY TO HAVE CRIMINAL HISTORIES, WHICH TRIGGER LONGER SENTENCES.

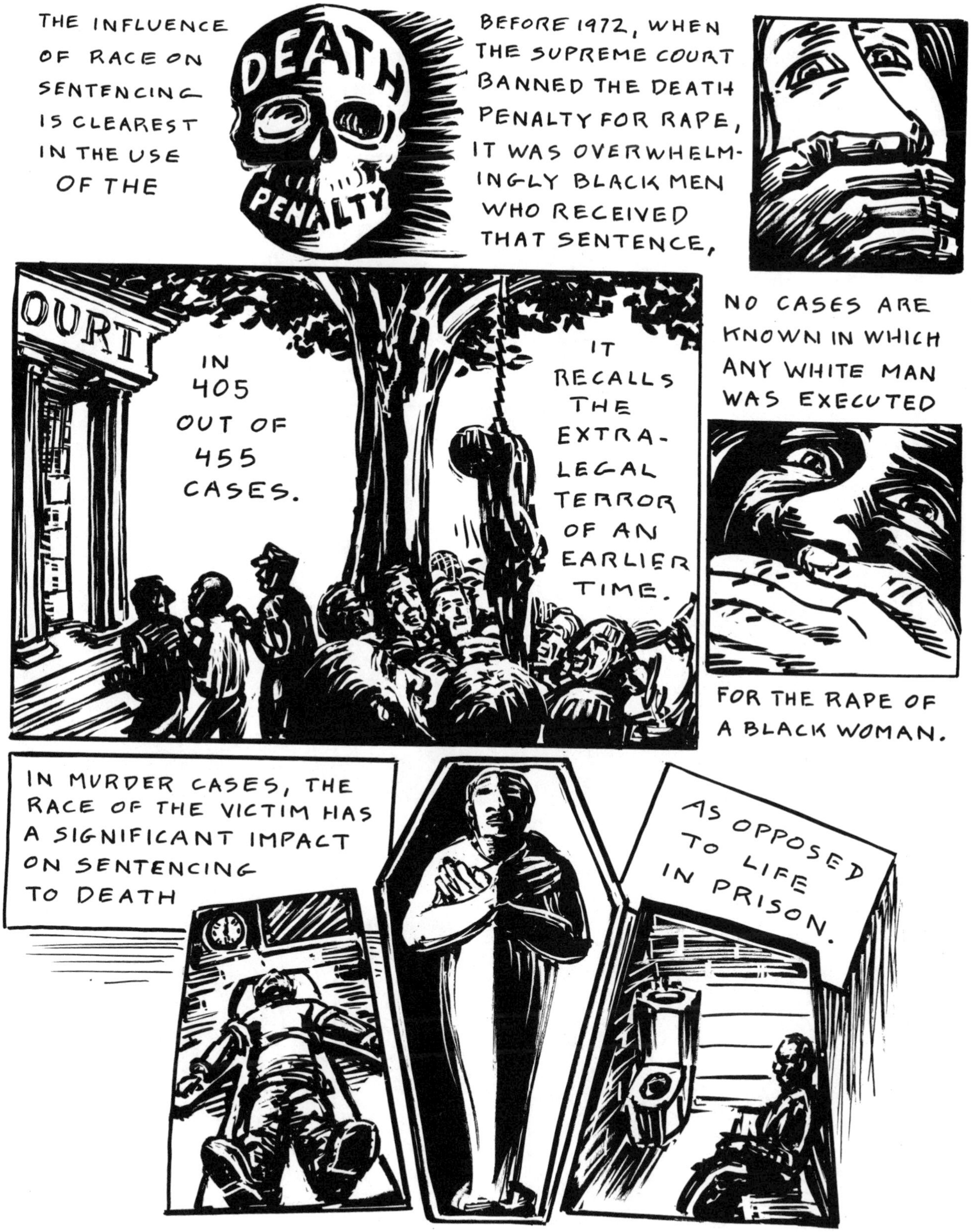
THE INFLUENCE OF RACE ON SENTENCING IS CLEAREST IN THE USE OF THE
DEATH PENALTY
BEFORE 1972, WHEN THE SUPREME COURT BANNED THE DEATH PENALTY FOR RAPE, IT WAS OVERWHELMINGLY BLACK MEN WHO RECEIVED THAT SENTENCE,
OURT
IN 405 OUT OF 455 CASES.
IT RECALLS THE EXTRA-LEGAL TERROR OF AN EARLIER TIME.
NO CASES ARE KNOWN IN WHICH ANY WHITE MAN WAS EXECUTED
FOR THE RAPE OF A BLACK WOMAN.
IN MURDER CASES, THE RACE OF THE VICTIM HAS A SIGNIFICANT IMPACT ON SENTENCING TO DEATH
AS OPPOSED TO LIFE IN PRISON.

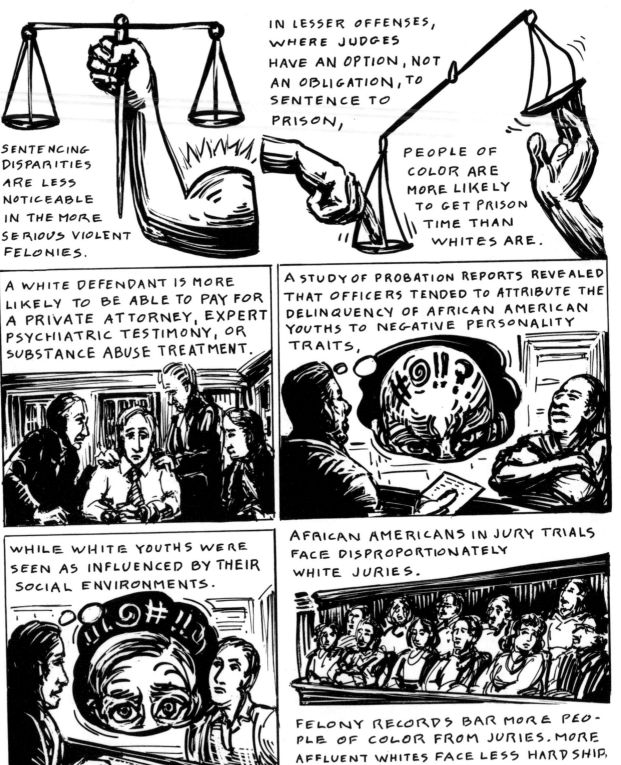

SENTENCING DISPARITIES ARE LESS NOTICEABLE IN THE MORE SERIOUS VIOLENT FELONIES.

IN LESSER OFFENSES, WHERE JUDGES HAVE AN OPTION, NOT AN OBLIGATION, TO SENTENCE TO PRISON,

PEOPLE OF COLOR ARE MORE LIKELY TO GET PRISON TIME THAN WHITES ARE.

A WHITE DEFENDANT IS MORE LIKELY TO BE ABLE TO PAY FOR A PRIVATE ATTORNEY, EXPERT PSYCHIATRIC TESTIMONY, OR SUBSTANCE ABUSE TREATMENT.

A STUDY OF PROBATION REPORTS REVEALED THAT OFFICERS TENDED TO ATTRIBUTE THE DELINQUENCY OF AFRICAN AMERICAN YOUTHS TO NEGATIVE PERSONALITY TRAITS,

WHILE WHITE YOUTHS WERE SEEN AS INFLUENCED BY THEIR SOCIAL ENVIRONMENTS.

AFRICAN AMERICANS IN JURY TRIALS FACE DISPROPORTIONATELY WHITE JURIES.

FELONY RECORDS BAR MORE PEOPLE OF COLOR FROM JURIES. MORE AFFLUENT WHITES FACE LESS HARDSHIP IN REPORTING FOR JURY DUTY.

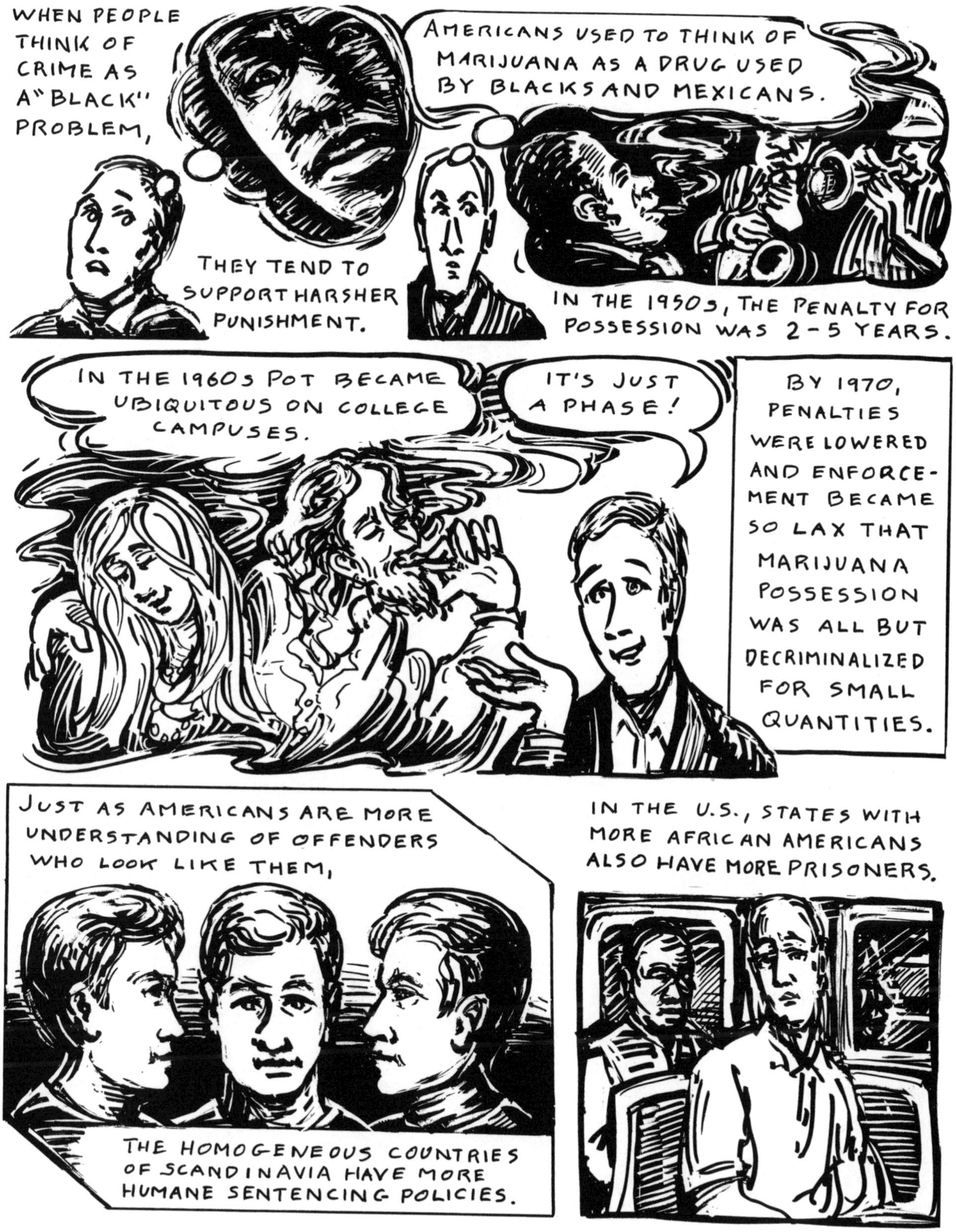
WHEN PEOPLE THINK OF CRIME AS A "BLACK" PROBLEM,
THEY TEND TO SUPPORT HARSHER PUNISHMENT.
AMERICANS USED TO THINK OF MARIJUANA AS A DRUG USED BY BLACKS AND MEXICANS.
IN THE 1950S, THE PENALTY FOR POSSESSION WAS 2-5 YEARS.
IN THE 1960S POT BECAME UBIQUITOUS ON COLLEGE CAMPUSES.
IT'S JUST A PHASE!
BY 1970, PENALTIES WERE LOWERED AND ENFORCEMENT BECAME SO LAX THAT MARIJUANA POSSESSION WAS ALL BUT DECRIMINALIZED FOR SMALL QUANTITIES.
JUST AS AMERICANS ARE MORE UNDERSTANDING OF OFFENDERS WHO LOOK LIKE THEM,
THE HOMOGENEOUS COUNTRIES OF SCANDINAVIA HAVE MORE HUMANE SENTENCING POLICIES.
IN THE U.S., STATES WITH MORE AFRICAN AMERICANS ALSO HAVE MORE PRISONERS.

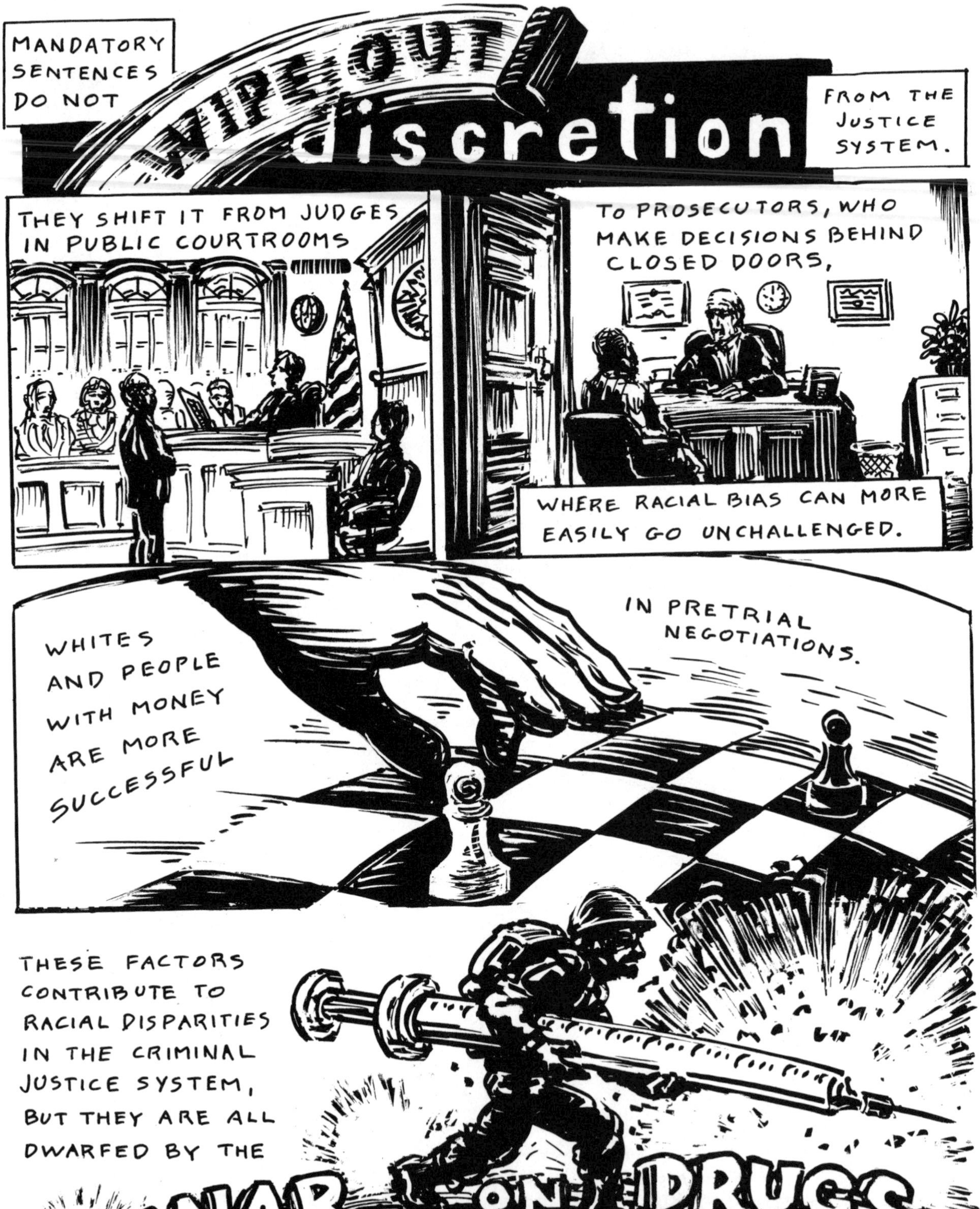
MANDATORY SENTENCES DO NOT
WIPE OUT
discretion
FROM THE JUSTICE SYSTEM.
THEY SHIFT IT FROM JUDGES IN PUBLIC COURTROOMS
TO PROSECUTORS, WHO MAKE DECISIONS BEHIND CLOSED DOORS,
WHERE RACIAL BIAS CAN MORE EASILY GO UNCHALLENGED.
WHITES AND PEOPLE WITH MONEY ARE MORE SUCCESSFUL
IN PRETRIAL NEGOTIATIONS.
THESE FACTORS CONTRIBUTE TO RACIAL DISPARITIES IN THE CRIMINAL JUSTICE SYSTEM, BUT THEY ARE ALL DWARFED BY THE
WAR ON DRUGS

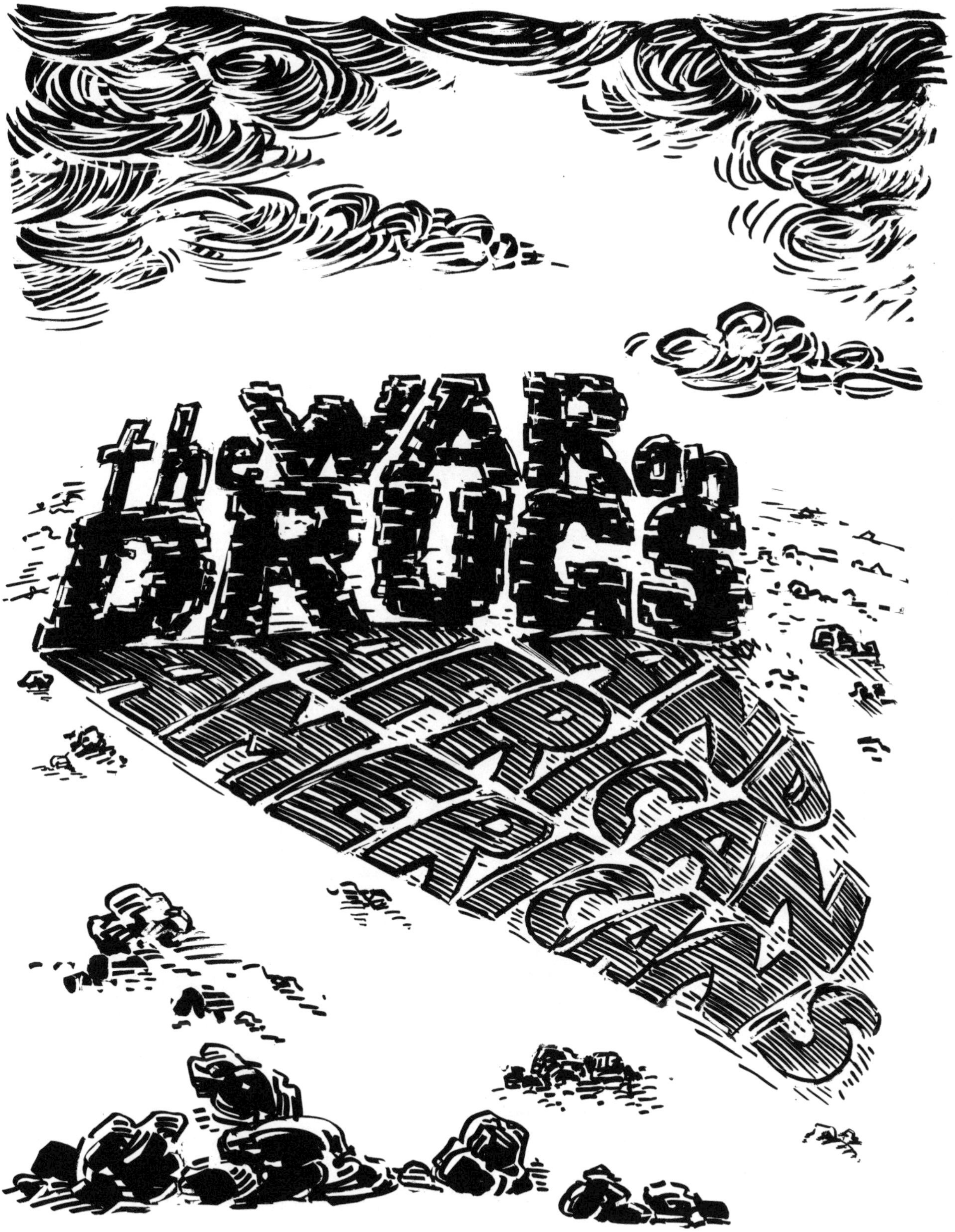
the WAR on DRUGS
AFRICAN AMERICANS

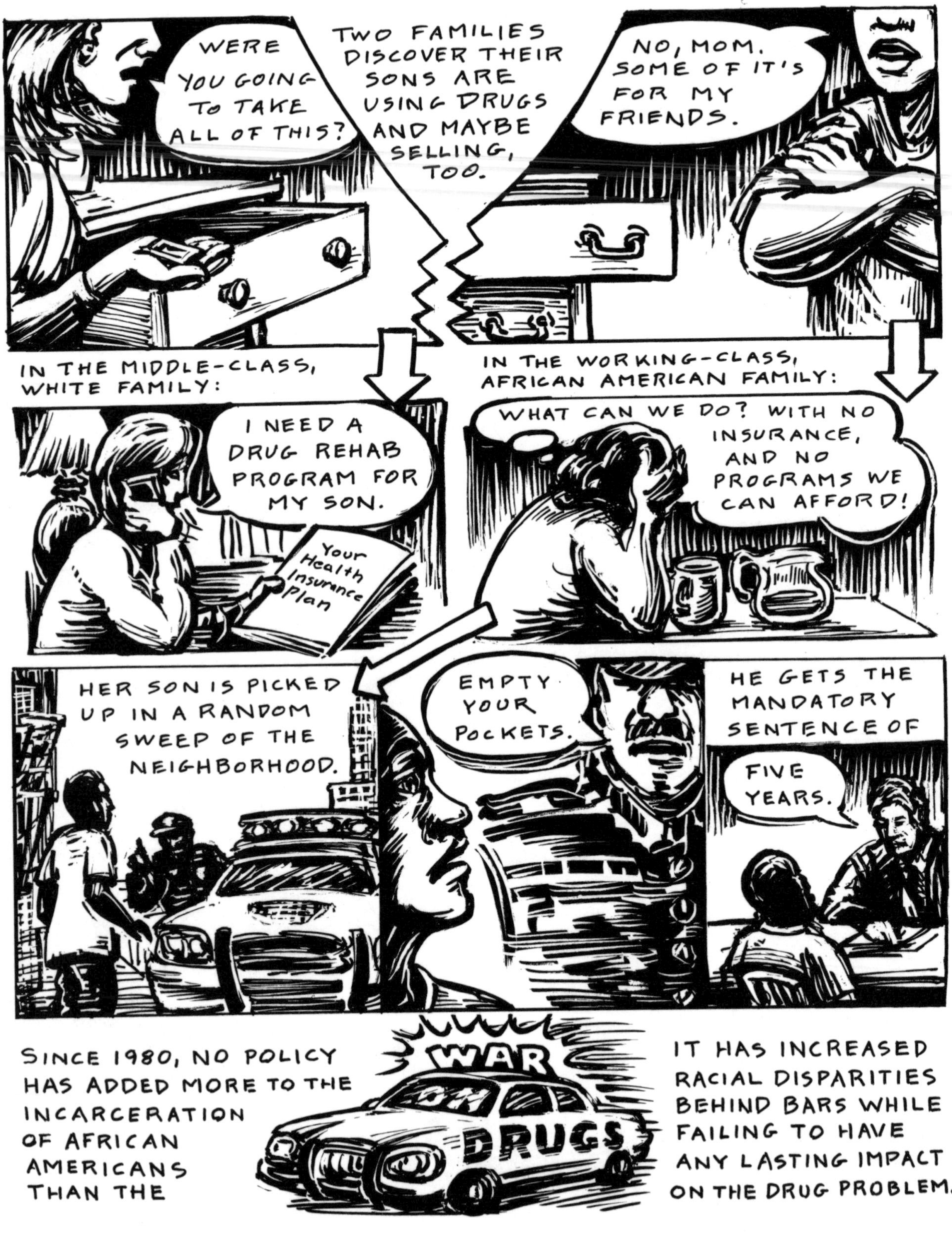
TWO FAMILIES DISCOVER THEIR SONS ARE USING DRUGS AND MAYBE SELLING, TOO.
WERE YOU GOING TO TAKE ALL OF THIS?
NO, MOM. SOME OF IT'S FOR MY FRIENDS.
IN THE MIDDLE-CLASS, WHITE FAMILY:
I NEED A DRUG REHAB PROGRAM FOR MY SON.
Your Health Insurance Plan
IN THE WORKING-CLASS, AFRICAN AMERICAN FAMILY:
WHAT CAN WE DO? WITH NO INSURANCE, AND NO PROGRAMS WE CAN AFFORD!
HER SON IS PICKED UP IN A RANDOM SWEEP OF THE NEIGHBORHOOD.
EMPTY YOUR POCKETS.
HE GETS THE MANDATORY SENTENCE OF
FIVE YEARS.
SINCE 1980, NO POLICY HAS ADDED MORE TO THE INCARCERATION OF AFRICAN AMERICANS THAN THE
WAR ON DRUGS
IT HAS INCREASED RACIAL DISPARITIES BEHIND BARS WHILE FAILING TO HAVE ANY LASTING IMPACT ON THE DRUG PROBLEM.

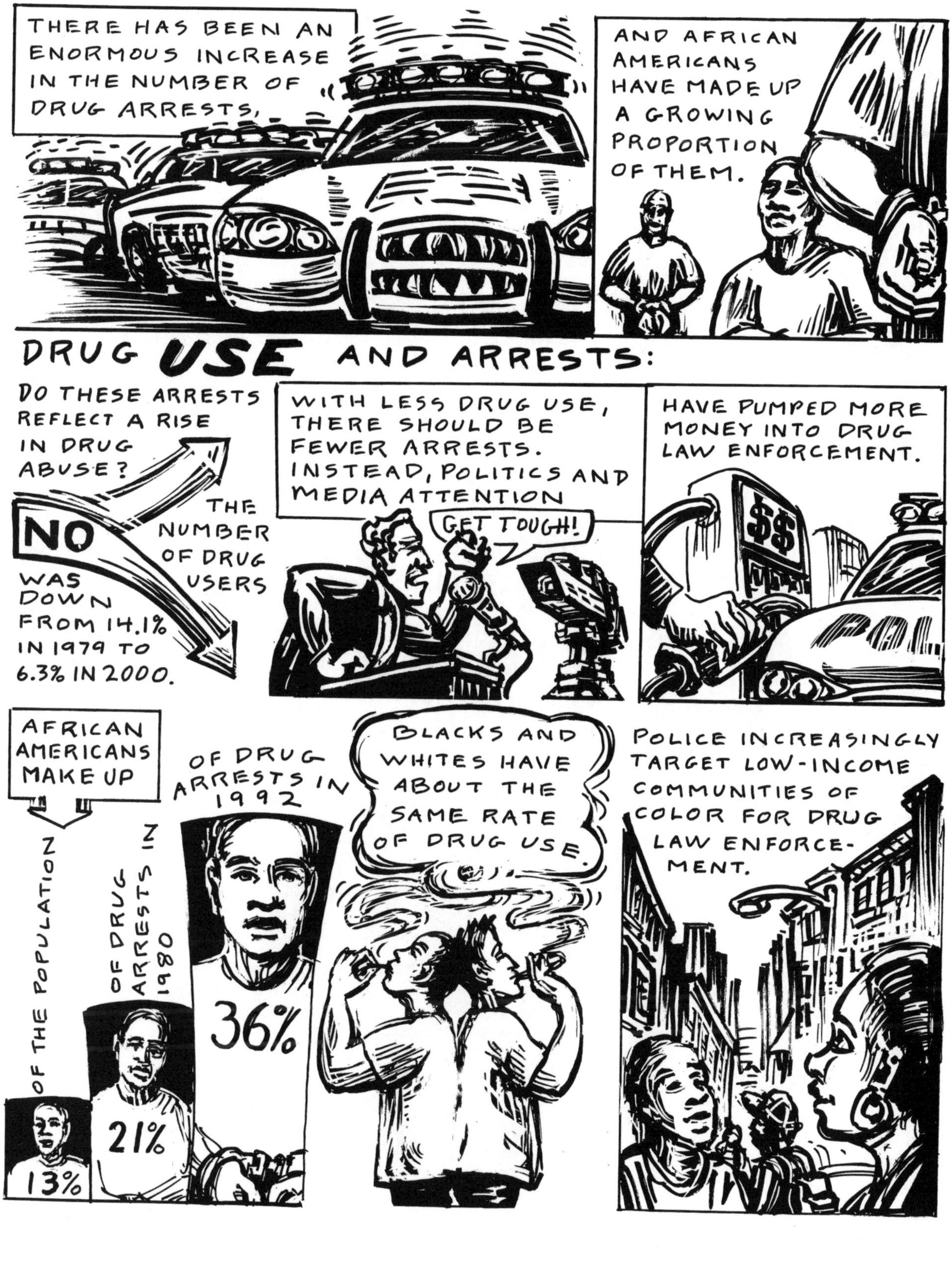
THERE HAS BEEN AN ENORMOUS INCREASE IN THE NUMBER OF DRUG ARRESTS,
AND AFRICAN AMERICANS HAVE MADE UP A GROWING PROPORTION OF THEM.
DRUG USE AND ARRESTS:
DO THESE ARRESTS REFLECT A RISE IN DRUG ABUSE?
NO
THE NUMBER OF DRUG USERS WAS DOWN FROM 14.1% IN 1979 TO 6.3% IN 2000.
WITH LESS DRUG USE, THERE SHOULD BE FEWER ARRESTS. INSTEAD, POLITICS AND MEDIA ATTENTION
GET TOUGH!
HAVE PUMPED MORE MONEY INTO DRUG LAW ENFORCEMENT.
$$
POL
AFRICAN AMERICANS MAKE UP
OF THE POPULATION
13%
OF DRUG ARRESTS IN 1980
21%
OF DRUG ARRESTS IN 1992
36%
BLACKS AND WHITES HAVE ABOUT THE SAME RATE OF DRUG USE.
POLICE INCREASINGLY TARGET LOW-INCOME COMMUNITIES OF COLOR FOR DRUG LAW ENFORCE-MENT.

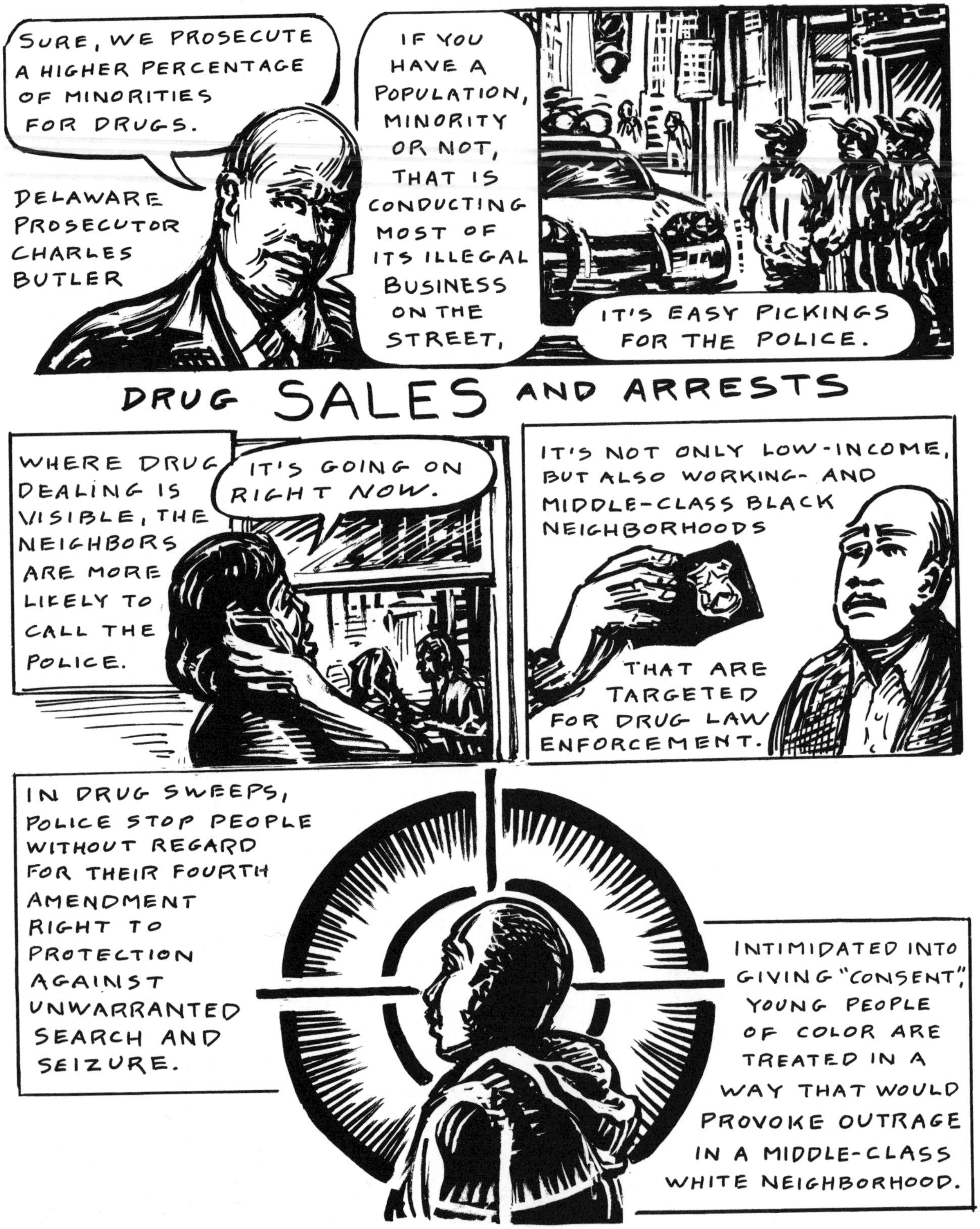
SURE, WE PROSECUTE A HIGHER PERCENTAGE OF MINORITIES FOR DRUGS.
DELAWARE PROSECUTOR CHARLES BUTLER
IF YOU HAVE A POPULATION, MINORITY OR NOT, THAT IS CONDUCTING MOST OF ITS ILLEGAL BUSINESS ON THE STREET,
IT'S EASY PICKINGS FOR THE POLICE.
DRUG SALES AND ARRESTS
WHERE DRUG DEALING IS VISIBLE, THE NEIGHBORS ARE MORE LIKELY TO CALL THE POLICE.
IT'S GOING ON RIGHT NOW.
IT'S NOT ONLY LOW-INCOME, BUT ALSO WORKING- AND MIDDLE-CLASS BLACK NEIGHBORHOODS
THAT ARE TARGETED FOR DRUG LAW ENFORCEMENT.
IN DRUG SWEEPS, POLICE STOP PEOPLE WITHOUT REGARD FOR THEIR FOURTH AMENDMENT RIGHT TO PROTECTION AGAINST UNWARRANTED SEARCH AND SEIZURE.
INTIMIDATED INTO GIVING "CONSENT," YOUNG PEOPLE OF COLOR ARE TREATED IN A WAY THAT WOULD PROVOKE OUTRAGE IN A MIDDLE-CLASS WHITE NEIGHBORHOOD.

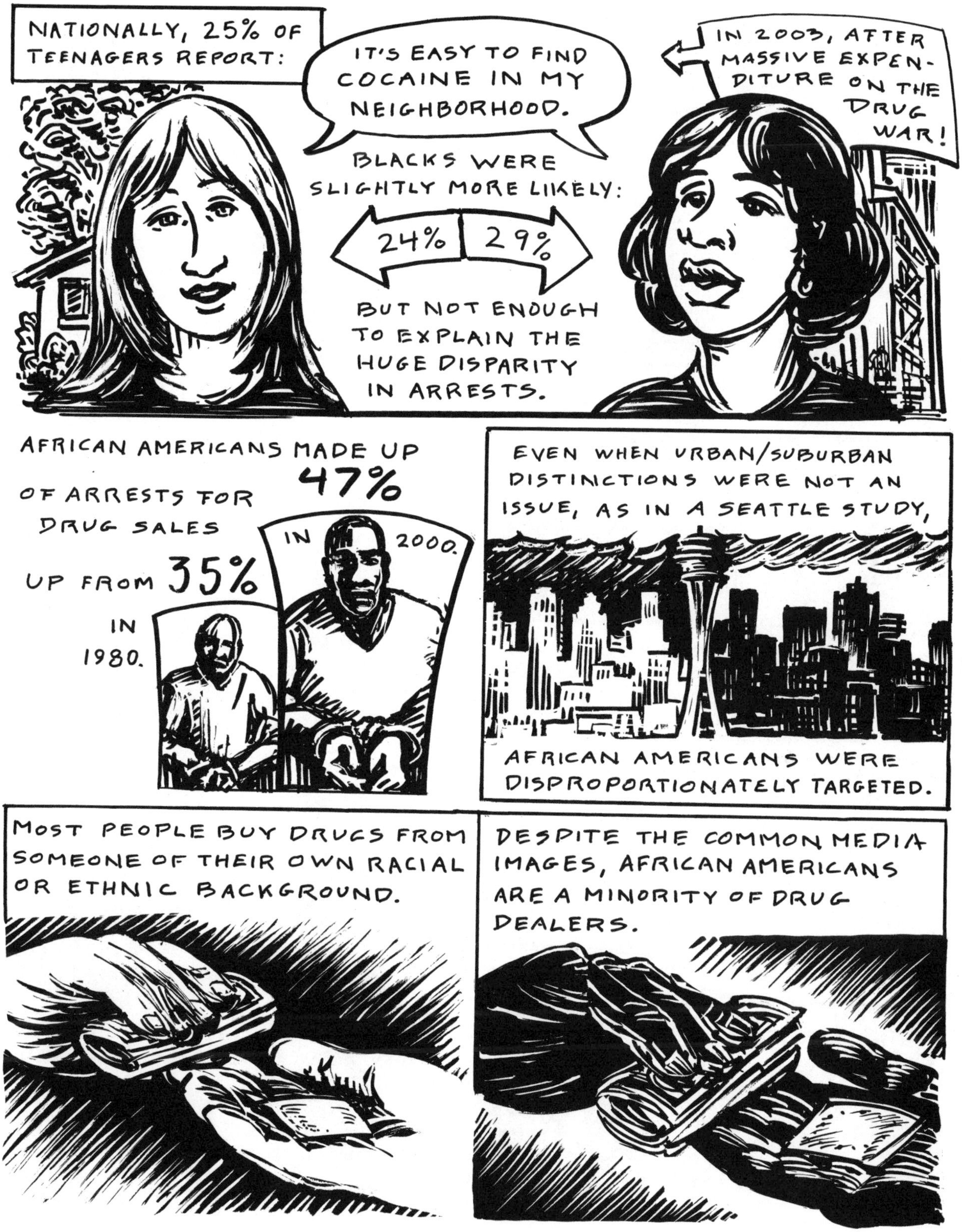
NATIONALLY, 25% OF TEENAGERS REPORT:
IT'S EASY TO FIND COCAINE IN MY NEIGHBORHOOD.
BLACKS WERE SLIGHTLY MORE LIKELY:
24%
29%
BUT NOT ENOUGH TO EXPLAIN THE HUGE DISPARITY IN ARRESTS.
IN 2003, AFTER MASSIVE EXPENDITURE ON THE DRUG WAR!
AFRICAN AMERICANS MADE UP 47% OF ARRESTS FOR DRUG SALES
IN 2000.
UP FROM 35% IN 1980.
EVEN WHEN URBAN/SUBURBAN DISTINCTIONS WERE NOT AN ISSUE, AS IN A SEATTLE STUDY,
AFRICAN AMERICANS WERE DISPROPORTIONATELY TARGETED.
MOST PEOPLE BUY DRUGS FROM SOMEONE OF THEIR OWN RACIAL OR ETHNIC BACKGROUND.
DESPITE THE COMMON MEDIA IMAGES, AFRICAN AMERICANS ARE A MINORITY OF DRUG DEALERS.

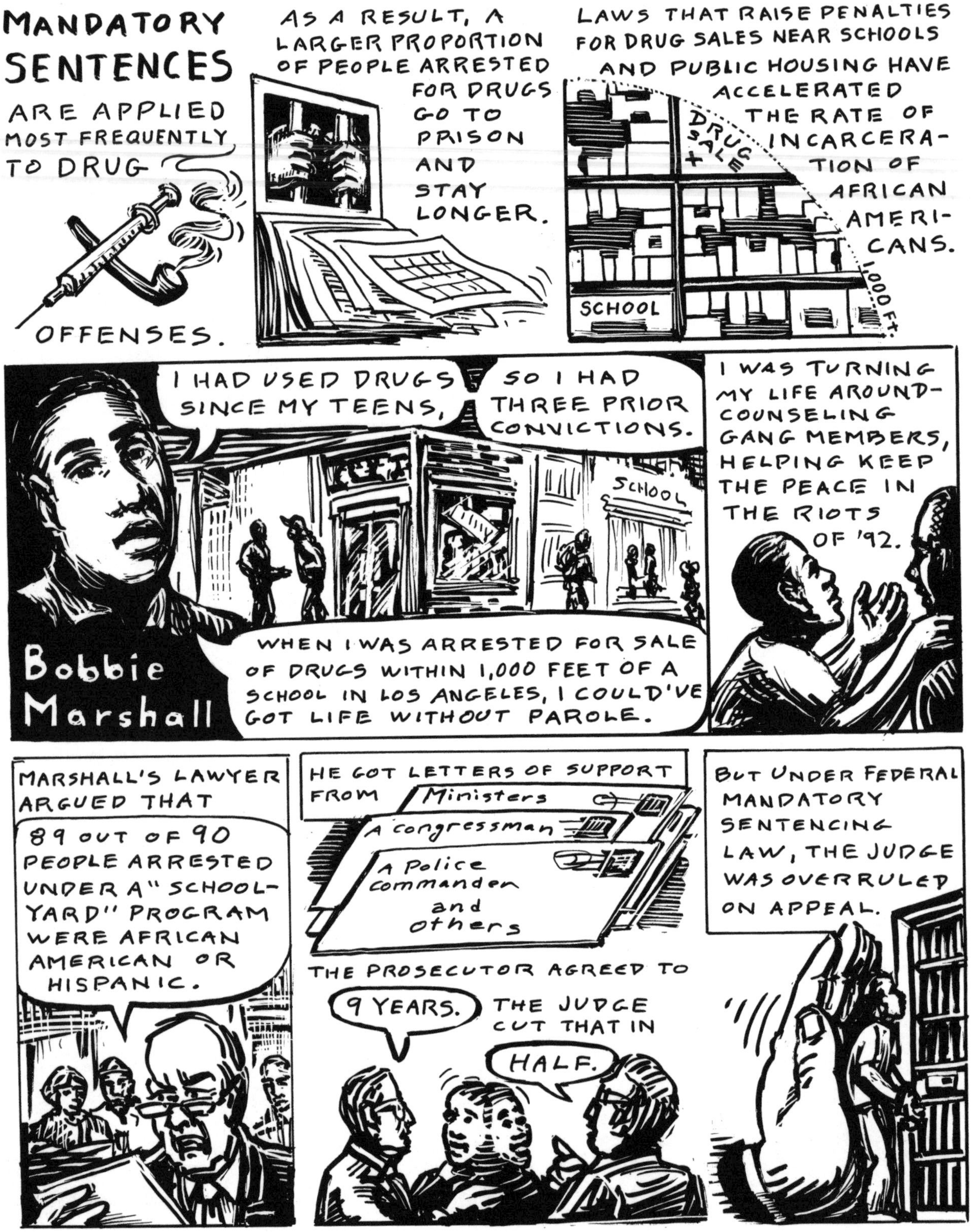
MANDATORY SENTENCES ARE APPLIED MOST FREQUENTLY TO DRUG OFFENSES.
AS A RESULT, A LARGER PROPORTION OF PEOPLE ARRESTED FOR DRUGS GO TO PRISON AND STAY LONGER.
LAWS THAT RAISE PENALTIES FOR DRUG SALES NEAR SCHOOLS AND PUBLIC HOUSING HAVE ACCELERATED THE RATE OF INCARCERATION OF AFRICAN AMERICANS.
DRUG SALE
SCHOOL
1,000 FT.
I HAD USED DRUGS SINCE MY TEENS,
SO I HAD THREE PRIOR CONVICTIONS.
SCHOOL
Bobbie Marshall
WHEN I WAS ARRESTED FOR SALE OF DRUGS WITHIN 1,000 FEET OF A SCHOOL IN LOS ANGELES, I COULD'VE GOT LIFE WITHOUT PAROLE.
I WAS TURNING MY LIFE AROUND— COUNSELING GANG MEMBERS, HELPING KEEP THE PEACE IN THE RIOTS OF '92.
MARSHALL'S LAWYER ARGUED THAT
89 OUT OF 90 PEOPLE ARRESTED UNDER A "SCHOOL-YARD" PROGRAM WERE AFRICAN AMERICAN OR HISPANIC.
HE GOT LETTERS OF SUPPORT FROM
Ministers
A congressman
A Police commander and others
THE PROSECUTOR AGREED TO
9 YEARS.
THE JUDGE CUT THAT IN
HALF.
BUT UNDER FEDERAL MANDATORY SENTENCING LAW, THE JUDGE WAS OVERRULED ON APPEAL.

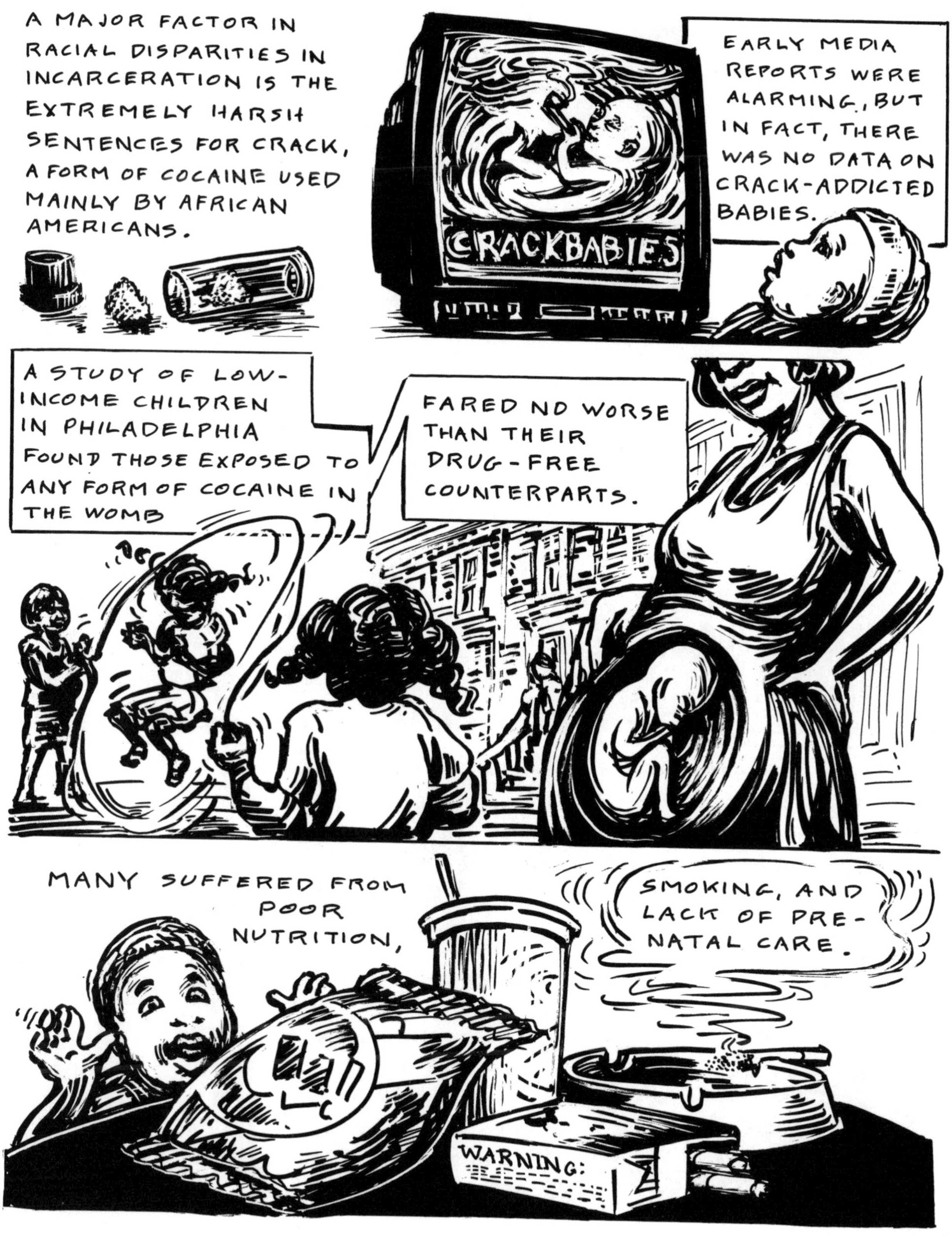
A MAJOR FACTOR IN RACIAL DISPARITIES IN INCARCERATION IS THE EXTREMELY HARSH SENTENCES FOR CRACK, A FORM OF COCAINE USED MAINLY BY AFRICAN AMERICANS.
CRACKBABIES
EARLY MEDIA REPORTS WERE ALARMING, BUT IN FACT, THERE WAS NO DATA ON CRACK-ADDICTED BABIES.
A STUDY OF LOW-INCOME CHILDREN IN PHILADELPHIA FOUND THOSE EXPOSED TO ANY FORM OF COCAINE IN THE WOMB
FARED NO WORSE THAN THEIR DRUG-FREE COUNTERPARTS.
MANY SUFFERED FROM POOR NUTRITION,
SMOKING, AND LACK OF PRE-NATAL CARE.
WARNING:

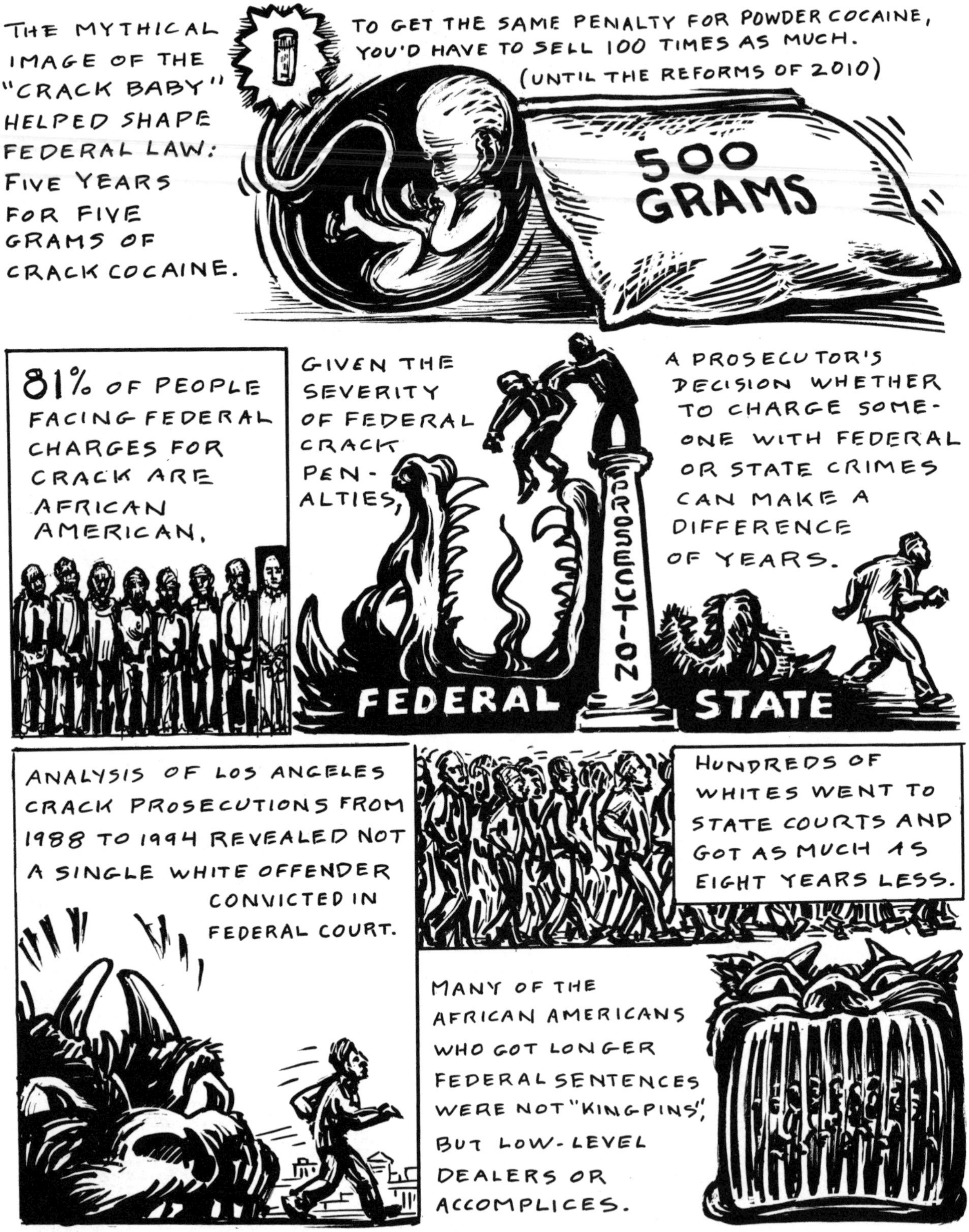
THE MYTHICAL IMAGE OF THE "CRACK BABY" HELPED SHAPE FEDERAL LAW: FIVE YEARS FOR FIVE GRAMS OF CRACK COCAINE.
TO GET THE SAME PENALTY FOR POWDER COCAINE, YOU'D HAVE TO SELL 100 TIMES AS MUCH.
(UNTIL THE REFORMS OF 2010)
500 GRAMS
81% OF PEOPLE FACING FEDERAL CHARGES FOR CRACK ARE AFRICAN AMERICAN.
GIVEN THE SEVERITY OF FEDERAL CRACK PEN-ALTIES,
A PROSECUTOR'S DECISION WHETHER TO CHARGE SOME-ONE WITH FEDERAL OR STATE CRIMES CAN MAKE A DIFFERENCE OF YEARS.
PROSECUTION
FEDERAL
STATE
ANALYSIS OF LOS ANGELES CRACK PROSECUTIONS FROM 1988 TO 1994 REVEALED NOT A SINGLE WHITE OFFENDER CONVICTED IN FEDERAL COURT.
HUNDREDS OF WHITES WENT TO STATE COURTS AND GOT AS MUCH AS EIGHT YEARS LESS.
MANY OF THE AFRICAN AMERICANS WHO GOT LONGER FEDERAL SENTENCES WERE NOT "KINGPINS", BUT LOW-LEVEL DEALERS OR ACCOMPLICES.

THE IMPACT OF LONG SENTENCES:

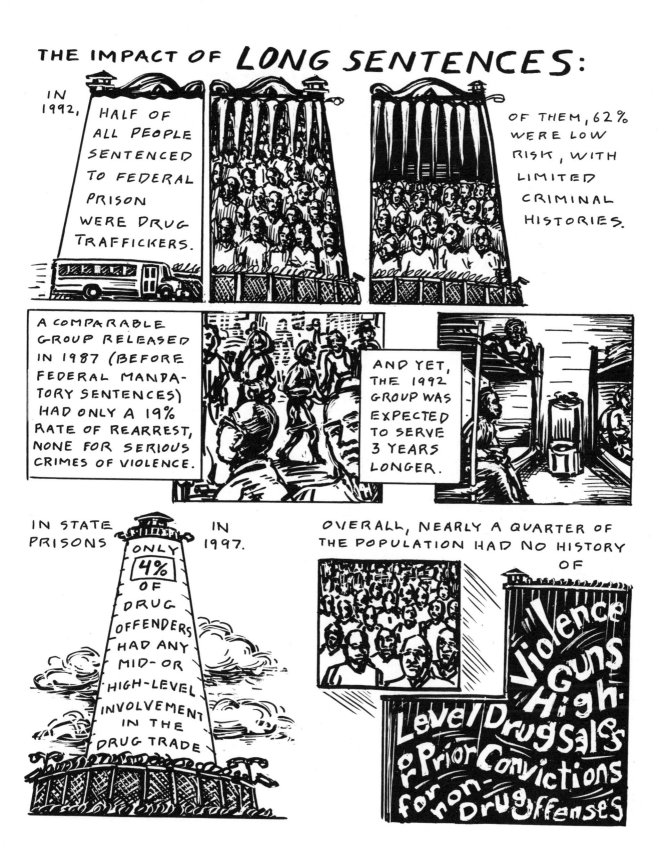

IN 1992, HALF OF ALL PEOPLE SENTENCED TO FEDERAL PRISON WERE DRUG TRAFFICKERS.

OF THEM, 62% WERE LOW RISK, WITH LIMITED CRIMINAL HISTORIES.

A COMPARABLE GROUP RELEASED IN 1987 (BEFORE FEDERAL MANDATORY SENTENCES) HAD ONLY A 19% RATE OF REARREST, NONE FOR SERIOUS CRIMES OF VIOLENCE.

AND YET, THE 1992 GROUP WAS EXPECTED TO SERVE 3 YEARS LONGER.

IN STATE PRISONS IN 1997. ONLY 4% OF DRUG OFFENDERS HAD ANY MID- OR HIGH-LEVEL INVOLVEMENT IN THE DRUG TRADE

OVERALL, NEARLY A QUARTER OF THE POPULATION HAD NO HISTORY OF

Violence Guns High-Level Drug Sales o Prior Convictions for non-Drug Offenses

97

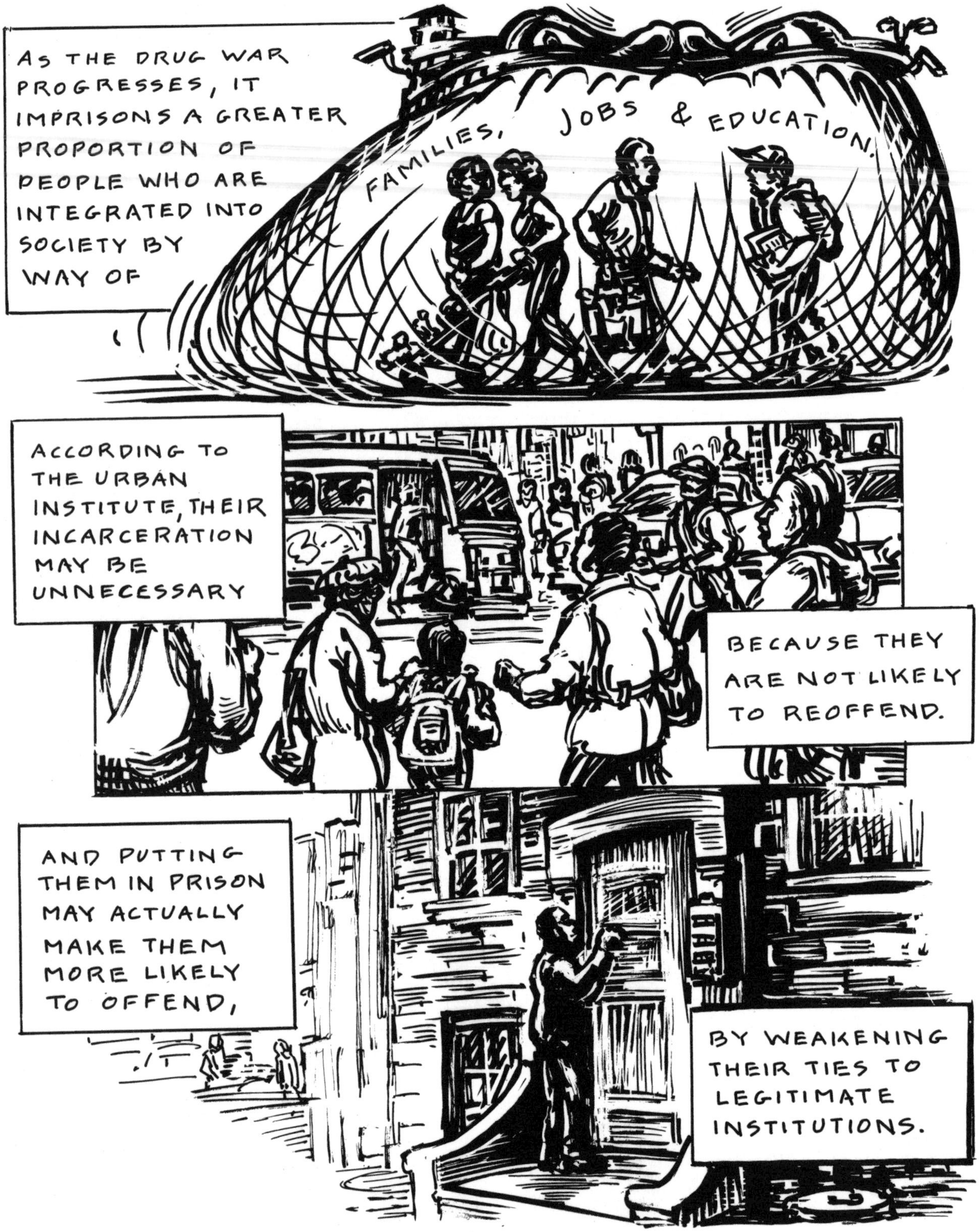
AS THE DRUG WAR PROGRESSES, IT IMPRISONS A GREATER PROPORTION OF PEOPLE WHO ARE INTEGRATED INTO SOCIETY BY WAY OF
FAMILIES, JOBS & EDUCATION.
ACCORDING TO THE URBAN INSTITUTE, THEIR INCARCERATION MAY BE UNNECESSARY
BECAUSE THEY ARE NOT LIKELY TO REOFFEND.
AND PUTTING THEM IN PRISON MAY ACTUALLY MAKE THEM MORE LIKELY TO OFFEND,
BY WEAKENING THEIR TIES TO LEGITIMATE INSTITUTIONS.

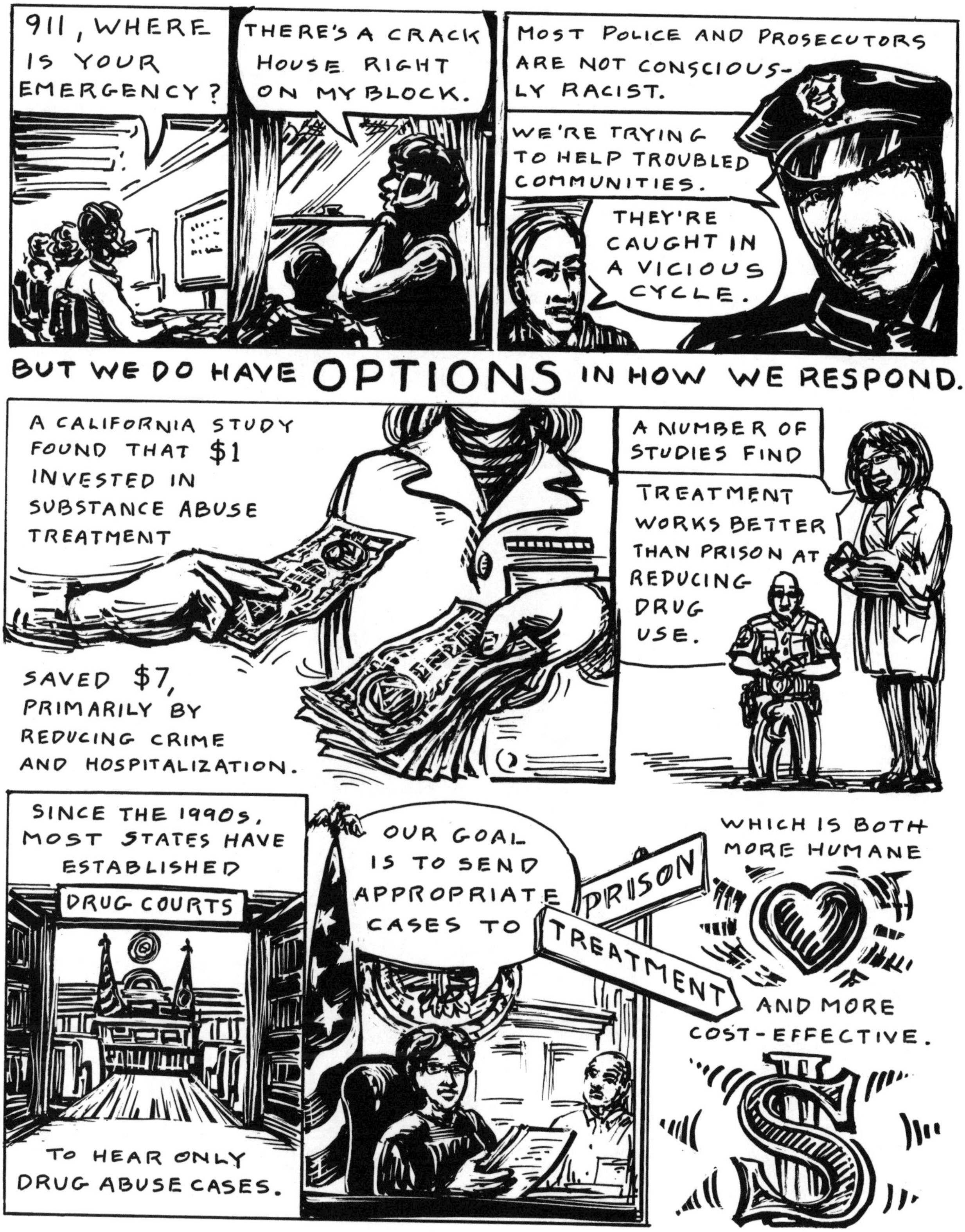
911, WHERE IS YOUR EMERGENCY?
THERE'S A CRACK HOUSE RIGHT ON MY BLOCK.
MOST POLICE AND PROSECUTORS ARE NOT CONSCIOUS-LY RACIST.
WE'RE TRYING TO HELP TROUBLED COMMUNITIES.
THEY'RE CAUGHT IN A VICIOUS CYCLE.
BUT WE DO HAVE OPTIONS IN HOW WE RESPOND.
A CALIFORNIA STUDY FOUND THAT $1 INVESTED IN SUBSTANCE ABUSE TREATMENT
SAVED $7, PRIMARILY BY REDUCING CRIME AND HOSPITALIZATION.
A NUMBER OF STUDIES FIND
TREATMENT WORKS BETTER THAN PRISON AT REDUCING DRUG USE.
SINCE THE 1990s, MOST STATES HAVE ESTABLISHED
DRUG COURTS
TO HEAR ONLY DRUG ABUSE CASES.
OUR GOAL IS TO SEND APPROPRIATE CASES TO
PRISON
TREATMENT
WHICH IS BOTH MORE HUMANE
AND MORE COST-EFFECTIVE.

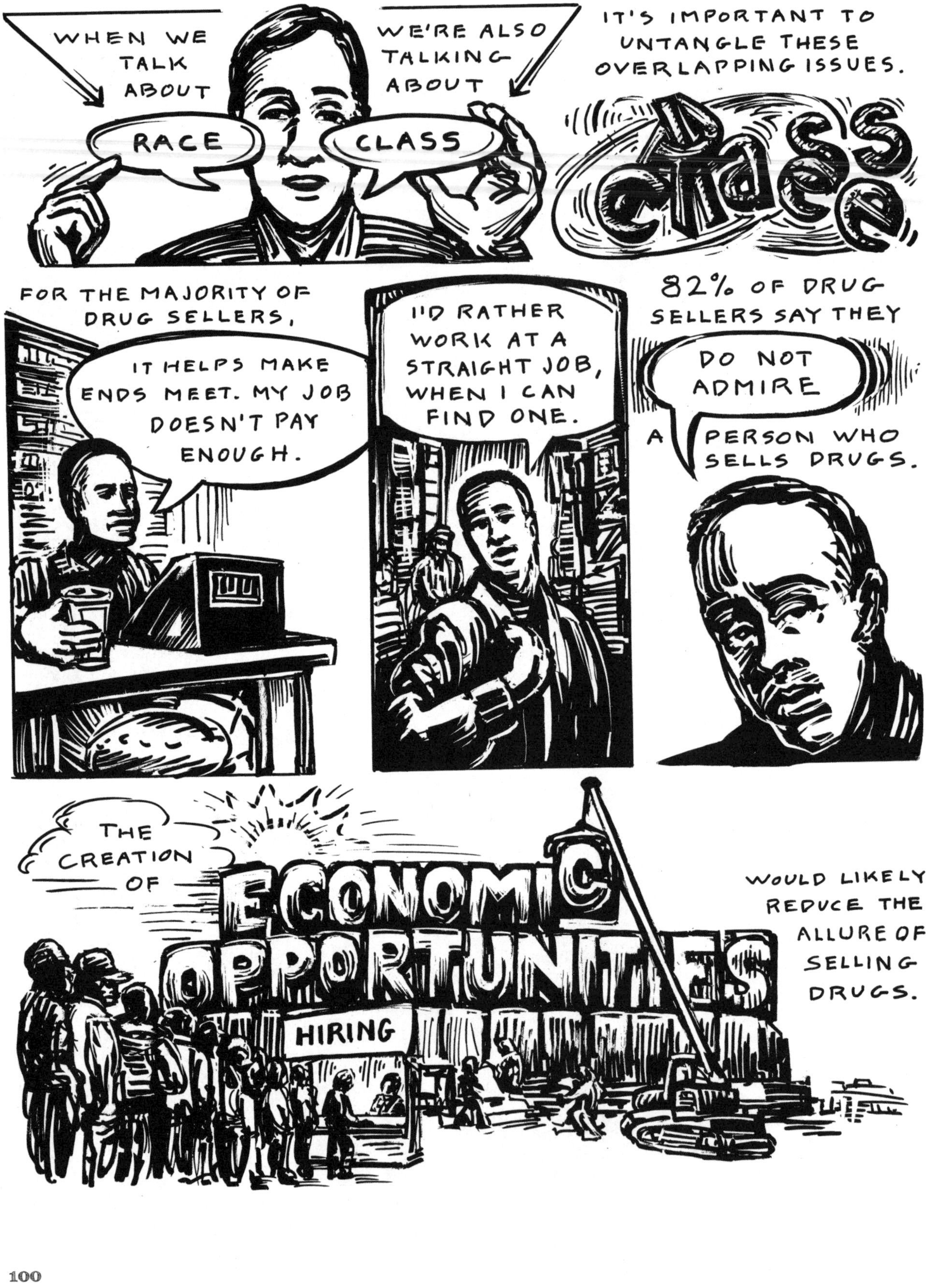
WHEN WE TALK ABOUT
RACE
WE'RE ALSO TALKING ABOUT
CLASS
IT'S IMPORTANT TO UNTANGLE THESE OVERLAPPING ISSUES.
FOR THE MAJORITY OF DRUG SELLERS,
IT HELPS MAKE ENDS MEET. MY JOB DOESN'T PAY ENOUGH.
I'D RATHER WORK AT A STRAIGHT JOB, WHEN I CAN FIND ONE.
82% OF DRUG SELLERS SAY THEY
DO NOT ADMIRE
A PERSON WHO SELLS DRUGS.
THE CREATION OF
ECONOMIC OPPORTUNITIES
HIRING
WOULD LIKELY REDUCE THE ALLURE OF SELLING DRUGS.

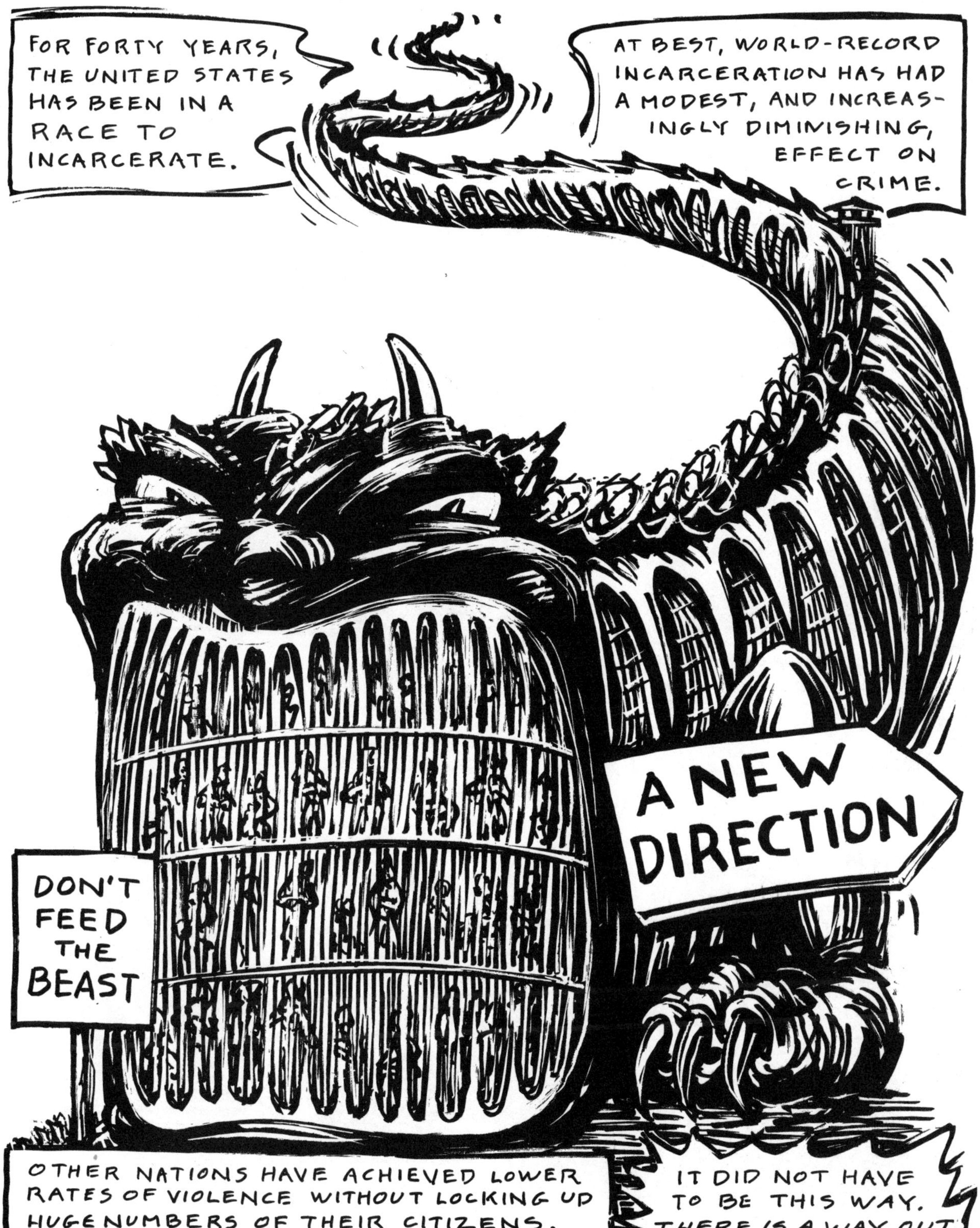
FOR FORTY YEARS, THE UNITED STATES HAS BEEN IN A RACE TO INCARCERATE.
AT BEST, WORLD-RECORD INCARCERATION HAS HAD A MODEST, AND INCREASINGLY DIMINISHING, EFFECT ON CRIME.
A NEW DIRECTION
DON'T FEED THE BEAST
OTHER NATIONS HAVE ACHIEVED LOWER RATES OF VIOLENCE WITHOUT LOCKING UP HUGE NUMBERS OF THEIR CITIZENS.
IT DID NOT HAVE TO BE THIS WAY. THERE IS A WAY OUT.

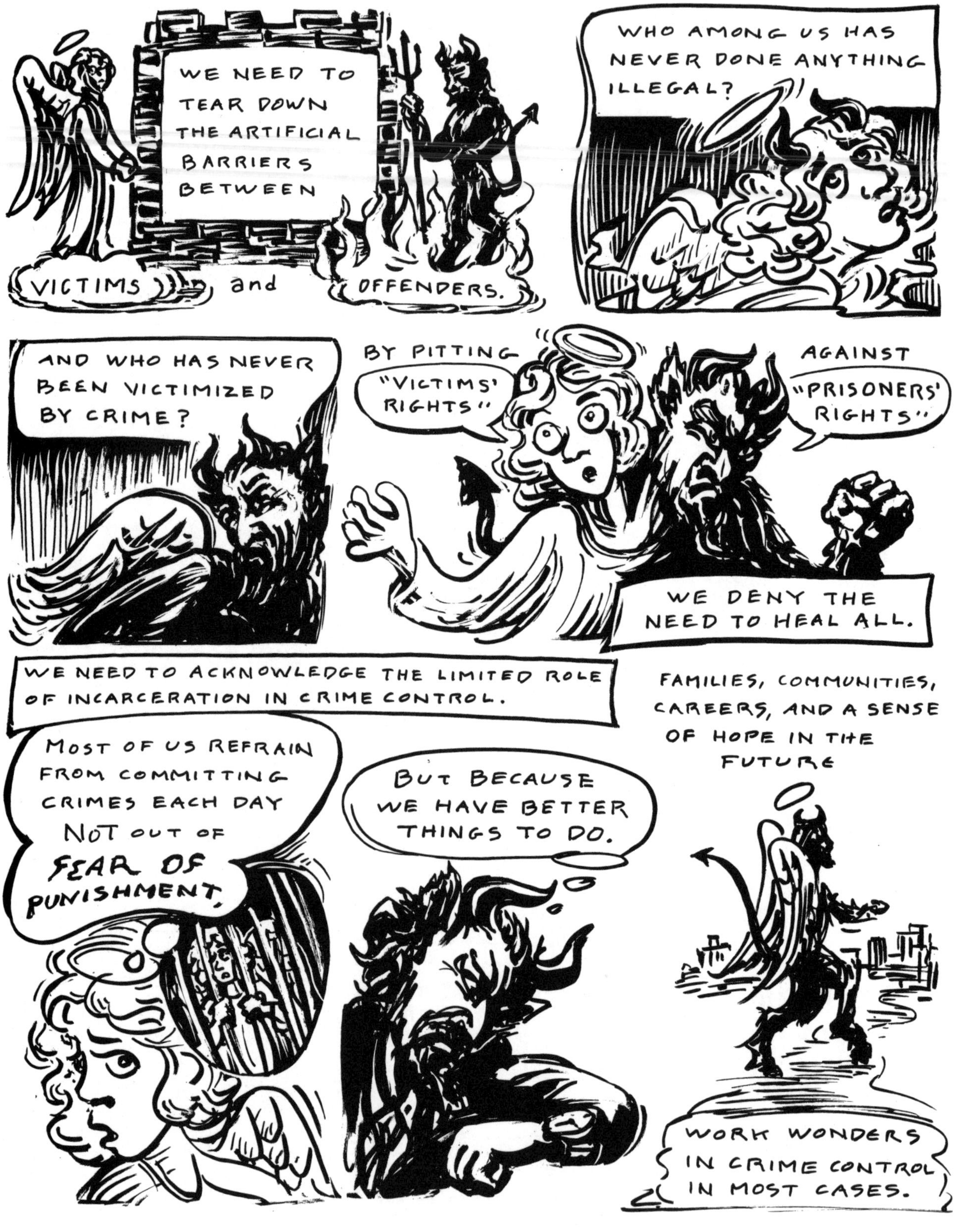
WE NEED TO TEAR DOWN THE ARTIFICIAL BARRIERS BETWEEN
VICTIMS and OFFENDERS.
WHO AMONG US HAS NEVER DONE ANYTHING ILLEGAL?
AND WHO HAS NEVER BEEN VICTIMIZED BY CRIME?
BY PITTING
"VICTIMS' RIGHTS"
AGAINST
"PRISONERS' RIGHTS"
WE DENY THE NEED TO HEAL ALL.
WE NEED TO ACKNOWLEDGE THE LIMITED ROLE OF INCARCERATION IN CRIME CONTROL.
MOST OF US REFRAIN FROM COMMITTING CRIMES EACH DAY NOT OUT OF FEAR OF PUNISHMENT,
BUT BECAUSE WE HAVE BETTER THINGS TO DO.
FAMILIES, COMMUNITIES, CAREERS, AND A SENSE OF HOPE IN THE FUTURE
WORK WONDERS IN CRIME CONTROL IN MOST CASES.

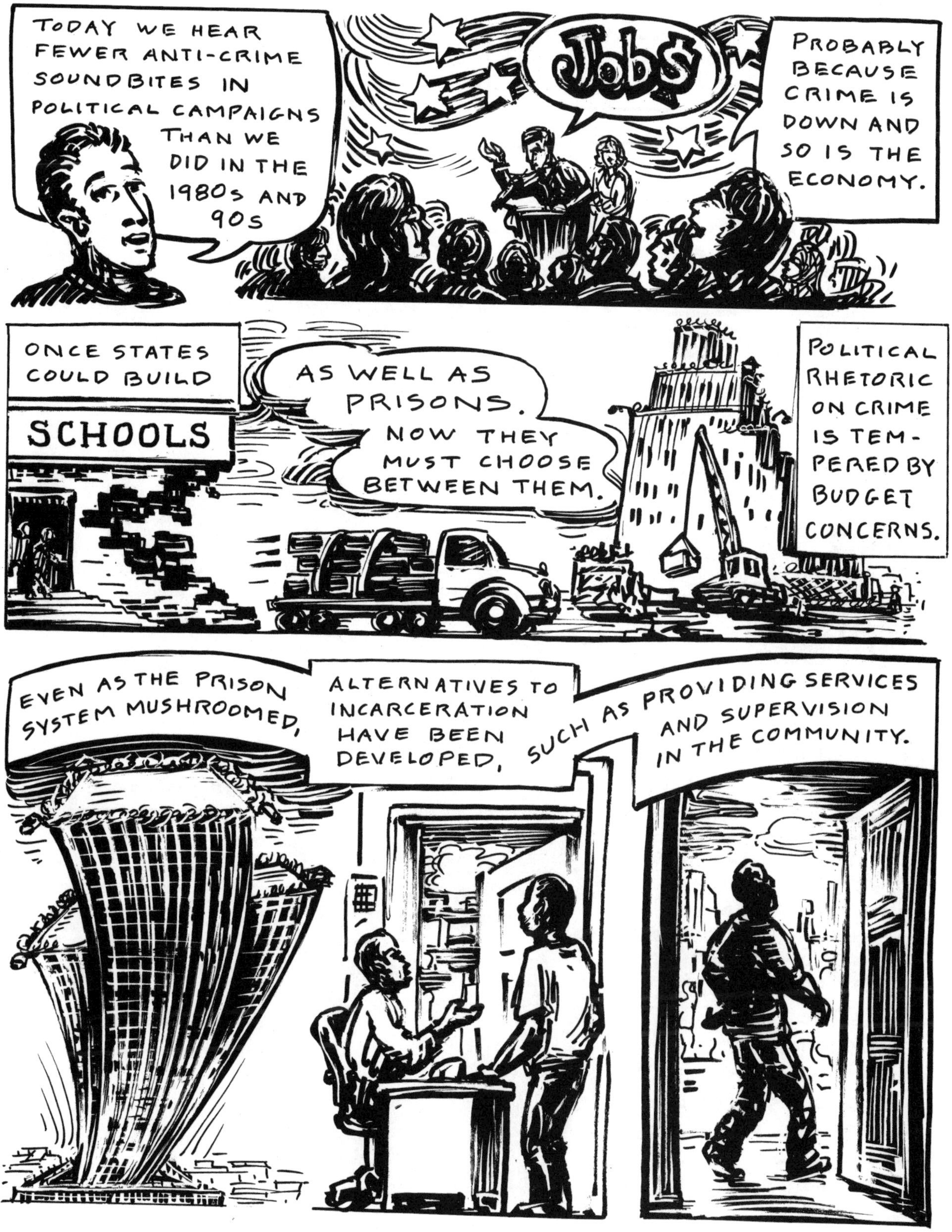
TODAY WE HEAR FEWER ANTI-CRIME SOUNDBITES IN POLITICAL CAMPAIGNS THAN WE DID IN THE 1980s AND 90s
JOBS
PROBABLY BECAUSE CRIME IS DOWN AND SO IS THE ECONOMY.
ONCE STATES COULD BUILD
SCHOOLS
AS WELL AS PRISONS. NOW THEY MUST CHOOSE BETWEEN THEM.
POLITICAL RHETORIC ON CRIME IS TEMPERED BY BUDGET CONCERNS.
EVEN AS THE PRISON SYSTEM MUSHROOMED,
ALTERNATIVES TO INCARCERATION HAVE BEEN DEVELOPED,
SUCH AS PROVIDING SERVICES AND SUPERVISION IN THE COMMUNITY.

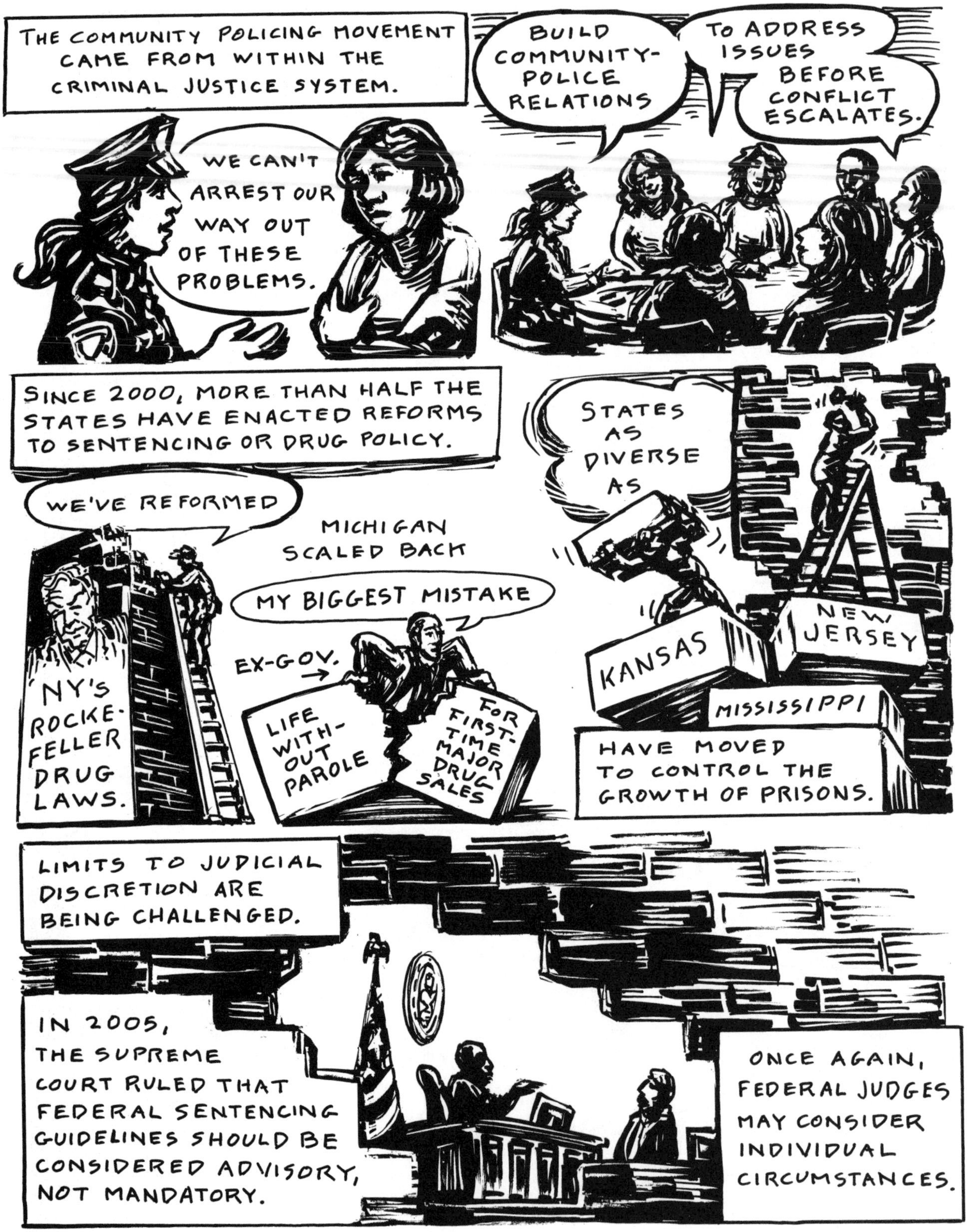
THE COMMUNITY POLICING MOVEMENT CAME FROM WITHIN THE CRIMINAL JUSTICE SYSTEM.
WE CAN'T ARREST OUR WAY OUT OF THESE PROBLEMS.
BUILD COMMUNITY-POLICE RELATIONS
TO ADDRESS ISSUES BEFORE CONFLICT ESCALATES.
SINCE 2000, MORE THAN HALF THE STATES HAVE ENACTED REFORMS TO SENTENCING OR DRUG POLICY.
WE'VE REFORMED
NY'S ROCKEFELLER DRUG LAWS.
MICHIGAN SCALED BACK
MY BIGGEST MISTAKE
EX-GOV.
LIFE WITHOUT PAROLE
FOR FIRST-TIME MAJOR DRUG SALES
STATES AS DIVERSE AS
KANSAS
NEW JERSEY
MISSISSIPPI
HAVE MOVED TO CONTROL THE GROWTH OF PRISONS.
LIMITS TO JUDICIAL DISCRETION ARE BEING CHALLENGED.
IN 2005, THE SUPREME COURT RULED THAT FEDERAL SENTENCING GUIDELINES SHOULD BE CONSIDERED ADVISORY, NOT MANDATORY.
ONCE AGAIN, FEDERAL JUDGES MAY CONSIDER INDIVIDUAL CIRCUMSTANCES.

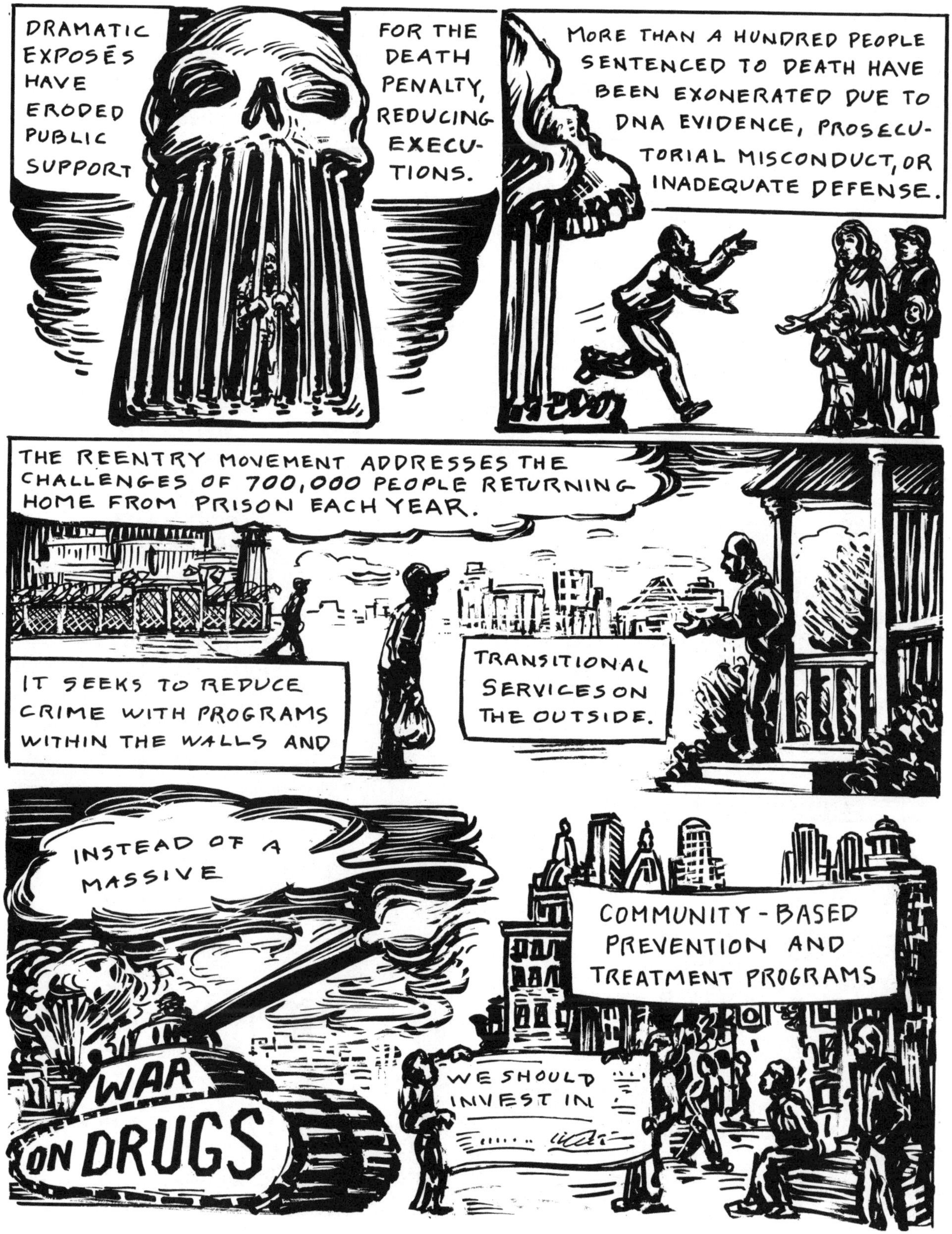
DRAMATIC EXPOSÉS HAVE ERODED PUBLIC SUPPORT
FOR THE DEATH PENALTY, REDUCING EXECU-TIONS.
MORE THAN A HUNDRED PEOPLE SENTENCED TO DEATH HAVE BEEN EXONERATED DUE TO DNA EVIDENCE, PROSECU-TORIAL MISCONDUCT, OR INADEQUATE DEFENSE.
THE REENTRY MOVEMENT ADDRESSES THE CHALLENGES OF 700,000 PEOPLE RETURNING HOME FROM PRISON EACH YEAR.
IT SEEKS TO REDUCE CRIME WITH PROGRAMS WITHIN THE WALLS AND
TRANSITIONAL SERVICES ON THE OUTSIDE.
INSTEAD OF A MASSIVE
WAR ON DRUGS
WE SHOULD INVEST IN
COMMUNITY-BASED PREVENTION AND TREATMENT PROGRAMS

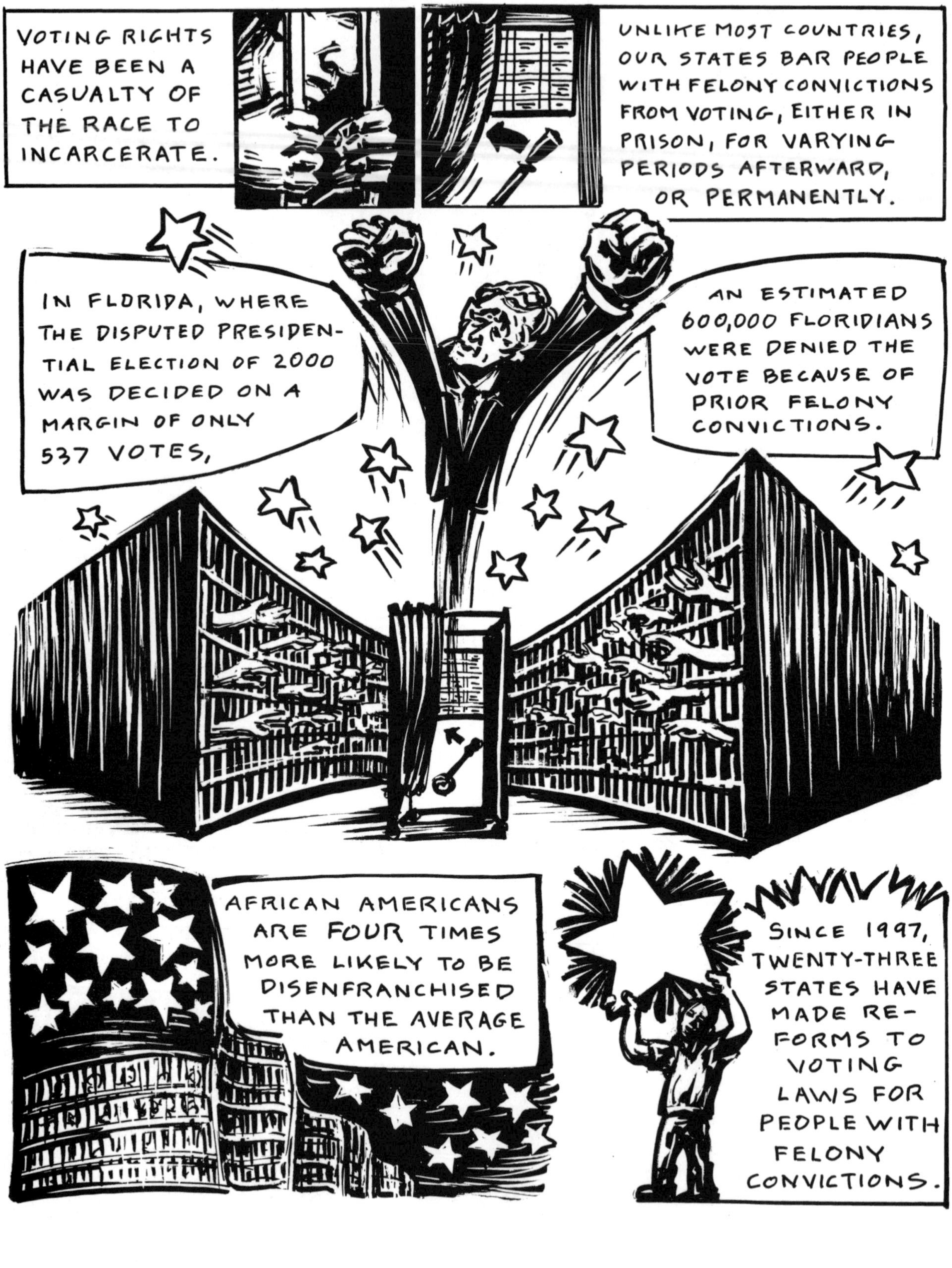
VOTING RIGHTS HAVE BEEN A CASUALTY OF THE RACE TO INCARCERATE.
UNLIKE MOST COUNTRIES, OUR STATES BAR PEOPLE WITH FELONY CONVICTIONS FROM VOTING, EITHER IN PRISON, FOR VARYING PERIODS AFTERWARD, OR PERMANENTLY.
IN FLORIDA, WHERE THE DISPUTED PRESIDENTIAL ELECTION OF 2000 WAS DECIDED ON A MARGIN OF ONLY 537 VOTES,
AN ESTIMATED 600,000 FLORIDIANS WERE DENIED THE VOTE BECAUSE OF PRIOR FELONY CONVICTIONS.
AFRICAN AMERICANS ARE FOUR TIMES MORE LIKELY TO BE DISENFRANCHISED THAN THE AVERAGE AMERICAN.
SINCE 1997, TWENTY-THREE STATES HAVE MADE REFORMS TO VOTING LAWS FOR PEOPLE WITH FELONY CONVICTIONS.

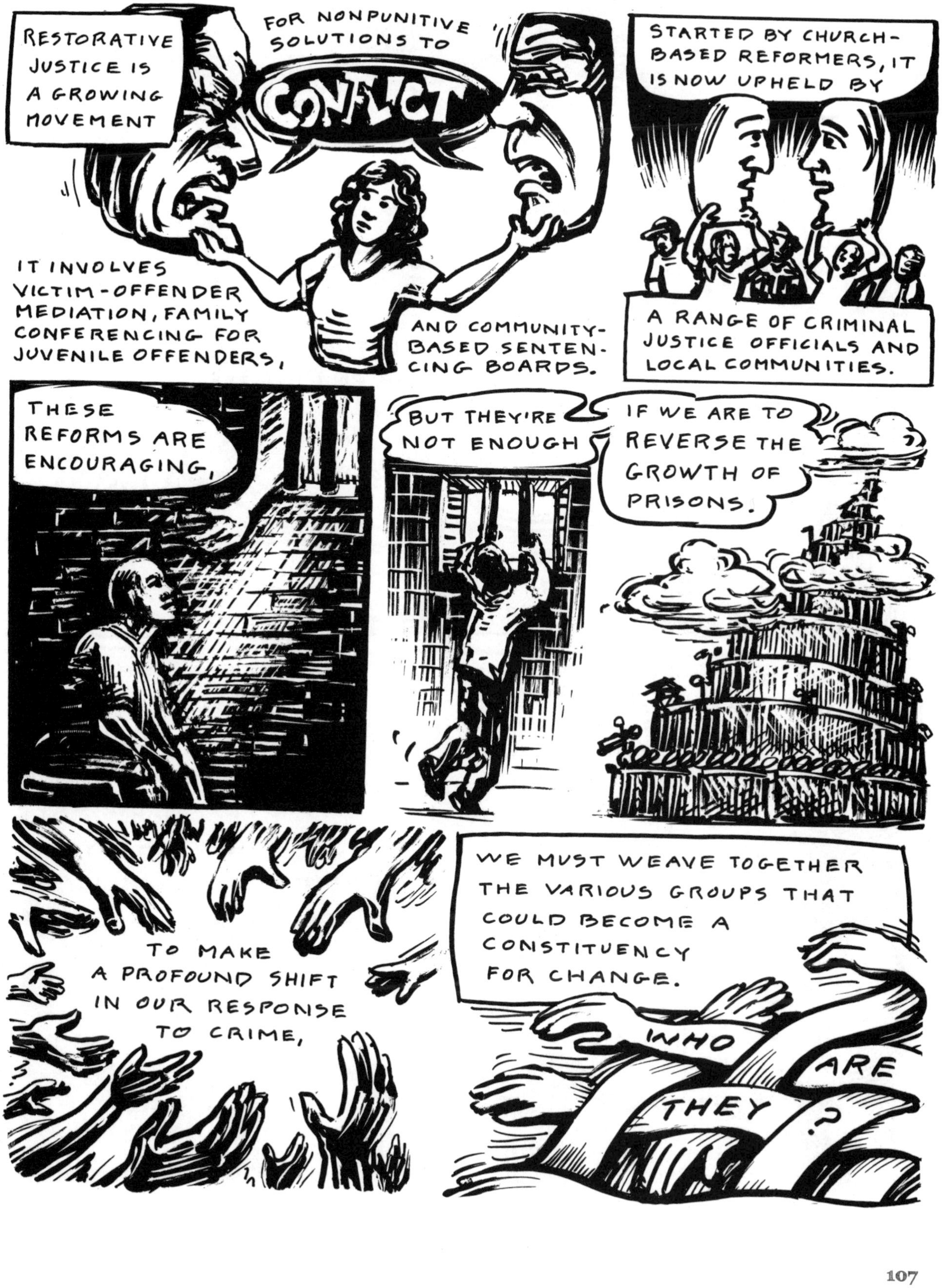

RESTORATIVE JUSTICE IS A GROWING MOVEMENT
FOR NONPUNITIVE SOLUTIONS TO
CONFLICT
IT INVOLVES VICTIM-OFFENDER MEDIATION, FAMILY CONFERENCING FOR JUVENILE OFFENDERS,
AND COMMUNITY-BASED SENTENCING BOARDS.
STARTED BY CHURCH-BASED REFORMERS, IT IS NOW UPHELD BY
A RANGE OF CRIMINAL JUSTICE OFFICIALS AND LOCAL COMMUNITIES.
THESE REFORMS ARE ENCOURAGING,
BUT THEY'RE NOT ENOUGH
IF WE ARE TO REVERSE THE GROWTH OF PRISONS.
TO MAKE A PROFOUND SHIFT IN OUR RESPONSE TO CRIME,
WE MUST WEAVE TOGETHER THE VARIOUS GROUPS THAT COULD BECOME A CONSTITUENCY FOR CHANGE.
WHO ARE THEY ?

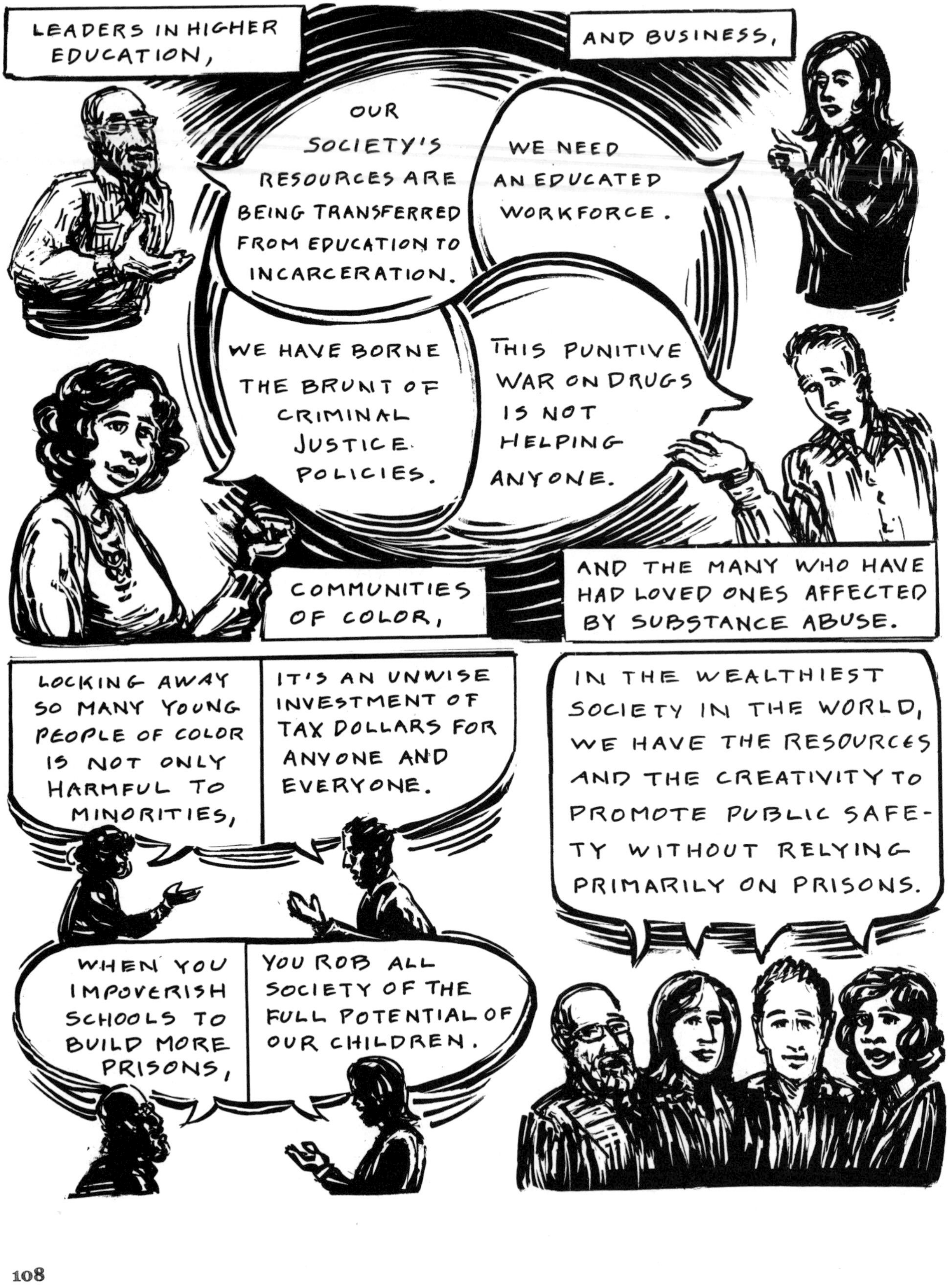
LEADERS IN HIGHER EDUCATION,
AND BUSINESS,
OUR SOCIETY'S RESOURCES ARE BEING TRANSFERRED FROM EDUCATION TO INCARCERATION.
WE NEED AN EDUCATED WORKFORCE.
WE HAVE BORNE THE BRUNT OF CRIMINAL JUSTICE POLICIES.
THIS PUNITIVE WAR ON DRUGS IS NOT HELPING ANYONE.
COMMUNITIES OF COLOR,
AND THE MANY WHO HAVE HAD LOVED ONES AFFECTED BY SUBSTANCE ABUSE.
LOCKING AWAY SO MANY YOUNG PEOPLE OF COLOR IS NOT ONLY HARMFUL TO MINORITIES,
IT'S AN UNWISE INVESTMENT OF TAX DOLLARS FOR ANYONE AND EVERYONE.
IN THE WEALTHIEST SOCIETY IN THE WORLD, WE HAVE THE RESOURCES AND THE CREATIVITY TO PROMOTE PUBLIC SAFE-TY WITHOUT RELYING PRIMARILY ON PRISONS.
WHEN YOU IMPOVERISH SCHOOLS TO BUILD MORE PRISONS,
YOU ROB ALL SOCIETY OF THE FULL POTENTIAL OF OUR CHILDREN.

Coda by Carnell Hunnicutt

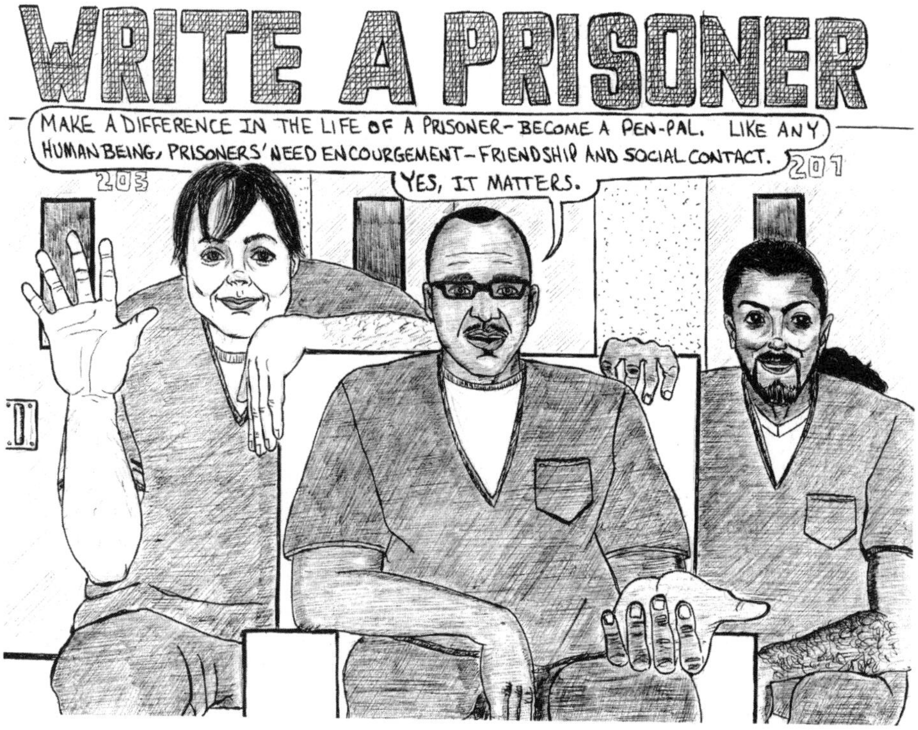
WRITE A PRISONER
MAKE A DIFFERENCE IN THE LIFE OF A PRISONER- BECOME A PEN-PAL. LIKE ANY HUMAN BEING, PRISONERS' NEED ENCOURGEMENT- FRIENDSHIP AND SOCIAL CONTACT.
YES, IT MATTERS.
203
201

CARNELL HUNNICUTT

Some suggested resources for donating books to prisoners.

Appalachian Prison Book Project

LOCATION: Morgantown, West Virginia

SENDS TO: Kentucky, Maryland, Ohio, Tennessee, Virginia, and West Virginia

FOUNDED: 2004

BOOK DONATIONS: Drop off or mail

WEBSITE: aprisonbookproject.wordpress.com/

NOTES: See website for instructions on dropping off books or volunteering. Financial contributions are accepted online, by mail, or in person. Donations of office or packaging supplies can be dropped off or mailed.

MAILING ADDRESS:
Appalachian Prison Book Project
PO Box 601
Morgantown, WV 26507–0601

Books to Prisoners

LOCATION: Seattle, Washington

SERVING: All states except California

FOUNDED: 1973

BOOK DONATIONS: Drop off or mail

WEBSITE: www.bookstoprisoners.net

NOTES: BTP sends books across the United States at no charge to the prisoner. Due to financial limitations BTP does not send to male prisoners in California. BTP only accepts requests by snail mail. Book donors should check the BTP website before sending books. BTP's books are all donated, so they do not always have books on every subject or genre. BTP is always in need of financial donations, which can be made online or by mail. Donations of office or packaging supplies can be dropped off or mailed.

MAILING ADDRESS:
BTP
92 Pike St, Box A
Seattle, WA 98101–2025

Books Through Bars

LOCATION: Philadelphia, Pennsylvania
SENDS TO: Delaware, Maryland, New Jersey, New York,
Pennsylvania, Virginia, and West Virginia
FOUNDED: 1989
BOOK DONATIONS: Drop off or mail
WEBSITE: booksthroughbars.org
NOTES: See website for instructions on dropping off
books or volunteering. Financial contributions can be
made online, by mail, or in person. Donations of office or
packaging supplies can be dropped off or mailed.
MAILING ADDRESS:
Books Through Bars
4722 Baltimore Ave
Philadelphia, PA 19143–3503

Chicago Books to Women in Prison

LOCATION: Chicago, Illinois
SENDS TO: Women's correctional facilities in Arizona,
California, Connecticut, Florida, Illinois, Indiana, Kentucky,
Mississippi, and Ohio
BOOK DONATIONS: Drop off or mail
WEBSITE: chicagobwp.org
NOTES: See website for instructions on dropping off books
or volunteering. Financial contributions can be made online
or by mail. Book requests and donations of packing tape
can be mailed.
MAILING ADDRESS:
Chicago Books to Women in Prison
PO Box 14778
Chicago, IL 60614–8524

Prison Book Program

LOCATION: Quincy, Massachusetts
SENDS TO: All states except California, Illinois, Maryland,
Michigan, Nevada, and Texas
FOUNDED: 1972

BOOK DONATIONS: Drop off or mail
WEBSITE: www.prisonbookprogram.org
NOTES: See website for instructions on dropping off
books or volunteering. Financial contributions can
be made online or by mail. Other items that can be
donated include: packing materials, especially Tyvek
envelopes; brown paper bags; packing tape; laptop
computers; shipping tape dispensers; Sharpies;
photocopying services; office chairs; and gift
certificates to OfficeMax, Staples, and other
office supply stores.
MAILING ADDRESS:
Prison Book Program
c/o Lucy Parsons Bookstore
1306 Hancock St, Suite 100
Quincy, MA 02169–5112

*Some suggested resources for finding a pen pal in
prison.*

Black and Pink

FOCUS: LGBTQ
COST TO INCARCERATED PEN PAL: Free
COST TO PEN PAL ON THE OUTSIDE: Free
MINIMUM AGE: 18
WEBSITE: www.blackandpink.org/prison-penpals/

Christian Pen Pals

FOCUS: Christian
COST TO INCARCERATED PEN PAL: $24 annual membership
COST TO PEN PAL ON THE OUTSIDE: $24 annual membership
MINIMUM AGE: None
WEBSITE: christianpenpals.com
NOTES: Christian Pen Pals is a general pen pal website
with a small subset of users who are incarcerated.
It costs $2 per month to become a member (a full
year must be paid at once) and get access to other
users' email addresses, but there is no fee to post
an ad listing. It is not required that pen pals be
Christian.

Denver Anarchist Black Cross

FOCUS: Political prisoners

COST TO PEN PAL ON THE OUTSIDE: Free

WEBSITE: denverabc.wordpress.com/prisoners-dabc
-supports/political-prisoners-database/

Jewish Pen Pals

FOCUS: Jewish

COST TO INCARCERATED PEN PAL: Free

COST TO PEN PAL ON THE OUTSIDE: Free

MINIMUM AGE: 18

NOTES: All of the incarcerated individuals in the registry are
Jewish, but it is not required that pen pals on the outside
be Jewish.

WEBSITE: www.jewishpenpals.org

Lost Vault

COST TO INCARCERATED PEN PAL: $5 annually

COST TO PEN PAL ON THE OUTSIDE: Free

MINIMUM AGE: 18

WEBSITE: lostvault.com

Prison Inmates Online

COST TO INCARCERATED PEN PAL: $50 for a lifetime membership

COST TO PEN PAL ON THE OUTSIDE: Free

MINIMUM AGE: 18

NOTES: Prison Inmates Online also hosts an online
community of family, friends, and pen pals of incarcerated
individuals to share knowledge, experiences, and support.

WEBSITE: www.prisoninmates.com

Prisoner Correspondence Project

FOCUS: LGBTQ

COST TO INCARCERATED PEN PAL: Free

COST TO PEN PAL ON THE OUTSIDE: Free

MINIMUM AGE: 18

WEBSITE: www.prisonercorrespondenceproject.com

Celebrating Independent Publishing

Thank you for reading this book published by The New Press. The New Press is a nonprofit, public interest publisher. New Press books and authors play a crucial role in sparking conversations about the key political and social issues of our day.

We hope you enjoyed this book and that you will stay in touch with The New Press. Here are a few ways to stay up to date with our books, events, and the issues we cover:

- Sign up at www.thenewpress.com/subscribe to receive updates on New Press authors and issues and to be notified about local events
- Like us on Facebook: www.facebook.com/newpressbooks
- Follow us on Twitter: www.twitter.com/thenewpress

Please consider buying New Press books for yourself; for friends and family; or to donate to schools, libraries, community centers, prison libraries, and other organizations involved with the issues our authors write about.

The New Press is a 501(c)(3) nonprofit organization. You can also support our work with a tax-deductible gift by visiting www.thenewpress.com/donate.